GREAT HOUSES OF
AUSTRALIA

GREAT HOUSES OF
Australia
50 homes with a story to tell

Text by Denis Gregory
Photography by Alf Manciagli

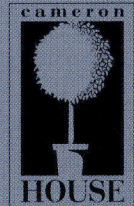

cameron
HOUSE

Contents

Abercrombie House

It's the middle of the night. An owl is looking for his tucker as a carriage going at a furious pace races up the wooded driveway of Mount Pleasant estate, near Bathurst, in central western New South Wales. Seconds later, inside the house, doors slam and crockery breaks. It's an inexplicable appearance of the celebrated ghost of Strath, said to happen before the death of a member of the family.

Present owner of the magnificent Mount Pleasant mansion, now called Abercrombie House, is educator and author Rex Morgan and, although he hasn't seen the ghost, he admits to other supernatural phenomena. One night he woke suddenly, aware someone was nearby. His wife Mary, already awake, told him a figure had walked to his side of the bed and then gone away. Another night, his secretary saw a shadowy figure under a fir tree; and former residents have told him they often heard the grand piano being played although nobody other than them was in the house at the time.

When Mr Morgan first visited the 120-year-old house in 1968, his decision to buy it was influenced by the ghosts of the former owners. It had not been lived in for around 25 years — a prerequisite for a psychic occurrence — and had fallen into disrepair.

Mr Morgan stood in the entrance hall and looked at the portraits on the wall of Major General William Stewart, a Bathurst pioneer and early lieutenant governor of New South Wales; and his son, James Horne Stewart, who built the 52-room, granite home in the 1870s on the then 6000-hectare estate. Major General Stewart was born in Scotland in 1769 and died at Bathurst in 1854. He was the son of William Stewart of Caithness, Scotland, and grandson of Donald Stewart of Appin, one of Prince Charles

Edward's (the Young Pretender's) officers. He married Isabella Innes and had one son, James. The major general was appointed a member of the Legislative Council in 1823 and was lieutenant governor from 1823 to 1827. He was acting governor in 1825 for thirteen days.

Mr Morgan believed both Stewarts seemed to urge him to buy the house: 'What was more significant was that they both appeared pleased, knowing that I would look after it.

'I'm glad to say I heeded their advice and have no reason to believe they are not still pleased with the restoration and, more importantly, that we are living in the house and sharing its beauty and splendour with others.'

Rex Morgan travels regularly but lives in Abercrombie House when he is home. He was the founder of the Pittwater House group of schools in Sydney, was headmaster and is still chairman of the board. In recent years he has become a guest lecturer at universities and does a lot of work in China.

Abercrombie House has a National Trust 'A' classification and is listed in the National Estate Register of Australia. It is likely to be listed in the New South Wales' Register as well.

The house was built on a 1200-hectare land grant given to Major General Stewart by the Duke of York in 1827 as a reward for services in the Peninsular War. He chose the land on the Evans Plains Creek. He also bought 4800 hectares of adjoining land and used convict labour to build a house known as Strath.

Major Stewart's son James began building the main house on four levels — a basement, two main floors and an attic — in 1870 and it took paid workers eight years to finish. Excavating the granite on the site was a two-year job.

The 52 rooms include ten bedrooms, two dining rooms, a ballroom, library and study. There are seven staircases and 30 marble fireplaces. There are seven stone outbuildings, including a dairy, coach-house, stable block and blacksmith shop. All the paddocks are bordered by a mild-steel fence put up in the 1890s.

The Stewarts established a big open-cut sawpit, now called Sawpit Creek, and cut all their own hardwood on the property. All the structural timber, floor joists and roof beams are local hardwood. The floors are Baltic pine except for the entrance hall, which is parquetry made in England. All the joinery is Australian red cedar.

The roof is slate that came from the Bangor Quarry in Wales. The quarry ran out in 1925 so the only source of replacement slate now is from other buildings being demolished. Some replacement slate on Abercrombie House came from the old police station in Bathurst.

The verandah has about 130,000 hand-laid mosaic tiles from Campbells Brick and Tile company in England, and the front entrance has tiles from Minton. The pink and black marble for the fireplaces came from various quarries.

James Stewart died in 1920 when he was 96, and his son Athol lived there for seven years before he moved away, selling all the contents. The house was not used again as a

THE STAFF QUARTERS.

family home until Mr Morgan bought it in 1969. There had been different caretakers, and during World War II the Women's Land Army used it as a base.

In the 1950s Professor James Stewart, a nephew of Athol and an archaeologist at Sydney University, turned the house into a research outpost. He made some structural repairs as well as putting up new wallpaper, fluorescent lights and built-in wardrobes.

More recently, Rex Morgan's son Christopher, who also lives on the estate with his wife Xanthe, has done much of the restoration work.

'After my father bought it, the house became the great family project,' he said. 'I was six when we first moved here and I have a brother and sister as well so we were three little children racing around in this massive empty house.

'Our childhood was playing hide and seek and looking for ghosts and doing all those sorts of things. My parents set out on the huge project of restoration and as children we became involved. We all grew up with a great love of the house, a great interest in its history and a great desire to see it restored.'

Chris Morgan studied archaeology at the University of Sydney and then did a post-graduate museum studies diploma so that he would have the qualifications to help with the restoration. When he finished the course he went home and began the final push.

'I spend a lot of time restoring rooms and furniture and working with my father who is a great collector.'

Much of the now-restored furniture was bought from clearing sales. 'My father used to stop people on the way to the dump to get old furniture from them in the 1970s when everyone was throwing it away,' Chris Morgan said.

THE SITTING ROOM FIREPLACE.

The Morgans have done all the restoration work themselves, with the help of a carpenter who is employed full-time. They've replaced the 1950s wallpaper, ripped out the built-in wardrobes and upgraded electrical fittings.

'My wife Xanthe and children Julia and Henry are helping, so now the third generation of our family is becoming involved. The kids are good gardeners and do their part,' remarked Mr Morgan.

'We've all learnt trades. I can be a slate-layer, bricklayer, carpenter, painter and can restore marble fireplaces. My wife is an expert wallpaperer. But in a sense, the job will never be finished. It will go on forever because the maintenance on a house this size requires constant attention, although we are coming to the end of the major work.'

The latest addition in a back section of the house is an exhibition of royal memorabilia. Rex Morgan is a great collector with a particular passion for monarchy souvenirs. The family decided to put them together to form an exhibition covering the reign of the nine kings and queens since Australia was colonised. There is also an archives section that can be used by researchers and students.

'We wanted to show material associated with the monarchy so that, regardless of the choice people might make about becoming a republic, we will have resource material for future generations,' Chris Morgan explained.

A covenant in the sale to the Morgans required a change of name for the house, known locally as Mount Pleasant, Stewart's Mount, Stewart's Castle and The Castle. The family selected Abercrombie because at the time it was situated in Abercrombie Shire, now part of Bathurst, and the name had Scottish connections going back to the Stewarts.

Abercrombie House now sits on only 20 hectares but the family keeps horses and chickens and there is also an orchard. However, the main family enterprise is to ensure the house survives.

The large formal gardens are separately listed in the National Estate Register. 'We have lots of mature trees that were planted by James Stewart in 1870. Bunya pines were brought down from the south coast of Queensland, there are lots of Arizona and Scotch pines and some Italian pines called *Pinus ponderosa* that were popular in Rome in 1870.

'There were a lot of ornamental willows but people are now taking them out. We also have lots of original roses. An apple tree on the property was planted by a convict in 1834, which makes it one of the oldest still growing.

'A grapevine in the garden came from a cutting the original pioneer General William Stewart brought in 1824 from the famous grapevine at Hampton Court in England that was planted by King Henry VIII.'

And the ghosts? 'I don't think there's any left. When we first came here as children we used to see people in the house whom we could never explain and we decided they were ghosts. And lots of times when people came here to stay they would come down to breakfast and say they heard someone walking around or in their room.

'Before we moved in, the house was deserted for a long time and became really derelict and overgrown, and a lot of young Bathurst people used to come to look and lots of ghost stories came from that. But it's pretty peaceful here now.'

A MIX OF GOTHIC AND BARONIAL ARCHITECTURE.

Bedervale

LEFT: BEDERVALE HOMESTEAD.

BOTTOM LEFT: THE ORIGINAL
SECTION OF THE HOUSE.

BOTTOM RIGHT: THE SITTING
ROOM.

BELOW: OLD KITCHEN ITEMS.

Captain John Coghill, master of the convict ship *Mangles*, certainly knew his way between England and the new colony of New South Wales. He made nine voyages, transporting around 2000 convicts.

But the opportunities in the colony attracted him and, after selling his share of the ship in 1826, he brought out his wife Jane, their son and two daughters to settle on the land. At the time, he was in partnership in a property called Kirkham at Camden with surveyor general John Oxley and that's where he and his family first lived.

Captain Coghill was born at Wick in Scotland in 1785, and in 1814 became master of the transport ship *Martha*, later acquiring a half share in the *Mangles*. Dr Thomas Braidwood Wilson was his ship's surgeon and his journals show Coghill lost only one convict and he was sick when put on board.

Both Captain Coghill and Dr Wilson took up grants in the colony around the same time. Captain Coghill took up 2000 acres (810 hectares) in 1822 on the east bank of the Wingecarribee River near Berrima, which his brother William looked after while he was at sea. William later bought it.

In 1826 Captain Coghill, now a new settler, was prompted by Oxley to make his selection of land and take instant possession. With former ship's surgeon David Reid, who lived near Goulburn, he rode through the little-known southern district near present-day Braidwood and selected a 5600-acre (2268-hectare) block below Mt Jillimatong, which he later called Bedervale. Two years later he was running 300 cattle and by 1833 had added a mob of sheep.

The grant required an amount of land to be cleared each year and a house had to be built. The original cottage is in the Bedervale courtyard.

In 1836 Coghill commissioned architect John Verge to design a homestead and he presented his bill, totalling £16, in May 1837. Verge was also the architect for Camden Park House, Elizabeth Bay House and Tuscullum.

Work probably did not begin for several years after John Verge drew the plans. All the bricks had to be made on the property by convicts. The walls are double brick and were rendered on the outside with plaster and lime to make them look like stone. That also preserved the bricks because they weren't fired at a high temperature and were inclined to fret, which has happened in the courtyard.

All the cedar was cut in the Tudor Valley towards the New South Wales south coast along with the hardwood floors and black ash columns. The sandstone and marble were quarried from Bundanoon and Drayton near Marulan, on the Hume Highway.

Generally, the bigger the room, the higher the ceiling — 13 feet (4 metres) in the main rooms. In some of the smaller rooms, including the hallway, the ceilings are lower. The skirting boards are wide and the windows quite plain, although more ornate in the main rooms.

The builder is not known, although records show a carpenter named Alexander Fairlie was employed for 40 shillings a week and rations for 128 weeks. In 1836 Coghill paid a J. Poulteney for brickmaking, and in 1838 paid a John Kent for bricklaying. A plasterer named Richard

Wilson was employed in 1841 and the house was believed to have been finished around 1842.

Other payments were made for large quantities of sawn timber, including cedar, French polish, white lead, sheet lead, glass, linseed oil, putty and paint brushes. Large quantities of nails and flooring brads were also bought.

Coghill became a member of the Legislative Council in 1843 but resigned in 1845 to take his family to England while he sorted out problems with the Bank of Australia, which had collapsed. He was a director of the bank and wanted to raise £18,000. The bank's fall helped bring about the 1840s depression.

Coghill's only son David looked after Bedervale while his father was away, but he died on the property in 1847 at the early age of 31. One of Coghill's daughters was killed at only nineteen when she fell from a carriage. She and her brother, and Captain Coghill and his wife are all buried on the Bedervale property.

While in England, Coghill's second daughter Elisabeth met Robert Maddrell, who was studying medicine at Giessen University in Germany. They were married in London in 1849 and the Coghill family returned to Bedervale the same year. When Captain Coghill died in 1857, Bedervale went to Robert Maddrell. Under his supervision the property was increased in size to 33,000 acres (13,365 hectares). His descendants lived there until 1972, six generations in 136 years, until Roger and Margaret Royds bought the house and its original contents.

They had lived at Jinglemoney, a property about 16 kilometres from Braidwood. Mrs Royds said they had always believed it was 'all jingle and no money … We realised we needed more land because we wanted to educate our children who had to go to boarding school and we wanted them to experience city life. We bought two blocks adjacent to Bedervale. One block almost came to the house so it seemed sensible to buy Bedervale when Rob Maddrell wanted to sell it,' Mrs Royds explained.

'The question of money was a big item but we had worked in Sydney for three years doing up old houses and had that real estate as a deposit. Income from the land was poor and land prices dropped so the equity of our loan wasn't good enough and we were advised to sell our real estate, which was the biggest mistake we ever made.

'But we bought Bedervale in 1972 from Robert Maddrell, walk in walk out. He went to Queensland and we moved in. My family and friends helped tidy things up.'

The Royds did a lot of research and cataloguing because they thought they might find themselves in a financial situation where they would have to sell up. To secure the house they applied to the federal government for a national estate grant. In return, they offered the contents of the house, because they thought the family collection from the Coghills to the Maddrells was the most important to save. After two years, great persistence, and many visits by politicians, they eventually received approval for the grant. They had to nominate public ownership so they nominated the National Trust.

Robert Maddrell also left family portraits there and the Royds have since introduced their own family collection.

Mrs Royds revealed they have done a tremendous amount of research and have built up a story about the house and the people who had lived in it. 'Because it was always the older family who came in here, there weren't a lot of fashion changes. Everything could have been painted white or the old furniture thrown out. In fact, the iron beds were thrown out but not away and were in an old bathroom in the courtyard so we restored them and brought them back. We also connected electricity and water, put in a new bathroom, extended the kitchen and built a family room,' she said.

THE DINING ROOM.

THE OLD KITCHEN.

gentleman's residence and also had to show he was well educated so he had all the right books.

The Royds brought up their four children in Bedervale: Victoria; Martin, who has a property in Braidwood; Rodney, who now runs the Bedervale property, which has had its original holding reduced to 1200 acres (486 hectares); and the youngest, Sonia, who now lives on the Royds' original property, Jinglemoney.

Mrs Royds commented that Bedervale was not an easy house for young children. It was a house designed for servants and needs lots of maintenance.

Today, the house has an entrance hall, drawing room, dining room, pantry, scullery and a verandah room, now the kitchen. There's a library; small sitting room, which was a main bedroom; a main bedroom, which was the original dining room; a butler's pantry; morning room; conservatory and eight bedrooms.

There are two small rooms on the end of the courtyard verandah. One was initially used as a bathroom and is now part of the kitchen and the other a stairwell to upstairs. A small room off the eastern end of the front verandah is now a bathroom. Office lamp rooms are now used for linen and as another bathroom.

The house reflects a high standard of preservation, including the original furniture and household utensils from pre-1840 to 1905. As a collection, the house contents reflect the changing tastes and social habits from Victorian to Edwardian times.

The roof was originally timber shingles, but in 1888 galvanised iron was put over the top. A second higher roof was added over the central valley to avoid drainage problems and the chimneys were extended to balance it all up.

The present dining room, which has the bay windows on the left at the front of the house, was added in 1905, and water and acetylene gas lighting were put in at the same time.

The stables at the back are flanked by two wings, forming a courtyard. These are the oldest buildings and comprise on one side the schoolroom, which was the original house, with added rooms above and the dry store. The kitchen, cool room and laundry are on the other side.

The stables enclosing the courtyard comprise a coach-house, horse stalls, harness room and grain silo with a loft above. Cellars run the full length of the house with entry from the back.

Bedervale has ten chimneys and seven fireplaces.

Mrs Royds said some of the doors had been painted so they had to be stripped, but fortunately the doors in the other rooms only needed to be polished. The bathroom when the family took over was outside the back door — which they considered was rather inconvenient — so it was moved. It had only a bathtub and a washing machine and the washing machine emptied into the bath. The water went into a brick drain down the courtyard, so the Royds borrowed money to put in a new drainage system.

'There was no laundry and I used to do the ironing in the hall, with 30 metres of cord to vacuum the house. So we applied to have the power connected but only in some rooms because there was only one transformer. We kept adding to that,' Mrs Royds said.

'The toilets were either down the yard or at the other end of the house. We also put in new gutters and downpipes and new doors on the stables. Nothing was ever thrown away and it was just a matter of locating it. So where they opened up the stables to make it into a garage, we had to re-brick and put the original door back.

'We moved bookcases back into what was originally the library but had been used as a bedroom. Behind one bookcase was framework and when we took it away we found it was a door. We got the bookcases back through there.'

The library contains several thousand books that were owned by Captain Coghill and Robert Maddrell. Mrs Royds said she thought the books were bought to impress people by a man who was setting himself up in the colony of New South Wales as a gentleman. He had to have the

Bishopscourt

Paul Howard MacGillivray graduated from the University of Aberdeen in Scotland with a master's degree in arts when he was seventeen. He was a brilliant student and looked set to follow his father, who was professor of natural history at the same university.

However, a year later in 1852 his father died and he put aside his interest in natural history, went to London and studied medicine. He was awarded his degree with distinction, so much so that when he was only 21 he was elected a member of the Royal College of Surgeons.

Dr MacGillivray took a job as a surgeon on ships carrying adventurers to the Victorian goldfields, and made two trips before he decided to stay in Australia and work as a medical officer for a naval volunteer brigade. In 1862 he accepted an appointment as resident surgeon at the Bendigo Goldfields Hospital, staying there for fourteen years.

Despite a busy professional life, Dr MacGillivray carried out a great deal of medical research, and in 1874 was elected president of the Victorian Medical Society. He also became a world authority on hydatids disease, an ailment caused by a tapeworm in the larval state that results in cysts.

In 1876, he decided to go into private practice and, needing his own consulting rooms and home, drew a sketch of what he wanted and gave it to architect John M. Brady. Mr Brady had designed railways, bridges and docks and was responsible for a scheme to divert water to Bendigo.

The home at the time was considered the largest private residence in Bendigo. The *Bendigo Advertiser* in April 1875 described the home on the corner of Forest and Rowan streets in great detail and said it 'spoke well for the confidence felt in the stability of the district that men like Dr MacGillivray and others do not hesitate to lay out large sums of money on buildings of a character superior to any yet erected in Bendigo'.

The newspaper noted that the frontage to Forest Street would be 45 feet long (14 metres) and would be the private entrance. There would be 'a handsome balcony continuing the whole length on this front'. The Rowan Street frontage 'will be 56 feet long [17 metres] on which there will be a porch entrance for patients. The whole of the exterior walls and chimney shafts are to be cemented; the windows, porch etc will have architraves, pilasters in the same material; the whole will be struck in imitation of ashlar blocks and all the angles of the building will have rusticated quoins ...'

The report went on to say that 'between the whole of the joists on the second storey halfway in their depth is inch boarding supported on strong battens and the spaces filled in with lime concrete to deaden sound, over which the floorboards are laid. The whole of the interior walls and ceilings will be stuccoed and ornamented in the usual manner. The whole of the rooms, lobbies and halls will have gas laid on.'

Dr MacGillivray renewed his interest in natural science and in 1880 was elected a fellow of the Linnean Society in London; later the University of Aberdeen awarded him an honorary Doctorate of Laws. He also formed the Bendigo Science Society.

Upon his death in July 1885, the flags flew at half-mast throughout Bendigo. Although he had achieved international

LEFT & BOTTOM RIGHT: THE SITTING ROOM.

BOTTOM LEFT: THE ELEGANT LINES OF BISHOPSCOURT.

BELOW: THE MAIN BEDROOM.

recognition, he had always maintained his role as a family doctor. A hall in the Bendigo TAFE College has been named after him.

One of the next owners of the MacGillivray residence was Mrs Edith Lansell, of Fortuna. The house was probably an investment of some sort as it's unlikely she lived there (see Fortuna Villa).

In 1921 she gave the house to the Anglican Church as a memorial to two nephews, Reginald Lansell Frew and Clive Balfour, who were killed in action in World War I in 1917. It was to be used as the residence of the Bishop of Bendigo and was named Bishop's Court, which would later become Bishopscourt.

The house was expensive to maintain but was used as the bishop's palace for 64 years until the church decided it wanted something more in keeping with present-day standards and sold it. A new bishop's residence was built in 1984 in Bendigo for around the same price as that obtained from the sale.

Beverley Leeson and her daughter and son-in-law Mark and Helen Lees bought Bishopscourt in 1999 from Phil Byrne, who was the local magistrate and then the Victorian coroner. Indeed, most of the house's owners since the church sold it have been professional people like magistrates and solicitors.

Although renovations had been carried out by some of the previous owners, Mrs Leeson and the Lees have done a good deal of work. The bathrooms were 1920s-style with the pipes running down the walls and covered by tin, so they were renovated. A lot of painting has been done and they have added light fittings and other decorative pieces in keeping with the period. They also did a great deal of work

PART OF THE LARGE GARDEN.

in the big garden, which at one stage incorporated a separate section for croquet.

The changes through the years have included the addition of bay windows at the back, while a balcony verandah on one side has been removed. Several of the fireplace surrounds and mantels are different to the original black marble. Some of the original plasterwork has also been replaced, along with the original iron roof, which is now tile. A second, smaller, staircase has been added at the back.

The dining room is situated at the front of the house and a sunroom leads off it. On the right is the formal lounge, which has a door through to the garden. The study is on the left. The entrance hall is huge and still has the original wallpaper, as does one of the bedrooms upstairs.

The second street entrance opens to a hall 18 metres long and 2 metres wide. The doctor's waiting room and a separate dispensary were on one side but these have been converted into a living room and scullery. The kitchen, cellar, bathroom and back verandah also open off the hall.

Upstairs was designed for Dr MacGillivray and his family and servants and included a drawing room and nursery, bedrooms and a bathroom. The layout has remained virtually the same, although some of the rooms are now used as extra bedrooms.

'It's our family home and we love living here,' Mrs Leeson said. 'We've done lots of work and there's still lots to do but it's well worth it. It's a lovely home.'

THE DINING ROOM.

In Memory Of

WILLIAM HAWKE

DIED JULY 18, 1902: AGED 56 YEARS.

ALSO

MARY WILKINSON

BELOVED WIFE OF THE ABOVE

DIED OCT. 29, 1896 : AGED 46 YEARS.

Bookanan

After the Blue Mountains were crossed in 1813, the colonial government banned settlers from going farther west than the Macquarie River at the new township of Bathurst. But when the ban was lifted in 1823, a small group of Cornish farmers were among the first to begin new lives in the Western Districts by selecting land in a picturesque valley on Lewis Ponds Creek.

Leading the charge was William Tom and his family, who selected 640 acres (259 hectares) he called Springfield. Other Cornishmen to settle in the same area were George Hawke, John Glasson and Richard Lane. They agreed to come together and establish an agricultural area, but later branched out into horticulture. George Hawke brought fruit trees to the region and was given credit for establishing a horticultural industry in the Orange district with apples, pears, stone fruits, figs and pomegranates. He also had an extensive vineyard.

It wasn't long before the valley became known as Cornish Settlement. The name was changed to Byng in the 1880s to honour Admiral Byng of the Royal Navy who took part in the early Napoleonic Wars in 1805. The community was predominantly Wesleyan and built a stone church.

When copper was discovered in the Byng Valley in 1849, there was an influx of Cornish miners and the settlement grew to about 500 people. The Carangara copper mine began operations in 1850 on Glasson's property and a smelting furnace was built. But there was never a police station or a hotel, and for a mining village in Australia, that was unique. Obviously the Cornish Wesleyanism was a major influence on the area.

When the first payable gold was discovered at nearby Ophir in 1851 by Parson William Tom, his brother James, and John Lister, most of the miners working at the copper mine left and it was impossible to find labour to load the drays. That was the end of the mine.

John Glasson and George Hawke had become partners in 1829 on one large holding, which Glasson received freehold title for in 1835. In 1838 George Hawke married, took over his own holding just down the road and built a home he called Pendarves.

Glasson had lived in a bark hut and then a small stone dwelling but, by 1840, after getting freehold title on the land, had built a new stone home he called Newton Vale. He later changed that to the house's present name of Bookanan.

In 1873, Glasson sold out to a Sydney foundry owner, Walter Friend, and went to New Zealand. Friend later sold to a Mr Randall.

George Hawke bought Bookanan in 1882 and it has been in the Hawke family since then. It was used as a farmhand's house for some years while Hawke still lived at nearby Pendarves. Initially, the Glasson–Hawke partnership survived by producing milk. They made butter and cheese and

THE FRONT VERANDAH.

LEFT: BOOKANAN HOMESTEAD.

BOTTOM LEFT: AN ANCESTOR'S GRAVE.

BOTTOM RIGHT: THE BYNG CHURCH.

OLD COOKING POTS ADD CHARACTER.

sent it to Sydney while they cleared the land of the big box and white gum trees. As they cleared, they planted wheat. Over the years, the property has weathered the usual economic problems, the Depression, droughts and war.

Current owner Will Hawke said his father leased out the property when he went to World War I. He returned in 1919 and told the tenants they would change over on 1 January 1920, but they said no. They wanted to abide by the terms of the lease and give the property back one year after the war had ended.

Will and Barbara Hawke moved to Bookanan as a young married couple in 1964. They raised two children: Fiona, an actress but now housewife and mother of two children; and son Philip, who works on the property.

Mr Hawke said that when they moved into the house it was a question of, 'Do we dump it, do we wreck it, do we pull it down or do we try to save it? Fortunately Barbara said let's have a go at it but it has been a labour of love.

'But we have enjoyed doing it. Even with the problems. It's a comfortable home and to us a very special place because of our long-term connection with it. Six generations have been associated with Bookanan. In 2004 we celebrated the 175th anniversary of the Hawkes' association with the Byng district.'

Will Hawke served twenty years in local government with Canobolas and Cabonne shire councils at Orange, and Mrs Hawke is very active in the community. They run mainly prime lambs and about 150 cattle along with producing some merino wool from sheep on the 920-hectare property's higher ground.

Bookanan was based on John Glasson's home in Cornwall. He had written to the family asking for dimensions and built it in the same style. It has a strong Georgian influence although Glasson added a verandah to provide shade and temperature control, something needed in the Australian conditions. The Georgian aspect is an interesting feature. It was unusual to have that style of house at such an early date in the central west of New South Wales because the Macquarie River wasn't legally crossed until 1823 and the Blue Mountains hadn't been crossed until 1813.

Bookanan has a dining room, sitting room, family room, breakfast room/kitchen, laundry, and what the Hawkes call a mud room, where they come in from the paddocks and clean up before going inside. A vestibule hall gives access to the dining room and sitting room.

Upstairs there are four bedrooms, a sewing room, office, and ensuite bathroom, which all have ceilings sloping into the roof.

'When we first moved in, there was no electricity, no bathroom, no telephone and no running water,' Will Hawke said. 'So we had to put those modern facilities in.

'In 1976 we did a major restoration. We changed the kitchen to make it more functional, opened up the old kitchen and laundry, which was a flagged area that hadn't been used. We took up the flags and put down a floor and installed another bathroom.

'The family room was renovated. Other than that, there were no major structural changes. Basically the house is the

THE SITTING ROOM.

same as it was in 1840. The roof was shingle but has been covered with corrugated iron, probably about 1900. We looked at putting shingles back on but that was not practical, financially or weather-wise.'

All of the materials were made by hand. The main posts and rafters were ironbark, cut from the property and shaped with axes. The cedar was all hand worked and the joinery is still quite fine and in good condition. At the time the house was built, Glasson recorded that he had assigned servants (convicts) working on the property, which was not unusual. He was pleased with the quality of the cedar work and joinery but wasn't as impressed with the stonework. He noted that he thought the masons could have done a better job.

The two main cedar doors were made so that a cross was formed. This was as a way of introducing Christian symbols into the house during the era in England when false idols were not permitted. The cross was a technique used in joinery at the time.

The staircase is cedar. It is not in the best condition and creaks loudly but the Hawkes plan to have it repaired. The flooring is ironbark planks butt-jointed together. The workmanship is good and there are no cracks.

The inside walls are plaster and lath with a hair finish. The outside walls are stone. The front verandah is stucco but the rest is random-laid stone.

All the stone, including the outside flagging, was cut from a quarry on the property. It is the same stone that was used to build other Byng Valley homes, including Springfield,

Pendarves, Willow Cottage and the church. It resembles sandstone but is actually a hard sedimentary rock.

Today, the walls move constantly, but there are no major problems. As the soil dries out, cracks open up, but as the soil becomes damp, the cracks close up again.

Stone walls at the back of the house once formed part of a building for carriages and a feed room for horses. Initially it was an accommodation area replacing Glasson's bark hut.

The house surrounds have a strong English influence with lots of oaks and elms and particularly the hawthorn trees originally planted as a fence. But when rabbits became common at the turn of the century, they attacked the new seedlings and the hedge failed. The amount of work that would have been required to keep the hedge in order was simply too much, and the trees are now leftovers of the English countryside that have been 'Australianised'.

FAMILY PHOTOGRAPHS LINE THE STAIRCASE.

THE STONE STABLES.

Borambola

While most people living on a farm usually move into town at semi-retiring age, Basil and Anne McMullen — who had lived in an urban area all their life — did the opposite and moved out. They bought a 123-year-old historic homestead on a 42-hectare property and carried out a full restoration, including the addition of a few comforts like new heating and cooling. At the same time, with the help of their two sons, they established a vineyard, something totally new to them, and are selling wine under their own label.

Their Borambola homestead, 25 kilometres from Wagga Wagga in New South Wales' Riverina, is one of the most impressive homes in the district but it has taken a great deal of hard work to restore the house to its former glory. At one stage a previous owner used the dining room to store hay for his cows.

The early days of Borambola — a name derived from the Aboriginal word *bora bora* and referring to the initiation of boys into manhood — is pretty sketchy. Borambola, also the district name, was apparently taken up in the 1830s by George Macleay, the son of the colonial secretary at the time, Alexander Macleay, who built Elizabeth Bay House in Sydney. The run was then known as Tarcuttah.

THE PAINTED FACE-BRICK FAÇADE OF BORAMBOLA.

George Macleay, later Sir George, was manager of his father's 6070-hectare Brownlow Hill estate at Camden, but in 1829–30 went with Charles Sturt on his second exploration down the Murray and Murrumbidgee rivers. The government rewarded him with a squatting lease of 437 hectares for his voluntary service with Sturt. Reports say the grant was Toganmain, a property on the lower Murrumbidgee between Hay and Narrandera, several hundred kilometres from Borambola.

It is unclear how long Macleay owned the property, but a correspondent in the *Town and Country Journal* in September 1872 wrote an account of his trip on horseback from Hay to Wagga Wagga and Toganmain (an Aboriginal word meaning 'I am cold'), which was then owned by a John Dow. The next 10-mile (16-kilometre) stage of his trip was to Kerarbury Station, which he wrote was owned by 'Messrs Clarke and Macleay, the latter gentleman is member for the district.'

He was probably referring to William John Macleay, George Macleay's cousin, who was a member for Lachlan and Lower Darling from 1855 to 1856 and from 1877 to 1891. History records he took up the Karrabory squatting run, later Kerarbury, in 1839 'adjacent to that of George Macleay on the lower Murrumbidgee …' Records say it was the source of his wealth.

George Macleay had considerable land in the district and was the member of parliament for Murrumbidgee from 1851 to 1856. He returned to live in England in 1859 and was knighted in 1869. William John Macleay was also knighted, in 1889.

The second owner of Borambola around 1851 was a John Gordon but there's little known about him. A John Donnelly bought Borambola in 1865 and he commissioned Wagga Wagga man Charles Hardy to build the Borambola homestead in 1878.

While Donnelly owned the property, bushranger Captain Moonlite was in the district, raiding Wantabadgery station, just to the north-east of Borambola. Moonlite, christened Andrew George Scott, was a lay preacher, poet, an excellent horseman, civil engineer, sailor and prison reformer. He also robbed the Victorian Mt Edgerton bank and tried to put the blame on the manager, but was later found guilty and spent seven years in Pentridge Gaol in Melbourne.

There he made friends with a young James Nesbitt and, when freed in November 1879, they set off on a tour lecturing about prison reform and gathering young supporters as they went, including Augustus Wernicke, Thomas Rogan and Thomas Williams.

They walked into New South Wales and across the Borambola station to Wantabadgery where they asked for work, but were refused by the new manager. They returned several days later and again asked for work and cover from rain for the night, but were again refused.

The next day Moonlite and his friends bailed up the station and took 35 hostages, including visitors who arrived there in the three days the gang held siege. In a shootout with police, Nesbitt and Wernicke were killed as well as police officer Senior Constable Edward Bowen, who was allegedly shot by Moonlite.

Nesbitt and Wernicke were buried in Gundagai cemetery and Moonlite was hanged in Sydney and buried in Rookwood cemetery. In a letter he wrote an hour before his

THE SUNROOM AND ITS ADJUSTABLE CEILING LOUVRES.

23

death, Moonlite said his last wish was to be put to rest in the grave of his friend Nesbitt.

In 1994, two Gundagai women, Christine Ferguson and Sam Anderson Asimus, took up the challenge and at last obtained permission to have Moonlite's body exhumed and reburied at Gundagai in January 1995 next to where they believed Nesbitt was buried.

There are claims Moonlite and his gang raided Borambola station as well, taking some of its horses and shooting up the stables when they left. That could well have been between the time they left Wantabadgery the first time and when they returned several days later, but this can't be verified.

A succession of droughts put the Donnelly family through hard times, and after being declared bankrupt in 1890, the property was taken over in a foreclosure by rural company Goldsborough Mort. The company appointed a J.A. Gunn manager, believed to be the grandfather of the one-time giant of the Australian wool industry Sir William Gunn, and he ran Borambola until it was sold to a Mr Simpson.

Around 1910 it was subdivided and, after several more owners, was gradually whittled away through the years from its original 500,000 hectares. After the war the property was cut into 320-hectare lots for soldier settlement.

One of the property's many owners was Melbourne financier W.F. Hughes who bred racehorses there, including Hiraji who won the Melbourne Cup in 1947 with J. Purtell on board.

Borambola was further cut down in later years and now the McMullens have only 42 hectares.

The McMullens moved to Borambola with the idea of renovating the homestead and having a place with plenty of room for their grandchildren to visit from Sydney. Mr McMullen had been in business at Wagga Wagga for 45 years in menswear, travel and the development of residential land.

'Moving to a property was completely new to us,' Mr McMullen said. 'It was a whole new way of life.'

Mrs McMullen had misgivings about being that far out of town but when the property came up for auction, things 'just happened and we bought it. But it's worked well, it's peaceful here, we have lots of visitors and the space to look after them.'

The dominant architectural features of Borambola include two steep gables and bay windows on each side and a bullnosed verandah between, which is supported by paired timber columns. There are also wide verandahs at one side and at the back. The roof is corrugated iron.

THE MAIN BEDROOM.

Structurally, the painted face-brick homestead was sound when the McMullens bought it but needed lots of work. The McMullens almost froze the first winter there because of the high 4.3-metre ceilings, so installation of good heating became a priority. They used a geothermal system that takes the heat out of the ground in the winter and puts it back into the ground in the summer. The system has twelve pipes that descend 50 metres to where the temperature is a

THE DINING ROOM.

THE LOUNGE ROOM.

The kitchen has also had some modern facilities added, as Mrs McMullen believes that nowadays kitchens have to be functional. The workspace, which opens into a family room, retains its large fireplace and iron Aga stove. The Australian pine dresser holds a collection of Royal Doulton Norfolk scenes, and the cedar table was an old office desk.

Mrs McMullen has always had an interest in antiques and refurbishing but said Borambola was a big job, although she had some help with colours and fabrics from an interior designer.

Paintings by Norman Lindsay and Brett Whiteley hang on the walls along with works by local artists Joy Scherger and Greg Hansell. There is also a glass piece by Yass artist Peter Crisp.

There are two cellars underneath. Mr McMullen thinks one would have been for the kitchen to keep food cool. 'You can walk down into it but the other one has a trapdoor to go through,' he explained.

In the grounds, the original stables are still there but the only work done to them was applying a new coat of paint on the outside.

The National Trust has visited Borambola and given the renovations the thumbs up.

The garden still has trees planted by the early owners. A bunya pine stands on one side of the home and a large palm on the other. There is also a palm in the centre of an expanse of lawn surrounded by the original circular driveway at the front of the house. Roses form a border. Other trees include white cedars, elms, weeping cherries and crab apple.

Initially there was no intention of putting in a vineyard but the McMullens' sons Anthony and Tim had ideas about becoming involved in the wine industry. 'There was a paddock on the western side of the property where they wanted to grow some chardonnay and we sold the first vintage from there to friends,' Mr McMullen said.

'Then we decided to grow more so we put in another 2 hectares of chardonnay in 1995, 3.5 hectares of cabernet sauvignon in 1998 and 4 hectares of shiraz, and had our first vintage from that in 2001.'

The wine was originally made by Charles Sturt University but it ceased contract winemaking in 2002, so the McMullens went with a local firm whose chief winemaker was a lecturer in wine science at Charles Sturt. The wine is made to their specifications and two sections of a three-car garage have been converted into a cellar door.

constant 16 to 18 degrees Celsius, and water flows through them into two furnaces located in the roof. Heat is ducted into every room.

Two bathrooms were modernised and an atrium with glass roof built. The atrium was previously a courtyard and rooms were joined by a corridor. The new room, now a suntrap with adjustable louvres under the glass roof, functions well because it connects part of the house.

The hall is 25 metres long and running off it is a lounge room, dining room, sitting room, office, entrance hall and four bedrooms. The front door is original but has new white leadlights, which provide shimmering light.

The lounge room is spacious. The fireplace has its original wooden chimney piece and one of the room's features is a Victorian English mahogany wall clock and a William IV mahogany work table.

The dining room is filled with fine furniture, with the Regency mahogany dining table surrounded by eighteenth-century ladder-back chairs taking pride of place. A George III mahogany bookcase is filled with a collection of glass and china.

The main bedroom is papered with a sea of ribbons and roses. A cedar Victorian dressing table sits in the corner. The old fireplace has been replaced.

The main bathroom is believed to have been a mail sorting room when the homestead had the dual role of being the district post office. The two bathrooms in the house have been redone and now have a mixture of antique and modern fittings.

Boree Nyrang

Boree Nyrang's original homestead, owned by Robert and Emily Barton, was the setting for the marriage in 1863 of their daughter Rose Isabella Barton and Andrew Bogle Paterson. The son they had the following year, Andrew Barton (Banjo) Paterson, went on to write some of Australia's best-loved ballads, like *Waltzing Matilda*, *The Man From Snowy River* and *Clancy of the Overflow*.

The Bartons had a house on the creek but subdivided the property in 1865. John Smith of Gamboola, Molong, bought 17,000 acres (6885 hectares) of the original 66,560-acre (26,960-hectare) holding. Boree Nyrang was regarded at the time as one of the best sheep stations in the colony.

John Smith's eldest son controlled the property until 1904 when 6000 acres (2430 hectares) of Boree Nyrang were sold to Sir Norman Kater MLC, who built the present homestead.

Dr Kater, a prominent grazier and businessman, was also the honorary medical clinical assistant at Royal Prince Alfred Hospital from 1901 until 1902. He practised in College Street. In partnership with his father, Henry Edward Kater, he also owned Yanganbil and Egelabra stations in the Warren district in western New South Wales. Dr Kater, a member of the New South Wales Legislative Council from 1923 until 1955, was a foundation member of the Universal Service League in 1915, a director of Colonial Sugar Refining Company Limited from 1924 until 1949 and a director of Grazcos Co-operative Limited from 1919 until 1965. He was also involved in other companies, like the Globe Worsted Mills Pty Ltd, Liverpool and London and Globe Assurance Company Limited, Newcastle Wallsend Coal Company Pty Ltd and Peko-Wallsend Investment Ltd.

He was a councillor on the Graziers' Association from 1911 until 1965 and president from 1922 until 1925; and was a councillor on the Sheepbreeders' Association from 1927 until 1965, president from 1940 until 1944, and life governor in 1961. He was also a councillor on his local Boree Shire Council from 1915 until 1920.

Dr Kater sold Boree Nyrang in 1918 to George Rutherford of Bathurst, the son of James Rutherford who established the Cobb and Co stagecoach company in Australia. Dr Kater wanted to buy Eenaweena station but later bought Mexborough, which adjoined Egelabra.

In 1924, Dr Kater inherited Mount Broughton in the Southern Highlands from his father Henry Edward Kater. He extensively modified and expanded the house there in 1926, creating a baronial great hall in the centre of the house and adding a two-storey wing and several bedrooms upstairs. The house is now Peppers Manor House.

Dr Kater was knighted in 1929 for services to the pastoral industry. He died in August 1965 at Darlinghurst. He had two marriages. The first was to Jean Gaerloch Mackenzie in 1901 and they had two daughters and four sons. He married a second time to Mary Wade in 1938.

Boree Nyrang homestead was built for Dr Kater by four Italian craftsmen and is regarded as one of the finest examples of Australian architecture and construction. The Italian tradesmen initially built a workers' cottage, which later became the schoolhouse, and they lived there while they built Boree Nyrang.

The bluestone was quarried on the property and brought to the home site on drays. It was also split on site and there are still shards underneath the house.

The 36-room house is reflective of neo-colonial architecture of the late federation era. It has an area of 120 squares. There are six downstairs bedrooms, six upstairs rooms, six bathrooms and fourteen fireplaces. The living rooms comprise a large vestibule leading to a grand dining room and adjacent wine cellar.

When George Rutherford bought Boree Nyrang, which is an Aboriginal word meaning 'little meeting place', he used it as a freight stopover for his coaches. The stables and livery are still on the property.

Boree Nyrang stayed in the Rutherford family until the 1970s. Around 1972 Dr Lucas from Orange bought it. He

LEFT: BOREE NYRANG, BUILT FROM BLUESTONE BLOCKS.

BOTTOM LEFT: THE FRONT ENTRANCE.

BOTTOM RIGHT: THE HAYSHED.

only owned it for a short time but carried out a great deal of restoration work. Dr Lucas also subdivided some of the land and then sold in 1975 to a Mr Sullivan. He apparently was unable to maintain the house and in 1980 it was sold again to a Dr John Brain, an Anglican priest and psychologist. Dr Brain had ideas of turning it into a retreat but this didn't go ahead. He did, however, renew the guttering, water-collection pipes and tanks.

In 1996 Stephen Sykes and business partner Greg Urbanski bought the property from Dr Brain. By then the house hadn't been lived in for around seven years and need-ed a considerable amount of conservation work. The wall-paper was peeling and the ceilings were coming down. The new owners had a plan prepared by a heritage architect and set to work.

Stephen Sykes, whose daughters Philippa and Julia grew up in the house, said it was originally designed around the relationship between Dr Kater and the servants. The down-stairs servants, who lived upstairs in two rooms, had no access to the rest of the first floor. The downstairs servants had an exit from the back stairs to their living quarters. A door into the kitchen was put in about 1930 but before that it was just a servery. To get from the kitchen into the main part of the house required going out through one door and then back in through another because the downstairs ser-vants were never allowed into the main part of the house.

The kitchen has a built-in oven that nowadays would be called a wood-fired pizza oven. The kitchen also had a water heating system, which was considered advanced technology for that period.

Because Boree Nyrang was a working property, there are no ornate cornices and the original power was gas made from a coking shed at the back. The only lights were near the fireplaces but the Rutherfords installed a generator for 12-volt lighting. Electricity was connected in 1932.

Mr Sykes explained that Boree Nyrang also had a septic system, which comprised a bluestone tank about 100 metres from the house. He found it after almost falling in. It had been covered by old iron that had rusted away over time.

Boree Nyrang's living area is compact. To the left of the vestibule is the large lounge room and straight ahead is the grand dining room with adjacent wine cellar.

The first room on the right is the ladies parlour. When Mr Sykes pulled up the old carpet and polished the floors, he found thousands of sewing needles in the carpet.

Obviously that was where the women did their sewing. The next corridor led to the men's bathroom and cloakroom. It had been changed with temporary walls and had a garden hose to supply water to the shower. This was clearly when times were difficult for the different families. Modern plumbing has since been installed.

Off the hall is the library. The main bedroom is also off the hall to the right and it has a connecting door to the youngest child's room. There is a linen press on the left towards the southern wing where there is another child's room, nanny's room and a bottle-wash room.

Mr Sykes believes the house was designed around status. The important rooms were the lounge, drawing room, entry, dining room, main bedroom and parlour, and as children grew older they moved to the less important rooms. The house, despite its 36 rooms, was also only ever designed for two children. When Dr Kater's wife had twins, one of the other children had to move upstairs.

Upstairs were the servants' quarters, a dormitory room, two more bedrooms, a box room and the original bathroom. Back in the main part of the house beyond the kitchen were the service quarters, pantry, storage room, servants' dining room and large laundry with open fireplace and original copper.

All the timber is Australian redwood. The floors are pine from New Zealand. The roof is lined with tongue and groove

THE FRONT VERANDAH.

THE DINING ROOM.

A DETAIL OF ONE OF THE SHEDS.

cypress pine and corrugated iron was put on top of that. The bird proofing is original and still stops birds getting into the ceiling.

Ancillary buildings include the property's original coach-house, stables, shearing shed, schoolhouse, groom's cottage, milking bail and a machinery shed. The old clay tennis court has been rejuvenated with synthetic turf.

The shearing shed built in early 1900 still has the original six-stand fixtures, including a wool press, while the groom's cottage pre-dates the homestead. It has two bedrooms, a kitchen, living room, bathroom and closed verandah.

The present owners have planted a vineyard. The property had gone from 6000 acres (2430 hectares) to 148 acres (60 hectares) so intensive agriculture was the only option.

THE ENTRANCE HALL.

They put in 13 acres (5.25 hectares) of vines to produce a range of wines, including shiraz, cabernet sauvignon, ruby cabernet, sauvignon blanc, merlot, chardonnay, pinot noir and sangiovese. Wines produced from the vineyard are sold under the Barton Creek BC label.

The original 1.2-hectare homestead garden has an expansive lawn bordered by garden beds, deciduous and fruit trees, and pathways. Although retaining much of the original design, the garden has been restored in heritage style with the annual irises and jonquils supplemented with perennials like lavender and catmint. There is also a new rose garden.

Boree Nyrang is listed by the National Trust. Mr Sykes believes people can never really own a house like it. 'You just keep it in trust for future generations.'

A PEACEFUL BEDROOM CORNER.

Bunnamagoo

When the Paspaley pearling family bought the 1829 convict-built Bunnamagoo homestead on a 2040-hectare property at Rockley, near Bathurst, in 1992, it could have been described as little more than a pile of rocks under a roof. There were huge gaps in the old stone walls and the crude mortar that held everything together had been badly damaged by weather. But the Paspaleys wanted Bunnamagoo to continue as a working property — along with Thornthwaite at Scone, Kurrajong Park at Coolah and Eurunderee at Mudgee, which the family had also bought — and accepted that the homestead's restoration was a priority.

Bunnamagoo homestead was built by pardoned convict Thomas Pye, who somehow knew William Lawson, one of the three explorers who first crossed the Blue Mountains. Lawson saw the block and told Pye about it, and he, in turn, was able to get the land granted to him along with five convicts to work there. Pye came across the mountains and began building the house around 1821, finishing it in 1829.

It was a two-storey Georgian style with a roofed flagstone verandah running along the length of the front. It had a living area on the ground floor and three upstairs bedrooms.

THE CONVICT-BUILT
BUNNAMAGOO.

The kitchen was separate from the house but burned down in the early 1900s.

There was also an underground cellar with an outside entrance that is now used as a water tank but is also still being used to store wine. Access is from the inside of the house. Evidently the convicts were locked in the cellar at night and fed through an outside grille.

Pye's son William took over the property from his father and he was a reasonably successful farmer. But he enjoyed a drink or two and that was eventually his downfall.

In October 1863, after a daring raid on Bathurst two weeks earlier, notorious bushranger Ben Hall and gang members John Vane, Johnny Gilbert, Mick Burke and John O'Meally attacked the Dunn's Plains homestead, near Rockley, home of the assistant gold commissioner and magistrate Henry Keightley.

After a short gunfight, in which Burke was wounded and then shot himself in the head, Keightley surrendered and the bushrangers took him to a spot called Dog's Rocks, just east of Bunnamagoo. After arguing among themselves over his fate, Hall agreed not to harm Keightley provided they were paid a ransom of £500.

A VIEW TO THE VINEYARD.

Keightley's wife and a Dr Pechey, who had been staying at the homestead, went to Bathurst to get it. They returned the next day and the bushrangers kept their word, freed Keightley and left.

The story goes that, somewhere in the middle of all this, William Pye came across the bushrangers and they took a few shots at him. He apparently never recovered from the ordeal, began drinking heavily and lost Bunnamagoo in a card game to a Bathurst solicitor named McPhillamy. The family is still in business in Bathurst.

The Terry family, who were related to the McPhillamys, were probably the next owners. Bunnamagoo was then split into three because Mr Terry had two daughters and when they married he built them identical homes, one on the sub-divided section he called Laanecoorie and one on the section he called Kildrummie. The Paspaleys also bought Laanecoorie and incorporated it back into Bunnamagoo.

After the Terrys, Bunnamagoo had a string of owners and not all the gaps can be accurately filled, although the homestead was apparently vacant in the 1940s and 1950s and fell into disrepair.

The Paspaleys have an interest in historical homes and in rural Australia and bought Bunnamagoo in 1992, then owned by overseas investors who had employed an Australian company called Agricultural Investments to manage it for them. At the time, Peter Bracher looked after the Paspaley rural interests and he had no hesitation in going ahead with a major restoration.

The Paspaley Pearling Company is a family-owned enterprise that began in the remote north-west of Western Australia in the early 1930s. Nicholas Paspaley, born in Greece in 1914, migrated to Australia with his family in 1919. The family settled at Cossack, the ship's first port of call on the Indian Ocean coast, and was one of a handful of European families living there among the mainly Aboriginal and Asian population. Running water, electricity, shops and government services were non-existent.

Nicholas Paspaley began work at fourteen and at nineteen he had bought his own pearling lugger. It had no engines and air was pumped to the divers by hand pumps. When there was no wind for the sails, they rowed.

Growing over the years, the business has become the largest pearling company in Australia as well as venturing into other commercial pursuits. Employing more than 600 people, the company owns pearl farms on the north-west Australian coast between Broome and the Cobourg Peninsula, north of Darwin.

The farms produce Australian South Sea pearls, recognised as the best in the world, for markets in Japan, the US, Hong Kong and Europe. Paspaley also produces pearl-set jewellery which it sells through its retail outlets in Sydney, Darwin and Broome.

A fleet of modern ships and four sea-going aircraft support its pearling operations. It also has a subsidiary called Pearl Aviation, which operates Falcon and Cessna Citation jets, Beechcraft and Metroliners in a general aviation and medical retrieval business. Still family-operated, the business now has Nicholas Paspaley's son Nick as executive chairman.

Stuart Hughes, who had finished agricultural college before working as a jackeroo at Yass and a station hand at Bathurst, moved to Bunnamagoo to live in 1994 when Paspaley appointed him rural manager. His brief was simple: treat the property as if it were your own.

He and his wife Debbie lived through the total restoration of the 176-year-old homestead that was built from soapstone found on the property and roughly shaped by convicts. Besides putting up with living in two rooms — one a bedroom often cut off with builders' equipment — a makeshift laundry on the verandah, no kitchen for six months and dust everywhere, they had to cope with the birth of their daughter Emily. A son, Thomas, was also born at Bunnamagoo.

'But it was good to be on site because we could solve any problems the builders had by answering their questions straight away,' Stuart Hughes said.

The Paspaleys engaged Bathurst architect Henry Bialowas to look after the conservation side of the renovations at Bunnamagoo. Bialowas knew the brief would be a challenge. One of the stone walls in the original front section was leaning so badly it was in danger of collapsing.

THE DINING ROOM AND KITCHEN.

It was folded down and each stone was numbered by stonemasons and then put back up.

A chemical grout was pumped into the other walls through stainless steel tubes to stitch them back in place as well as sealing the inner render against the harsh weather conditions outside.

The inside walls and ceilings were replastered in the same free-form style as the original. The walls and corners are far from being straight and any attempt to rectify this would have destroyed the original.

A wing had been added in the 1970s to make the homestead T-shaped and it was unsympathetic to the original design. The Paspaleys decided to include the wing in the renovations to provide two extra bedrooms, bathroom and new kitchen. New doors, windows and timber joinery were put in and the walls were bag rendered and lime washed.

All the kitchen bench tops and bathroom vanities in the newer section are Italian marble. When the shipment arrived, it was taken to Orange to be cut. One of the employees was loading another job with a forklift and backed in too close to the marble, which was stacked against a wall. He saw it rocking before it fell to the ground and smashed, delaying the kitchen renovations. More marble

THE SITTING ROOM.

THE FRONT VERANDAH.

THE NEWEST ADDITION AT
THE BACK.

had to be found to complete the job.

Debbie Hughes noted that a lot of work had also been put into establishing new gardens. 'We brought in truckloads of topsoil and planted lawn. We had to move several pine trees and replaced them with elms.

'It's really a typical cottage garden with wisteria across the verandah, a weeping cherry at the front — which always flowers on the long weekend in October every year — lots of roses, lilac, lavender, honeysuckle box hedges, claret ash, Manchurian pears and lots of elms. But it's a challenge to grow anything because we get frosts down to −14.'

It's understandable that, after putting in so much work, the Hughes family would love Bunnamagoo, and, as Debbie Hughes explains, it's always been very dear to them.

'Stuart and I married when we were in our early twenties but I'm glad we did because we've spent our young energetic times at Bunnamagoo, moving here just after we were married. We first lived in a little cottage on the property but after three months we moved into the homestead.'

The homestead, among the first to be built west of the Blue Mountains, is now one of the state's finest historic homes and has won the Paspaley family acclaim. The National Trust awarded Bunnamagoo a heritage commendation and the restoration architect, Henry Bialowas, won an award for conservation architecture.

Wines now being produced there are also proving a winner. Stuart Hughes said they wanted to find ways to increase the cash flow because there was only a small margin in agriculture. 'We were sitting out on the front lawn with Paspaley director Peter Bracher, just thinking how we could increase things. We were having a glass of wine and some cheese and biscuits and I remember saying, "Why don't we do some of this?" pointing to the glass of wine.'

The pair had talked about growing flowers, sweet corn and cauliflowers before settling on the grapes, but wine grapes had never been grown in the frost-prone Rockley district. In fact, with frosts from March through to November, it was going to be a big challenge to get anything to grow.

'So we did some research, talked to some consultants and they came here and selected a site for us. We did some budgets and put a proposal to the Paspaley family and they decided to put in a trial block of 6 hectares.'

Mr Hughes, now the general manager of Paspaley Rural Properties, had run prime lambs, a few cattle and had grown irrigated lucerne on the property but knew almost nothing about viticulture.

They battled for several years with frosts and lost several vintages. After re-assessing everything they had done, it turned out the grapes on the side of a hill were probably in the wrong spot. They then had to find ways to protect the vineyard, so they looked at wind machines and smudge pots, which are now banned because of environmental laws, and finally installed a frost-protection spray system. The property had a river and an irrigation licence and they discovered they could protect the grapes down to about −7 degrees Celsius by spraying water on the vines at a certain temperature and stopping the frost damage.

Stuart Hughes said growing a grape vine was really no different to growing a rose. It was just a plant and he had to learn when to cut, water, fertilise and harvest it — and that's what people did in agriculture. Other than that, there was no rocket science in it, only hard work.

The perseverance paid off, and chardonnay, cabernet sauvignon and merlot wines under the Bunnamagoo label are now winning gold and bronze medals and selling well in 220 Sydney restaurants, as well as independent bottle shops.

Burrundulla

William Cox came to New South Wales in 1800 as officer-in-charge on the transport ship *Minerva*. He settled at Clarendon outside Sydney on the Hawkesbury River, became a successful farmer and later served as the Windsor magistrate.

In 1814 Governor Lachlan Macquarie appointed him to supervise the construction of a road over the Blue Mountains to the new settlement at Bathurst. Completing the job with a team of 30 convicts and eight soldiers in six months, he received as part payment a grant of land at Bathurst called Hereford.

His sons George and Henry were on the land at Mulgoa but, while looking after Hereford, they were encouraged by family friend Lieutenant William Lawson, who was commandant of the settlement at Bathurst, to have a look in the north at land along the Cudgegong River, near the present town of Mudgee.

James Blackman, a former principal overseer of government stock at Richmond and chief constable and pound-keeper at Bathurst, was the first to cross the Cudgegong River in 1821. Lawson had also been there and said it was

excellent grazing country, so George and Henry Cox headed off to see for themselves.

They became the first permanent European settlers on the Cudgegong River when they established the Menah Run, 3 kilometres north-west of present-day Mudgee, and it was here the first settlement developed with a police station and lock-up established in 1833.

The Coxes extended their holdings into the Gulgong area, near Mudgee, when they established the Guntawang cattle run in 1822, but continual conflicts with the local Aborigines resulted in them withdrawing. However, the Rouse brothers took cattle to the property and, in 1825, Richard Rouse was granted the station, upon which the village of Guntawang developed.

George and Henry Cox bought extensive tracts of land on the southern banks of the Cudgegong River, both upstream and downstream of the present site of Mudgee. In 1822 George Cox married Elizabeth Bell, daughter of Lieutenant Archibald Bell and Maria, née Kitchen, of Belmont, North Richmond. He returned to his Mulgoa property, Winbourne, and his Mudgee holdings were managed by overseers until 1845 when his eldest son, George Henry, turned 21 and was sent to take over.

George Henry looked after thousands of sheep taken there from Mulgoa and planted crops. He sold hay, made cheese and leased small sections of land to tenants. His busy life continued when, after marrying his cousin Henrietta, he was elected to the first New South Wales Legislative Assembly. He served four terms as mayor of Cudgegong and was active in various Mudgee organisations, including the Pastoral and Agricultural Society and Mechanics' Institute.

LEFT: BURRUNDULLA HOMESTEAD.

BOTTOM LEFT:
THE COURTYARD BELL.

BOTTOM RIGHT:
THE DINING ROOM.

BELOW: COLOURFULLY BOUND
OLD BOOKS IN THE LIBRARY.

One of several white marble fireplaces.

George had been living in a weatherboard cottage originally built by his father, but in 1864 he decided it was time to build a mansion house he called Burrundulla. The homestead is still occupied by George Henry Cox's descendants.

Jeremy Cox grew up on Burrundulla, now comprising 1700 acres (688 hectares) but went away to school and then to university where he studied agricultural economics followed by a diploma in finance. He worked in Sydney, mainly in investment management.

In 2002 he and his wife Petrina moved back to Burrundulla to get out of the city. She was a country girl, originally from the Armidale–Guyra district in northern New South Wales. Jeremy's father now lives on the coast but his two brothers still live on the property.

His father believed that maintaining a house like Burrundulla required lots of energy. As Jeremy explained, 'I don't think anyone was too keen to move into it at their age so we've moved in. We took on the task of trying to maintain the house and we're just taking a steady approach.

'We obviously can't do everything at once so it's a continual thing. We'll eventually get everything done and then it will be time to start again.'

It was George Henry Cox's son, Vincent Dowling Cox, who took over when George Henry died in 1901. George

Henry had left Burrundulla a few years earlier to return to Winbourne to live but went back to Mudgee after running into financial trouble. He leased the Winbourne vineyards and shut the house.

Vincent Dowling Cox was followed by his eldest son, also Vincent, but he was killed in the war at Alamein. 'That's how my grandfather Geoffrey Charles ended up with the property and he left it to his three sons. So it's now held by three arms of the family. I'm the seventh generation on the property and the sixth in the house because George didn't live here,' Jeremy Cox elaborated.

'The other three are my uncles. My father, his brothers, my brother and myself are small shareholders but how it transpires from here may be a different story. This is the first time it has ever been held by more than just one family member.'

Burrundulla homestead was designed by William Weaver from the firm Weaver and William Kemp and combines elements of Colonial–Georgian and Victorian style. Weaver had been an assistant to Colonial Architect Edmund Blacket before being appointed to the position himself in 1854. The job lasted only eighteen months before he resigned because the Colonial Secretary's Office refused to pay for extra work needed for a government building he had designed. Weaver said this amounted to a withdrawal of the confidence that had to be accorded to the head of the department. His designs had included a new Government Printing Office and a number of timber bridges in country areas.

Kemp had been articled to Blacket and later was appointed First Foreman of Works. He received significant recognition for his designs, particularly school buildings and technical colleges. Weaver and Kemp opened their own firm and had designed a new church at Mudgee which George Henry's father had helped found.

THE IMPOSING CENTRAL STAIRCASE.

Burrundulla was built by Henry Hudson. He was probably the same William Henry Hudson who arrived in Sydney from England via New Zealand in 1846, six years after the transportation of convicts to Australia ceased. He was a joiner, a craftsman in wood, and a vigorous and skilled worker in the classic Victorian style, making specialty timber items.

During the gold rush, Hudson prospered and in 1855 was able to set up a small shop in Botany Street, Redfern. By 1860, Hudson's Joinery was doing a roaring trade and many came to buy their furniture there.

His reputation attracted a large number of building contracts, including the magnificent woodwork in the Great Hall of the University of Sydney and the building of a railway bridge on the Liverpool–Campbelltown line. By then his three eldest sons had joined the business and by 1863 it was called Hudson and Sons.

In 1866, William Henry Hudson retired, and his sons bought machinery to turn their establishment into a steam joinery. Within ten years *The Sydney Mail* described the operation as 'perhaps the largest of its kind in the colonies'.

The company has had lots of ups and downs since then and a number of name changes but is still going. In May 2003 the company sold its merchandising branch network to focus on the manufacture of timber products and again changed its name, to Hudson Timber Products Limited.

William Weaver set down stringent specifications for Burrundulla, including the proviso that all bricks for the outside had to be carefully selected, of uniform colour, laid in mortar and finished with a neat ruled joint.

The specifications required all timber used in the building to be the 'best quality of the several kinds specified, sound, well seasoned, cut to the full dimensions ordered and free from veins, sap, knots, white ants or any other imperfections. The whole of the hardwood except the flooring boards and batons to be of ironbark or blue gum. The whole of the flooring boards are to be of stringy bark.'

The roof was originally split ironbark shingles but has since been replaced by corrugated iron. The shuttered sash windows on the ground floor were made with 'the best British plate glass' brought across the Blue Mountains by bullock wagons.

There are thirteen rooms in the house, and in the old servants' wings at the back there are another five, although they're not used for much now. Of the eighteen rooms, the five upstairs are all bedrooms except one, which was a walk-in robe. It has now been divided to make room for a bathroom. Jeremy Cox commented that moving from a one-bedroom apartment in Sydney to a house like Burrundulla was an entirely different lifestyle. The apartment would have fitted in the dining room and he and his wife found themselves shouting to each other from room to room and still getting no answer.

'But it didn't take us long to settle in and it's not a hard house to keep clean,' he said. 'We tend to use most of the rooms that we can. There's only one or two we don't use and we find it very functional. I don't think we could move back into something smaller.'

The dominating central section of the house is flanked on both sides by large single-storey rooms slightly set back with three-sided bays at each end. The dining room is on one side and has a circular ceiling. The 15-inch (38-centimetre) deep skirting boards and other woodwork, like that throughout the rest of the house, is mainly cedar. The 6-inch-wide (15-centimetre-wide) floorboards are made of ironbark and there is a black marble fireplace. Other fireplaces are made from white marble.

What is now the billiard room at the other end of the house was originally a bedroom and is almost a mirror of the dining room. Geoffrey Cox had a passion for recreational activities like billiards so he converted the bedroom into the billiard room. The floor could not be polished because the billiard table is dead level and would have been upset if it were moved, so Jeremy Cox decided to leave it be.

The drawing room, which has striped wallpaper and a pat-terned frieze, has family paintings on the walls. William Cox the road builder is there along with the unfortunate Charles Cox who was eaten by cannibals in the Fiji islands in 1813.

Jeremy Cox said his grandparents, and he assumed the other generations as well, lived downstairs in the summer because it was cool. When it became cold in the winter, the family then moved upstairs.

Furniture in the main entrance hall is original and includes two chairs with the family crest carved on the back. There's a painting of Burrundulla homestead and a district landscape done for George Cox by friend Conrad Martens.

The front door has leadlighting on each side. The archi-traves are cedar and two side tables are hand carved with grey marble tabletops

On the landing halfway up the staircase is a bust of Lord Byron. A stained-glass window with the Cox family crest —

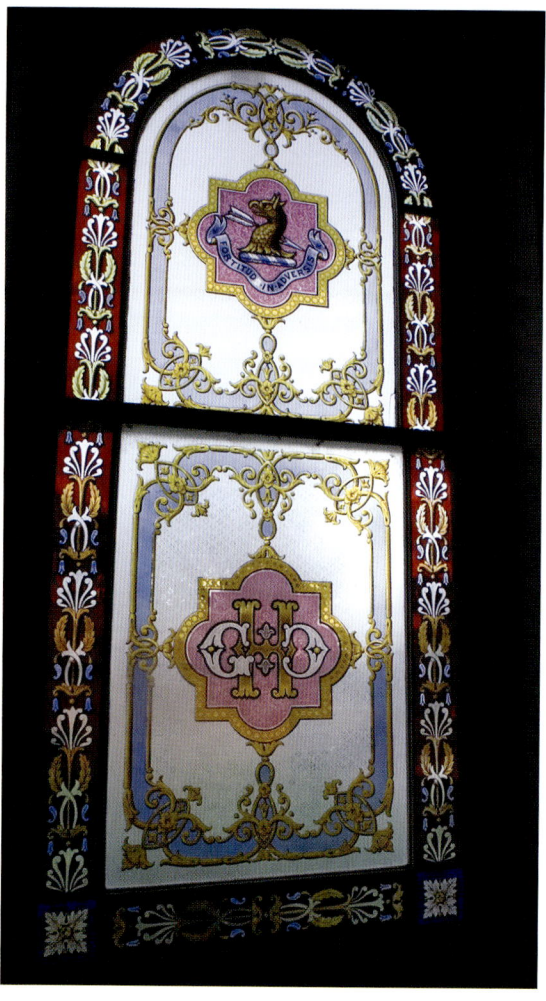

THE FAMILY CREST.

a griffin with an arrow through it to indicate 'Bravery and Diversity' — lights the staircase. On the bottom pane is George Henry Cox. The window had been pulled out for many years but was eventually restored.

The library is original, including the cedar bookcase and the colourfully bound old books. The collection includes 48 novels, pastoral and educational texts, dictionaries, a com-plete set of *Encyclopaedia Britannica*, every issue of *Punch* magazine dating from 1860 to 1892 and the *Illustrated London News*. There are also articles and photographs of war. Many of the books have been restored and show a strong per-sonal taste for discovery and exploration and natural history. Most of the books have George Henry's stamp on them.

When the ceiling collapsed in 2005, Jeremy Cox had the timber in the library restored. He said when builders were chipping away at the brickwork around the chimney, to replace it after the ceiling fell in, they found an old boot built into the brickwork.

People who were superstitious apparently used to leave artifacts or pieces of clothing to ward off the spirits, and

THE DINING ROOM'S WINE
CABINET.

they specifically put them in places like chimneys because that was where the spirits were supposed to come in.

Matching single-storey wings for a kitchen, servants' quarters and offices at the back of the house form a courtyard paved with rocks from the property. Underneath the courtyard is a well, which is still used. A pump takes the water to a tank in the roof.

A courtyard grapevine was planted around the same time that the house was built. It's a variety of table grape still quite common today.

A COSY CORNER.

The old gable-roof dairy is now a meat cool room. There is still an old butter churn there which was built with the house. Stables next door have fallen into disrepair and need a lot of attention.

Burrundulla now comprises about 1700 acres (688 hectares), 600 (243) on the river flats and 1100 (445) on higher ground. Of that, 165 acres (67 hectares) are devoted to grapes. One of Jeremy Cox's ambitions was to start their own wine label, which he has now done. He had an interest in wine because in his old job one of the sectors he had to analyse was beverages, and he subsequently learnt quite a bit about it and met many high-powered people in the wine industry.

'We knew quite a while beforehand we were going to make [wine] back here so I did a course through Adelaide University by correspondence in wine marketing and learnt a lot through that as well. We had the first vintage from our grapes made in 2003 under the Burrundulla label.'

George Henry also tried to grow grapes but was unsuccessful. Jeremy Cox thinks he probably planted them on the river flats. 'I have grapes now in the high country so I suppose back then it was very hard to irrigate up there. Now we've got the technology of being able to pump from the river to where the vineyard is because it's nowhere actually near the river itself.

'It's only early days but the grapes are going quite well. We're just waiting until we get the product right and then we'll get on to the distribution.

'This is all grazing land. At its peak we can run about 1400 head of cattle plus a couple thousand sheep to graze the land the cattle can't get to, but it's mainly cattle and vineyards nowadays and hopefully wine is something I've got to grow.'

Jeremy Cox has also put in infrastructure to agist racehorses. 'We'll spell them here on other people's behalf so we're starting to utilise the land a bit more efficiently,' he explained. 'We've really got to intensify [use of] the land. It's good land and you can never be zoned residential because it's in the flood plain.'

The house is on a slight rise in the Cudgegong Valley and overlooks lucerne paddocks. When there is lots of rain there are fairly extensive pools of water but it never actually floods.

Nobody knows for sure but, apparently, Burrundulla is derived from the Aboriginal word for the reeds that would have been found on the flood plains of the property.

THIS WAS THE HOME
-OF-
THE Rt HON. J. B. CHIFLEY
A NATIVE OF BATHURST
WHO WAS
PRIME MINISTER OF AUSTRALIA
FROM 1945 TO 1949.

10 Busby Street

Former prime minister Ben Chifley valued the country lifestyle of his home town of Bathurst in central western New South Wales higher than most other things. Chifley, who spent most of his youth living on his grandfather's farm, where he slept in a chaff-bag bed in a four-roomed wattle and daub shack with whitewashed walls and earth floor, went on to lead the country in the post-war years but never gave up his love for the town.

He was chairman of Bathurst District Hospital, a member of Abercrombie Shire Council and a director of the *National Advocate* newspaper. He was also a shrewd primer of parish pumps from Oberon to Orange.

Chifley and his wife Elizabeth (Lizzie) kept their modest semi-detached stone cottage at 10 Busby Street all their lives and never lost their Bathurst connections. The cottage, now a memorial, is the only remaining residence of a former Labor prime minister in New South Wales. It is listed on the state's Heritage Register.

Ben Chifley came from a strong Irish-Catholic background. His grandfather had left Tipperary after the Irish famine and migrated to New South Wales. When Ben Chifley was born at Bathurst in 1885, his father was working as a blacksmith and his grandfather had a small farm at Limekilns, just out of Bathurst.

When he was five years old, young Ben went to live on the farm to help his grandfather and aunt and attended the small local school. His grandfather died in 1899 when Ben was thirteen and he returned to his parents' home.

He went to a local Catholic school for a year before taking a job at a local store and then a tannery. His third job was as a shop boy at the Bathurst railway yards, just across the road from his parents' house.

Chifley became a fireman six years later, shovelling coal in locomotives by day, but at the same time keeping up his education at night classes. He was also an active member of the Federated Engine Drivers and Firemen's Association of Australasia and the Labor Party. In 1913 when he was 27, he became the youngest engine driver in the state. The following year Ben Chifley married Elizabeth McKenzie in the Presbyterian church in the Sydney suburb of Glebe. Neither family approved of the mixed-religion marriage, but

BEN CHIFLEY'S WORK ROOM.

Elizabeth's parents gave them the small cottage named Carnwath in Busby Street and they moved in.

Chifley, who had been at the centre of a prolonged six-week strike by engine drivers, coal miners and other workers, stood for Labor pre-selection for the New South Wales parliament in 1922 when he was 36. His platform was to right the wrongs that had been done to railwaymen at the end of the strike but he was unsuccessful when the state Labor executive stepped in and selected the candidates.

He stood for pre-selection for the 1924 state election but was unsuccessful. In 1925 he won pre-selection for the federal seat of Macquarie, which had been held by Labor, but failed to be elected.

Chifley again stood for the Macquarie seat in 1928 and this time was successful. Labor didn't win government but Chifley, a keen centralist, made his views known on making it easier to change the Constitution and a proposal to abolish the states.

In 1929 dissension in the Nationalist Party forced the then prime minister Stanley Bruce to call another federal election. Voters swept Labor into office under James Scullin, and Chifley was returned with a massive majority in Macquarie.

But the Scullin government had its share of problems and began to fall apart because of external economic pressures and internal bickering. Several government members set up their own party factions, and in Scullin's reshuffle of portfolios, Chifley became Minister for Defence.

The Scullin government was defeated in the December 1931 election. Chifley also lost his seat in Macquarie. The same year New South Wales Labor leader Jack Lang hatched a plan to have Chifley expelled from the Australian Federated Union of Locomotive Enginemen and was successful.

Without a seat in parliament, without union membership and without a job, Chifley had to look for new means of income. His earnings from the *National Advocate* newspaper were not a lot but they were supplemented by an inheritance his wife received on her father's death in 1931.

This inheritance enabled the Chifleys to make some improvements to their Busby Street house. The kitchen was joined to the house and gas heating installed in the dining room. The bathroom and toilet remained outside but a chip bathwater heater was replaced with a gas heater. With these modest comforts, Elizabeth's widowed mother and Ben Chifley and his wife lived a frugal existence in the house but, as Ben managed the McKenzie estate, they were comfortable.

Chifley attempted unsuccessfully to regain his seat at the 1934 federal election and in 1937 failed to gain party preselection. On the local level, Chifley was elected to Abercrombie Shire Council and became president in 1937.

In 1935, R.G. Casey, treasurer in the Lyons government, appointed Chifley to the Royal Commission into the banking

THE DINING ROOM.

system. When war was declared in September 1939, Robert Menzies' government acknowledged Chifley's economic expertise by appointing him to the Capital Issues Advisory Board. Then in July 1940 he was made director of labour supply and regulation in the Department of Munitions.

Menzies went overseas for four months rallying the troops, but when he returned, colleagues turned on him and he was forced to resign. Arthur Fadden, who had been acting prime minister, took over the job. But it was a short reign and in elections in 1941 Labor leader John Curtin became the third prime minister of the fifteenth parliament.

Chifley stood again for the seat of Macquarie. Illness hampered his campaigning but he was voted back, elected by Caucus to the Cabinet and then appointed treasurer by Prime Minister Curtin.

Late in 1942, he took on an additional role as Minister for Postwar Reconstruction and set the foundations for a new social order. The added portfolio made Chifley the most powerful minister after Curtin.

The strong political partnership between Curtin and Chifley helped Labor win a big majority in the federal election in August 1943. The government had gained support from voters to implement the nation-building measures put up by Chifley for a smooth transition to a progressive peacetime economy.

While staying at the Hotel Kurrajong in Canberra through the week, Chifley usually phoned his Bathurst home regularly to talk with his wife. Every second weekend, he would drive from Canberra to Bathurst, where he met constituents and kept up to date with the happenings at the *National Advocate* newspaper.

Curtin's health deteriorated, and in May 1945 it was Chifley who announced the end of the war in Europe. When Curtin died in July 1945 the new governor-general, the Duke of Gloucester swore in Deputy Prime Minister Frank Forde as interim prime minister. But it was Chifley who comfortably won the Caucus election for a new party leader the following week, becoming the sixteenth prime minister.

Chifley inherited economic problems and was forced to extend wartime austerity measures, including petrol rationing, which cost him dearly. He tried to nationalise the banks, provoking numerous protests. Menzies, who by now had formed the Liberal party, campaigned in the 1949 election on the slogan 'Tip out the socialists and fill up the bowsers'. The campaign worked and Menzies was swept into office.

Chifley's main tactical error was his plan to nationalise the banks. He also upset militant unionists by bringing in the army to work in New South Wales' coalfields when miners went on strike.

During his career he chalked up a number of major achievements. His government set up shipping, aluminium and atomic energy industries, began the Snowy Mountains hydro-electric scheme and took over telecommunications. Chifley was also a strong supporter of the birth of Australia's car, the Holden.

When Chifley became prime minister, his wife Elizabeth remained at their Bathurst home with her sick mother. Her first trip to Canberra as the prime minister's wife was in March 1946 when she stayed at the Lodge for a month and

THE MODEST KITCHEN.

attended functions associated with the opening of the parliamentary session.

When Chifley went to the conference of Commonwealth prime ministers in London in May, she returned home to Busby Street in Bathurst. Apart from a visit to New Zealand, she seldom travelled with him. She was a woman of gentle nature and loyalty and concealed her deeper feelings by self-control.

After Chifley lost office in 1949, he remained leader of the opposition and continued to spend much of his time in Canberra. When he died there in June 1951, Elizabeth Chifley fulfilled the final public demands on her, leading mourners at his big state funeral in Bathurst.

Elizabeth Chifley died at 10 Busby Street, her home for nearly 50 years, in September 1962. Much of her estate went to her Presbyterian church and a kindergarten was established from the bequest.

The late Victorian cottage was bought by Bathurst City Council in 1972 after a local campaign to save it. Proposals in the mid-1990s to relocate the house again prompted widespread community concern.

Today it is a house museum and visitors come from everywhere to look at the frugal nature of the Chifleys' lifestyle. During his lifetime, Chifley used it to develop an empathy with people across the nation who had experienced similar circumstances and to project an image of Ben Chifley as 'a plain man'.

Chifley in his policy speech in 1949 said it was the duty of the community to see that less fortunate people were protected and not left without hope. It was the beacon, the light on the hill, to which efforts should always be directed.

THE DINING ROOM MANTELPIECE.

Camden Park House

It was a bleak winter's day when the tiny, three-masted *Scarborough* battled her way through Sydney Heads and sailed slowly up Port Jackson. Rain squalls hid most of the shore's unfamiliar landscape of sheltered inlets, sandstone cliffs and grey-green eucalypt trees, a unique feature of the new penal colony of New South Wales.

The perilous voyage across the world had taken the hired merchant ship 228 days. Often for weeks on end she was pounded by heavy seas and howling winds or stuck solid in the doldrums. Supplies of fresh food, water and medicine were scarce and an alcoholic doctor had been of little use to relieve the suffering of those on board.

Of the original complement of 253 convicts jammed into the dingy holds of the 30-metre *Scarborough* at Portsmouth, England, only 180 had survived when First Fleet veteran Captain John Marshall dropped anchor in Sydney Cove on 28 June 1790. His free-settler passengers included members of the newly formed New South Wales Corps, who were hurriedly commissioned by the British army to relieve the detachment of marines sent to the colony in 1788 with Captain Arthur Phillip.

Among the corps members was a young, ambitious lieutenant of Scottish ancestry named John Macarthur. He had gambled his future on rapid promotion and ownership of land in the new settlement, which he believed would bring him much-wanted independence and security. Although only 21, he had studied law and farming practices and made up his mind to go to New South Wales after hearing the then exaggerated reports about land grants, the wonderful climate and the excellent conditions for growing crops, fruit and vegetables.

His attractive wife, Elizabeth Veale, was also keen for independence. She had been brought up in the sheltered environment of a vicarage in the Devon village of Bridgerule after her farming father died when she was six. Elizabeth, who had an eight-month-old son, Edward, shared her husband's enthusiasm for their new venture.

The Macarthurs spent their first winter in the colony in a cramped wattle and daub hut and, like everyone else, were restricted to the same government store rations of a few pounds of flour, some rice and chunks of old, salted meat.

THE DINING ROOM ALCOVE.

Times were tough. Most of the sheep brought out by the First Fleet had died, and two bulls and four cows had wandered away and become lost in the bush. Weevils destroyed much of the corn sent from England and small patches of vegetables were battling to survive in the unfertilised rocky ground. Governor Arthur Phillip, realising the serious shortage of food could see everyone starve, wrote to

LEFT: THE GEORGIAN FAÇADE OF CAMDEN PARK HOUSE.

BOTTOM LEFT: THE WINE CELLAR.

BOTTOM RIGHT: ONE OF SEVERAL OUTBUILDINGS.

England saying that if good settlers were sent out and the convicts divided between them to work fertile land on the banks of the Hawkesbury River, the settlement could eventually support itself. Otherwise he couldn't see it surviving.

The governor had already granted enterprising convict James Ruse an acre (0.4 hectares) of land near Parramatta, then called Rose Hill, to see what he could grow. He was later given another grant of 29 acres (11.7 hectares) because of his hard work.

Ruse cleared and hoed part of the land and became the first wheat and maize farmer in the colony. Because of his success, Governor Phillip was authorised to grant bigger, 100-acre (40-hectare) blocks, to non-commissioned officers so that more land could be cleared and cultivated. They were allowed to employ convicts to develop their holdings.

When Major Francis Grose took over in 1792 as lieutenant governor, after Phillip left to retire in England, he wasted no time in changing the role of the New South Wales Corps to give them effective control over the laws of the land. At the same time he promoted John Macarthur to a company commander and corps paymaster, which included a healthy pay rise and put him in charge of substantial government funds.

Major Grose also appointed Macarthur the Inspector of Public Works, a new administrative position with almost

unlimited powers over the colony's day to day affairs, as well as control of all government stores and convict labour. Another Grose initiative was to encourage corps officers to buy all the goods brought in by ship and re-sell them for a profit.

KITCHEN TEAPOTS.

John Macarthur was at last going places and more good news was on the way. In February 1793, Major Grose granted him 100 acres (40 hectares) of prime land at Parramatta, near the Ruse experimental farm and bounded on three sides by running water.

The Macarthurs, now with a new daughter they named Elizabeth, hired ticket-of-leave tradesmen to build the first stone farmhouse in the colony and moved there in November 1793. John Macarthur called the holding Elizabeth Farm after his wife.

In a letter to her mother, Elizabeth Macarthur wrote, 'It is an excellent brick building 68 feet [20.5 metres] in length, and 18 feet [5.5 metres] wide. The house has no upper storey but consists of four rooms on the ground floor, a large hall, closets, cellar and adjoining is a kitchen, with servants' apartments, and other necessary offices.' The main roof structure of this cottage still survives within the present

THE ORIGINAL KITCHEN.

roof of Elizabeth Farm house and it shows how thoroughly Macarthur's ticket-of-leave tradesmen did their job. Extensions were continually made, including more rooms, verandahs, wide openings and French doors. From being a late-eighteenth-century English cottage, it developed into the distinctive form of the colonial homestead and then to the status of a family mansion.

Elizabeth Farm has had a string of owners since it was sold by the Macarthur family in 1881 for £50,000 and is now maintained by the Historic Houses Trust of New South Wales.

Everything went smoothly for the Macarthurs for a few years. They received more land grants to add to Elizabeth

Farm, baby John was born, and Elizabeth Macarthur established a small thriving orchard and vegetable and flower gardens. John Macarthur, in a letter to his brother James, said he had sold £400 worth of produce in less than a year and had 1800 bushels of corn in his granaries. There were 20 acres (8 hectares) of fine wheat growing and 80 acres (32 hectares) prepared for crops of Indian corn and potatoes.

At the time, his stock comprised a horse, two mares, two cows, 130 goats, more than 100 hogs and an abundance of poultry. He made no mention in the letter of sheep, but nine years later noted that his flock had been raised from 30 Bengal Indian sheep and a coarse-wool Irish ram he bought from ships that called at Port Jackson in 1793. To that he had added eight or ten Spanish sheep.

Daughter Mary was born in 1795, and by the turn of the century after the birth of another son, James, who would become a competent farmer and explorer, John Macarthur owned 1610 acres (652 hectares) of land, most of which he had bought from other settlers. He ran 600 sheep and his herd of 100 cattle was the biggest in the colony.

But later that same year he decided to sell up and return to England. He offered the government his farm and livestock for £4000. New governor, Philip Gidley King, sent a recommendation to the colonial secretary that the offer be accepted, but before the reply came back telling King to buy only the English cattle and Spanish sheep, Macarthur found himself in trouble for wounding his commanding officer, Colonel Paterson, in a duel.

He was sent to England to face a court martial. It was November 1801, and only months earlier another son, William, had been born. Macarthur had also become the colony's biggest sheep farmer after he bought out Major Joseph Foveaux, who ran 1250 sheep on 1700 acres (688 hectares) at Toongabbie.

John Macarthur, who took daughter Elizabeth and son John with him on the ship to England to join their brother Edward at school, also packed samples of his best merino wool so he could promote its quality. Once in England, he used all his skills of diplomacy to avoid standing trial, and instead turned his trip into a major victory by convincing the Privy Council and influential garment manufacturers the colony could become a major wool exporter.

His fibres equalled the best from Spain in quality and softness, and price estimates put them around six shillings a pound. To cap things off, he received a grant of 5000 acres

(2025 hectares) of his own choosing and was allowed to resign from the army so he could pursue his fine wool development.

Elizabeth Macarthur meanwhile had run the Parramatta farm and supervised the breeding of the merinos, sharing her husband's view that wool was by far the best option for the future economic success of the colony. John Macarthur returned to Sydney in 1805 in his own ship, the *Argo*, and brought with him six rams and a ewe he had carefully selected and bought at a sale of some of King George III's merino flock.

Macarthur had convinced the secretary of state for the colonies, Lord Camden, that the land known as the Cow Pastures — where more than 40 cattle had bred from the four cows and two bulls that wandered away in 1788 — was the best available for his new wool industry. Although Governor King had wanted it left undisturbed, he was forced to go along with the higher authority in England. The grant was signed in January 1806, and Macarthur was now

fully committed to his dream. With the help of 34 convicts, he built rough shelters and transferred his stock.

A small slab hut with a gabled bark roof and a chimney on one side was the first house on the grant. A settlement grew up around the Cow Pastures and John Macarthur named it Camden because of the help given him by the secretary of state, Lord Camden. He called his own holding Camden Park.

But despite his important new project to establish a profitable wool industry, it wasn't long before John Macarthur was again in trouble with the colony's administration. Governor William Bligh, the infamous captain of the *Bounty*, had replaced King and he wasted no time launching a campaign to break up the rum trade and the lucrative commercial monopoly John Macarthur and officers of the corps were involved in.

Governor Bligh, who had no interest in the future of wool, wanted to take back the Cow Pastures and other land grants made to free settlers, and generally caused unrest in the

THE LIBRARY HAS MORE THAN 2000 BOOKS.

colony. The corps commander, Major George Johnston, was eventually persuaded by his senior officers and John Macarthur that Bligh should be removed from office.

Major Johnston marched on Government House on 26 January 1808, put Bligh under house arrest and assumed office as lieutenant governor. He appointed John Macarthur to the new position of secretary to the colony.

Life went on much as before while Major Johnston was in charge. However, John Macarthur knew there would be a day of reckoning and when Major Johnston was summoned to appear before a court martial back in England for overthrowing Bligh, he went with him. He wanted to support Johnston's actions and answer critics of the uprising, for which he was being blamed. They left Sydney in March, after the birth of another daughter, Emiline Emily.

Although John Macarthur wasn't on trial, he bore the brunt of the prosecution's case, which brought up all the disagreements and rows he had ever had with previous administrations of the colony. The court found Major Johnston guilty of mutiny against Bligh and dismissed him from service but allowed him to return to the colony to work his farm.

John Macarthur had to remain in England in exile because of an order in New South Wales that he be brought to trial for his part in the rebellion. Back in Camden, Elizabeth Macarthur was capably running their farm, and development of the colony was going ahead in leaps and bounds after Blaxland, Wentworth and Lawson had found a way across the Blue Mountains, which opened up vast new fertile plains.

John Macarthur and his sons James and William returned to Sydney in 1817 and brought with them vine cuttings, olive trees and farm equipment they had collected in Europe. He was allowed back on the undertaking he would have nothing to do with the affairs of the colony. The year he returned Elizabeth Macarthur had produced 6000 pounds (2725 kilograms) of high quality fine wool for export to England, where son John acted as the family's agent. James and William worked hard on the farm and carried on their mother's lead in the introduction of new ideas.

Their wool in 1821 brought record prices of up to 10 shillings a pound and was described as being superior to the best Saxon fleece, winning two gold medals from the Society of Arts. The Macarthurs planted the first vineyard with their imported cuttings and more than 600 fruit trees were

THE COALBROOKDALE PORCELAIN BOUGHT IN 1838.

thriving in the orchard. In addition, a dairy employed fourteen convict maids.

John Macarthur was appointed one of three non-official members of the Legislative Council in 1825 but he was suffering from long spells of depression and some of his actions were causing concern to his family. He died on 11 April 1834, in the small Belgenny Farm cottage where he lived on Camden Park.

Belgenny Farm is Australia's most important collection of rural buildings. The main buildings are grouped around a large courtyard which has as a central feature a plane tree and historic bell.

Belgenny Cottage, on the eastern side of the courtyard, was the Macarthurs' home and was built in several stages, the first around 1820. The centre section is brick-nog, a construction technique used in the first half of the nineteenth century, and is believed to be the oldest part. The back is a

Hudson kit home and was added in about 1920. William Hawkey, the farm manager, lived there.

It's generally thought the simple cottage was designed by architect Henry Kitchen, but researchers now believe that's unlikely because it bears no resemblance to his other work. They say its position near the courtyard and farm buildings is not in keeping with a main farmhouse and instead points to the likelihood it was the original kitchen block that served the farmhouse.

Construction of the buildings is generally of stud frame with weatherboard cladding and a verandah part of the way around. The front cottage has been in constant use for years and is in remarkably good condition.

For several years before his death John Macarthur planned and supervised the construction of the family's new mansion, later to be known as Camden Park House. Designed by colonial architect John Verge, it was a far cry from the wattle and daub hut the Macarthurs first lived in when they arrived in the colony but it never became their home. John Macarthur died before it was finished and Elizabeth decided to stay at Elizabeth Farm at Parramatta. The garden was begun in the 1820s and was well established before the house was completed in 1835.

Camden Park was then occupied by sons James and William. John was a barrister in London and Edward was in the army travelling the world.

William was a great horticulturist and was later knighted for his work. In 1838 he was the founding president of the Australian Floral and Horticultural Society, which in the 1870s became the Royal Agricultural Society.

James married Emily Stone in London in 1838 and they were the first permanent residents of Camden Park House.

In a letter to her aunt in England, Emily wrote, 'Even in England it would be deemed a very comfortable residence. Here there are few as good. The sitting rooms are of a good size, lofty and airy; the bedrooms, of which there are seven upstairs and one on the ground floor, are scarcely spacious enough; the walls are yet uncoloured, owing to the want of a painter, who, being a convict, was sentenced to punishment for a misbehaviour of some kind. He is now returned and we shall shortly have the discomfort of the smell of paint all over the house …'

James and William showed great enterprise running Camden Park. They imported expert workers to help them grow and market their wool, and assist them with improving their other agricultural enterprises. Among these were shepherds from Scotland, vinedressers from Germany and dairymen from Dorset.

They tried to breed silkworms and make olive oil, and they established Australia's biggest plant and tree nursery, which produced the best available collection of orchids and camellias in the country. William also put together a complete range of Australian timbers, which he catalogued in wall panels at the house.

The orchard was thriving. So too were the vineyards and the wine-making business. They exported the first Australian brandy in 1832. The brothers introduced silage and brought out three iron ploughs and a McCormick reaper.

James and Emily had a daughter Elizabeth, named after her grandmother. Elizabeth married Arthur Onslow in 1867

FAMILY PORTRAITS.

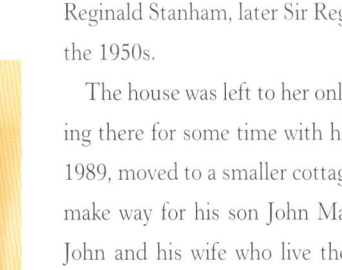

THE MARULAN MARBLE FIREPLACE IN THE DINING ROOM.

and had eight or nine children, leading to extra rooms being built upstairs.

William lived at Camden Park until his death in 1882.

Elizabeth Macarthur Onslow's son James lived there next, followed by his daughter, Helen, who in 1919 married Reginald Stanham, later Sir Reginald. They lived there until the 1950s.

The house was left to her only son Quentin who, after living there for some time with his wife Antonia, who died in 1989, moved to a smaller cottage on the property in 1990 to make way for his son John Macarthur Stanham. And it is John and his wife who live there now, together with their three children, William, Victoria and George.

Camden Park House is Australia's oldest private residence still occupied by the descendants of its founders. It and 1000 acres (400 hectares) of the surrounding land are still owned by the family.

John grew up in the house. After graduating from Sydney University with an economics degree and then earning a Masters in business administration, he worked in Sydney but is now a business consultant several days a week. The rest of the time he works on Camden Park, co-ordinating a dairy and chicken farm with his managers.

His wife Edwina, née Davidson, grew up west of Young in southern New South Wales and went to the small Stockinbingal Public School and then Frensham at Mittagong. Edwina, like her husband, also went to Sydney University where she completed a BA in languages. She travelled overseas and worked for a time in France. On her return she studied further in art at Sydney Technical College in screen prints and paintings. Now Edwina says she has a full-time job maintaining Camden Park.

Edwina Macarthur Stanham believes that while colonial architect John Verge designed the house, John Macarthur had some input because the family had found an old architectural plan that shows some changes.

The house is sandstock brick, stucco-covered, and built in the Palladian style of a central two-storeyed block flanked

by symmetrical pavilions. It is a particularly fine example of Georgian architecture.

It has sandstone columns on the eastern verandah and western portico. The window mouldings, porticos, parapets and the single-piece columns were made from local Hawkesbury sandstone, with the labour coming from convicts assigned to the Macarthurs.

Camden Park contains nearly 90 rooms; this includes the old servants' accommodation attached to the house in two wings. The second storey was added to the north-west wing in the 1890s for Elizabeth Macarthur Onslow's family. The floors throughout the house are all ironbark and the joinery and fittings are Australian cedar. The fireplaces are original with all the marble coming from Marulan, near Goulburn.

There is a large entrance foyer with stone floor and black marble inlays. The marble-topped cedar side tables and the hall chairs were made in Australia probably in the 1800s when the house was first furnished. The house still contains a lot of the original furniture.

To the left of the foyer is the 'wood passage', which features the display of wood samples put together by William Macarthur. He took a duplicate collection to the Paris International Exhibition in 1855 and also had three tables made to take; one is still in the house and the other two are in Government House in Sydney.

At the end of the wood passage is a cabinet with a Coalbrookdale porcelain service bought by James in 1838 from John Mortlock, 'China-man to Their Majesties Royal

Family', when he went to London to marry Emily Stone. It carries the Macarthur family crest, *Fide et Opera*, which means 'by faith and work'.

The dining room is notable for its unusual columned alcove, which provides structural support for the first floor. The room, which contains a collection of family portraits, is connected to the entrance hall by the 'book passage', where Verge put in a clerestory window to let in natural light, an architectural trick used by his English contemporary Sir John Soane.

From the book passage, the drawing room is off to the left. Here, a collection of watercolours by Conrad Martens is on display. He was a regular visitor to the house after his arrival in Australia in 1835.

The library has a wonderful collection of books, some going back to the 1600s, that reflects the family interests. It includes classical literature, biographies, scientific and agricultural texts, early Australian publications, and leather-bound copies of *Punch* and the *London Illustrated News*. The built-in cedar bookcases were originally at half-height but were extended over the years as the number of books grew. The library has an original argon lamp that ran on whale oil. Above the fireplace is the only portrait of John Macarthur in the house.

The private sitting room has an alabaster light shade that dates from around 1900 and marks the introduction of electricity. Argon lamps had been used in the entrance hall, dining room and library.

Rooms surrounding the courtyard were originally servants' quarters, a kitchen, laundry and an overnight stable. The housekeeper now occupies part of the area.

At the northern end of the courtyard is the tile room, which provided access to the cellar under the main house block for the people who brought in barrels of wine for bottling. Bays of original wine bottles are still there but the Macarthurs, who were pioneers in wine-making, ripped out their vines in 1872 after they were destroyed by phylloxera. They were never replanted. William had traded vine cuttings which were sent to the Barossa Valley to help establish vineyards there.

The four main living rooms, all in the front of the house, look out onto the garden through French windows. Plantings in the huge garden began in 1817, long before the house was built. James and William Macarthur brought back cuttings, seeds and vines collected on their trip to England and Europe with their father. William traded seeds all over the world and planted specimens in the garden while others from Camden Park were taken to the Botanic Gardens in Sydney.

It is still the largest intact nineteenth-century garden in New South Wales and demonstrates the informal picturesque style favoured at the time, despite having been overlaid by a later more formal gardenesque style.

William Macarthur introduced *Camellia japonica anenomiflora*, which is now the oldest surviving camellia in Australia. It continues to flourish in parts of the garden but some species have reached full maturity.

Current owner Edwina Macarthur Stanham said most of the garden maintenance was still mainly done by the family. 'The garden is old and parklands style with sweeping lawns

and established trees, many of them a rare species. Some of the trees include picconia from the Canary islands, Greek strawberry trees, old bunya pines and, of course, the Camden Park camellia, thought to be the oldest surviving in Australia being planted in 1834.

'We also have a bauhinia planted, they think, by explorer Ludwig Leichhardt on one of his visits here. We have the remains of the old hothouses in the garden, which had hot air pumped through them by donkey boilers.'

Croquet lawns are still used by Camden Park Croquet Club, and a cricket ground is used all summer on Saturdays by Camden Cricket Club and on Sundays by IZingari Cricket Club.

IZingari, Romany for 'the Wanderers', was formed in the 1850s at Cambridge University in England to play at other grounds all over the country. The Macarthur Onslows built the ground at Camden Park and nearly every English touring side played there.

Top Australian players, like Bob Simpson, Alan Davidson, Kerry O'Keefe, Doug Walters, Ian Craig and Jim Bourke have also played there, as well as legendary English captain W.G. Grace. In the early 1930s the ground was the star attraction in a number of Cinesound movies made by Ken G. Hall. Overseas teams still play at Camden Park.

Edwina Macarthur Stanham commented that, because the house had been in the family since 1835, every drawer pulled out resulted in a discovery. Lots of the original family papers have been donated to the Mitchell Library in Sydney. Two historians visit regularly and go through household items, often finding missing pieces that have come off something and putting them together. They found John Macarthur's fob watch in a box and an old map of the house.

More recently, Camden Park House became a popular location for film and fashion shoots for magazines. It was first used back in 1978 for the film *My Brilliant Career*, and other films have been made there since. However, it is still a working farm, producing 200,000 meat chickens, milking more than 200 cows a day and producing 2 million litres of milk a year.

'It's wonderful living in the house,' Edwina said. 'It's also a great privilege to live here. We love the house. It takes a lot of time to look after but we are lucky to have such a beautiful spot. It's a busy family house. We are very happy here.'

DAIRY COWS GRAZE THE SURROUNDING LAND.

Cliefden

LEFT: CLIEFDEN HOMESTEAD SEEN FROM THE SIDE.

BOTTOM LEFT: THE STABLES' ENTRANCE.

BOTTOM RIGHT: THE FRONT VERANDAH.

On 26 September 1863, four bushrangers, disguised in stolen police uniforms, bailed up Cliefden station on Limestone Creek, about 32 kilometres from the township of Canowindra. Ben Hall, Johnny Gilbert, John O'Meally and John Vane took owner William Montagu Rothery by surprise and tied him to a chair. Then they searched the house for loot but missed 500 gold sovereigns that had been hidden in a gumboot in the nursery. They also burnt down the hay shed.

The bushrangers rounded up Mr Rothery's horses and spent some time looking them over, finally choosing the best to take with them. They then ordered the cook to serve up a meal. After lunch the bushrangers helped themselves to Mr Rothery's finest wines from the cellar before they left for the nearby town of Canowindra. There they released the stolen horses, which found their way back to Cliefden.

Thomas Icely from Coombing had brought his two brothers-in-law, William Montagu Rothery and Frederick Rothery, to the colony in 1831 to be his neighbours on Cliefden. Icely's sister married the other large landholder in the district, William Lawson jnr, and his daughter Susannah Emily in 1855 married the Commander of the Fleet in the Australian Naval Station, Captain John Henn-Gennys, RN.

Icely was by far the biggest landowner in the district (*see* Coombing Park) and had up to 70 convicts working his land. More people lived on Coombing and Cliefden than in the nearby administrative town of Carcoar. Records show their occupations as labourers, groomsmen, gardeners, carpenters, servants, maids, overseers, brickmakers, coachmen, boundary riders and shepherds. Icely and the Rotherys registered their status as 'gentlemen'.

William Montagu Rothery was educated in France and England, becoming a barrister. He took up his 2960 acres (1200 hectares) but, by combining it with his brother's grant and buying more land, he increased his holding to around 24,700 acres (10,000 hectares). Frederick initially returned to England but came back during the gold rush.

William Rothery and his wife, Fanny Oceana Rothery, raised fine merino sheep and bloodstock horses and had a well-stocked store on the property from which they sold goods to other settlers. But, unlike other settlers, they had

THE OLD WOOL PRESS.

only one convict on Cliefden and he was the butler. All the other farm hands and servants came out from England and Scotland.

At one stage, 42 shepherds worked on the property. In a drought in the 1840s, William Rothery sent some of the shepherds in bullock teams over the mountains to the Nepean River to bring back couch grass to feed his bloodstock horses. He had a contract to supply the Indian Army with remounts.

A leading Anglican, William Rothery helped to build St Paul's Anglican Church at Carcoar in 1845. It was the second Anglican church west of the mountains and was designed by Edmund Blacket, who became one of the greatest nineteenth-century church builders. The church was unique in that it was built of brick. The Bishop of Australia, William Broughton, laid the foundation stone.

William Rothery's youngest son, Henry Alfred, together with the help of the other sons and daughters ran Cliefden after their father died in 1899. But in his will William Rothery stated the property was to be sold twenty years after his death.

In 1920 Edward Perrott, who owned land at Scone, bought Cliefden for £100,000, subdivided the property and put the blocks up for auction. Henry Alfred Rothery bought back 3865 acres (1565 hectares) for £9 an acre — more than double the £4 an acre the Rotherys had received when they sold to Perrott.

Henry Alfred and his wife, Marion Rivers Rothery, had nine children: two boys and seven girls. One girl, Audrey Sophia Augusta, lived in England for 25 years and then came back to Australia. She died in April 1987, aged 78.

The other girls were May Rivers, Gwendoline Doris, Caroline Rosetta Marion (Rose), Meta Wallace Lee and Laura Ada Loveday. The boys were Henry St George, who later managed the property, and Rex Albert.

Cliefden is now run by sisters Laura and Meta. They are only the third generation to live there since 1831 when William Montagu Rothery, their grandfather, established the property. Laura and Meta have lived at Cliefden all their lives apart from spending several years at college in Sydney after completing their primary education by correspondence. After their secondary schooling they returned to Cliefden and worked on the property.

The sisters still run sheep and Hereford cattle, and although they take on help when the sheep have to be shorn, they generally run the property themselves. Laura is also still a good shot with her Schneider rifle. Farming obviously runs in the blood as their older sister Rose topped the market at the weekly cattle sales with fifteen Herefords she bred just before she died in September 2005, aged 84.

Cliefden was built from bricks made on the property. The timberwork was cut on the property from box trees.

The house has around twenty rooms. A courtyard was covered in by William's youngest son, Henry Alfred, when he took over management of the property following his father's death in 1899. The covered-in area was used for entertaining and also housed a petrol generator, installed in later years to supply power, and a water tank.

The separate original kitchen was extended and a small window covered in, but it is still in the same place and the original wooden stove and hot water system (also run by wood) are still in use.

The drawing room and dining room are almost as they were when the house was built in 1831. A gold clock given to William Montagu by Governor Sir Charles Augustus Fitzroy, who stayed overnight at Cliefden on a visit to the

THE ORIGINAL KITCHEN IS STILL USED.

THE DRAWING ROOM.

THE DINING ROOM.

THE ENCLOSED COURTYARD.

The whitewashed stables, coach-house, woolshed and shearing shed were finished in 1842, four years after contractor John Pedley began work. Part of the deal was that he made the bricks on the property for 19 shillings a thousand and cut the wood and straw needed. An astute business-man, William Montagu also required Pedley to buy all his provisions from the Cliefden store.

The coach-house still houses many relics. The carriage in which William Montagu drove over the mountains is parked there. Bullet holes scar the shutters, the remnants of a gun-fight with bushrangers. A bushranger alarm bell stands on a post next to the bootmaker's hut and box room that was put

THE FAMILY CEMETERY.

district in 1846, sits on the mantelpiece of the drawing room. A silver service on the mantel in the dining room was given to William as a wedding present by King George IV. The chair William Montagu was tied to by the bushrangers is still there, just as if it had all happened yesterday.

Most of the other furniture is also original, including a spinet — a harpsichord with keyboard and mechanically plucked strings — that William Montagu had brought out from England.

There are seven bedrooms and all have fireplaces. Some windows have leadlighting while the doors and windows at the front have wooden shutters.

The roof was originally shingles but iron has been put on top. The bricks have a stucco finish.

up by William Montagu after the Ben Hall raid. He also installed loopholes in the wall so he could fire at anyone attempting to get to the stables where his stud horses were kept. Shearers kept rifles close by in the large woolshed.

The gardens at Cliefden won a string of awards when the *Sydney Morning Herald* garden competition was running. The competition ran statewide for more than 30 years and was recognised as one of the most prestigious awards to win. The core of the garden is still there but the sisters find it difficult to put aside the time needed to keep it at its best.

William Montagu Rothery and 22 of his descendants are buried on a peaceful hillside near the homestead.

Cook's Cottage

Cook's Cottage is the only eighteenth-century building in Melbourne. Often referred to as Captain Cook's Cottage, it was actually owned by his parents, James and Grace. It was originally built in 1755 in Yorkshire, England, but was bought by Sir Russell Grimwade in 1927 for £800, dismantled, all bricks numbered, sealed in cases and shipped to Australia in 1933.

The cottage was re-built in Fitzroy Gardens and presented to the people of Victoria by Sir Russell to commemorate Victoria's centenary. The two-storey cottage built from sandstone and brick has been carefully preserved ever since. The kitchen has an old ingle fireplace and dining table with plates and cutlery, while a wooden staircase leads to the main bedroom.

Originally standing on the edge of the village of Great Ayton, Yorkshire, the cottage was bought in 1755 by Cook's father, who had gone to Great Ayton to be a bailiff on Thomas Skottowe's farm, Airey Holme. With the bettering of his circumstances, the elder Cook made improvements to the building in which the family had lived since it had moved to Great Ayton from Marton-in-Cleveland. Indeed, it is possible that Captain James Cook lived there during his boyhood years from 1736 until 1745 when he left the village.

The original thatched cottage in which Cook was born at Marton was demolished in 1786 and so the Great Ayton family cottage is the only historical link Australia has with Captain Cook's origins.

In 1927 the last owner of the cottage, a Mrs Dixon, put it up for sale and Sir Russell Grimwade agreed to buy it and present it as a gift to the Victorian people. However, a difficulty arose when the patriotic Mrs Dixon decided the cottage should stay in Britain. She had already rejected offers from wealthy Americans for this reason, but she was eventually persuaded to agree to Victoria's claim as Australia was still in the Empire.

The cottage was shipped to Melbourne in 253 packing cases, arriving in April 1934. As the cottage had been altered considerably by a succession of owners following the Cook family's occupation, its Australian assemblers had the task of restoring it as accurately as research and guesswork would permit to its mid-eighteenth-century appearance.

The construction work was completed in six months, and the cottage was officially handed over to Lord Mayor H. Gengoult Smith by Sir Russell on 15 October 1934, during a centenary ceremony.

The cottage has subsequently undergone two restorations. The first was in the late 1950s and the most recent was in 1978, when a thorough effort was made to investigate and restore the building, furnish it with material appropriate to the period, and surround it with a garden of eighteenth-century character.

Cooksley's House

William John Farmer Cooksley was born at Wiveliscombe, Somersetshire, England, in 1836. His father was a builder and taught him the trade. Beginning work while young, he received little education but, when about seventeen, he decided to try a new life in Australia in the hope of being able to earn more money. His parents blocked his plans, however, and not wishing to defy them, he waited until he turned 21.

In June 1858, Cooksley left England and arrived at Moreton Bay in September 1858 with £1 in his pocket. Moreton Bay was a penal settlement on the Brisbane River, named by surveyor general John Oxley in honour of the then governor of New South Wales, Sir Thomas Brisbane.

Originally, free settlers were banned from going within 50 miles (80 kilometres) of the walled jail until authorities in England stopped sending convicts to Australia and the area was opened to everyone in 1842. The settlement grew into what is now Brisbane and in 1859 Queensland separated from New South Wales and became a state.

William Cooksley went to work as soon as he arrived at Moreton Bay, and he invested the money he earned in land at Sandgate, which he believed could be developed into a thriving area. He built a cottage for himself, but living there at the time was not without risk as Aborigines from Bribie and other adjacent islands made regular attacks. Only a rough track existed between Brisbane and Sandgate.

But Cooksley was determined to make Sandgate the premier watering place in the area and, with Hiram Wakefield, built a two-storey brick house on The Esplanade that was later converted into a hotel. He also built more cottages and campaigned strongly to have a decent road built to Sandgate.

Mr Cooksley was elected to the Sandgate council in 1881 after it became a municipality, and became mayor in 1885. But his health deteriorated and he declined another term. He also held a seat on the Toombul Divisional Board for two years and was a director of two of the most successful building societies in Brisbane. A staunch Liberal, he was asked several times to stand for parliament but again declined. He did take an active part in election campaigns.

Mr Cooksley married twice. His first wife died in March 1877 leaving him with six young children. He was married again in August 1877 to Kitty Cairns, the youngest daughter of Thomas Cairns.

In 1880, Mr Cooksley built another home in Queens Road, Hamilton, today an elite suburb of Brisbane, and called it Cairnsville after his wife. The land it was on extended to the Booroodabin Waterhole, the site of the present

LEFT: COOKSLEY'S HOUSE SEEN FROM THE BACK.

BOTTOM LEFT: LACEWORK ON THE BACK VERANDAH.

BOTTOM RIGHT: THE FRONT OF THE HOUSE.

THE FRONT VERANDAH.

Albion Park Racecourse. Originally the property extended all the way down to the Brisbane River and the present Cooksley Street was the driveway. Built on a pineapple farm, the house was one of the first two in Hamilton.

Now known as Cooksley's House, the bottom storey is built of locally quarried sandstone and the top from bricks with no cavity. The verandah columns are cast zinc and the iron lace railings are in Old Vienna pattern.

Acid-etched glass panels surround the doors and the original porcelain fingerplates are hand-painted with English flowers. The house has seven fireplaces, each with a different pattern.

It was designed by an unknown English architect while Mr Cooksley was on holidays in England in 1880. That probably explains why there were so many fireplaces, a feature certainly unsuited to a climate like Brisbane's. Verandahs were added to give it an Australian flavour.

A string of owners followed after William Cooksley died, and in the 1950s it was used as a halfway house for criminals. It was then converted into six residential flats, which necessitated the verandah being closed in on all sides with thin stucco sheeting, and rented until 1980.

When Cooksley's great grandson William Cooksley feared the house might be demolished for redevelopment, he bought it and carried out some restoration, including taking out the flats. Then he sold the property to a Stephen Moss in 1987. The present owner, Dr Archie Lamb, bought it in 1989 and put on a new roof and installed new plumbing and electrical wiring.

The house appears to be single storey from the front but it is actually two storeys. The lower floor is below ground level at the front, a feature designed to keep the house cool. The front retaining wall incorporates garden, and when it gets damp the moisture evaporates and cools the wall down. There is a gap of about a metre between the wall and the main front wall of the house.

The ceilings are 14 feet (4.3 metres) high and the house was originally gas lit. There are eight main large rooms, bathrooms and laundry. Nearly every room has an open fireplace — two double-sided ones upstairs, and a double-sided one and another single one downstairs. All the French doors opening out have cedar shutters.

There are three large bedrooms and two sleep-out bedrooms, a formal dining room on the top floor and a library. Downstairs there is a large kitchen with breakfast room and

TV room. A formal entrance hall runs the length of the house with doors at the front and back to catch cool breezes.

The staircase had been removed when the house was used for flats and the stairwell was covered with flooring. Since then a new staircase had been put in but Dr Lamb replaced that one with a Scottish antique he believed was more in

THE LIBRARY.

THE UPSTAIRS HALLWAY.

keeping with the house. Originally, a kitchen and servants' quarters were located at the back, but these burnt down.

Dr Lamb came to Australia from Scotland as a young doctor when he was 24 and settled in Brisbane, where he trained as an eye surgeon. Today, he has his own practice and lives in Cooksley's House with two teenage sons, James and Aidan.

The house was up for auction when Dr Lamb first became interested in buying it. It had been passed in but he had an inspection and fell in love with it, despite realising a great deal of work would be required to restore it to its former glory.

'I think, being Scottish, I'm not used to Australian houses. I don't like timber houses and this appealed to me because it was solid stone and had lots of history behind it,' Dr Lamb said. 'So, since 1989 I have been choosing pieces of antique furniture to complement the house.

'The staircase has a unique Georgian curved door that is 200 years old. I bought it and built the staircase around it. The balustrades are Scottish oak. I have sourced a lot of material from other houses through contacts in the antique trade and I've replaced most of the light fittings. The one in the breakfast room came from a friend's café in Paris.

'The two ex-gaslights in the upper floor came from Archbishop Mannix's house in Melbourne that were taken out when electricity was connected. They have been modified to take small globes.

'There's a whale oil lamp in the hall downstairs. You fill it and float a wick. It's a Georgian-type thing, mounted on chains and you pull it down, light it and push it back up.

'The lights in the downstairs verandah came from old Queensland rail carriages. In the formal dining room there's a large Waterford crystal chandelier.'

The library features a Georgian mahogany bookcase. An overmantel mirror is French, and a chair carrying the Glasgow coat of arms was originally owned by the chairman of the Glasgow Stock Exchange. All the floors are polished timber.

The top storey at the back has a balcony overlooking Albion Hill. The backdoor bell came from Innsbruck.

THE MAIN BEDROOM.

In the grounds, what were once stables at the back have now been converted into a garage, while the front garden features multiple rose bushes.

THE HOUSE SEEN FROM THE GARDEN.

Cooma Cottage

The only Australian-born colonial explorer, Hamilton Hume, who discovered the rich Yass plains back in 1821 before tramping around the countryside with English notables William Hovell and Charles Sturt, later retired to the southern New South Wales town of Yass and lived there for 34 years. Known as a 'currency lad' because he was native born, Hume ran a vineyard and orchard, made good wines, built the local flourmill, served as a magistrate, and donated land for the hospital and two churches.

Australia's busiest road, the Hume Highway, carries his name along with the Hume and Hovell walking track, which winds for 370 kilometres through the bush between Yass and Woomargama, near Albury, on the New South Wales–Victorian border.

Hume's expeditions were an important chapter in Australia's history. They were also central to the country's development as a nation.

He was born at Parramatta on 19 June 1797, and moved with his family to a 40-hectare land grant near Appin when he was fifteen. He spent a good deal of his time exploring the surrounding country, developing good bushcraft skills and learning Aboriginal customs and languages.

At seventeen, he set off on his first expedition to the Berrima district with younger brother John and an Aboriginal friend. In the next few years he made more expeditions into the same area and, in 1818 with James Meehan, discovered Lake Bathurst and the Goulburn Plains. Accompanied by his brother-in-law George Barber and neighbour William Broughton, Hume discovered the Yass Plains in 1821 and the following year reached the Clyde River.

THE COOMA COTTAGE COMPLEX.

THE ORIGINAL FRONT OF THE HOUSE, NOW THE BACK.

In 1824, Governor Brisbane asked Hume to find what lay between the Goulburn Plains and Bass Strait. With William Hovell, an English sea captain who knew little about the bush but was an excellent navigator, they set out with six assigned men, and in the following sixteen weeks made many important discoveries, including the Murray River, some of its tributaries and the grazing lands between Gunning and Corio Bay in Victoria. In 1829, Hume joined Sturt's expedition into the interior to explore the western rivers, following the Bogan, Darling, Castlereagh and Macquarie.

THE FRONT OF THE HOUSE TODAY.

Hume moved to Yass to live in 1839, buying a small four-room weatherboard cottage and 40 hectares of land for £600. The cottage had been built by convicts for Cornelius O'Brien in 1835. His brother Henry was one of the first white settlers in the Yass district.

In the next twelve years Hume made extensive additions to cater for dozens of regular visitors, including 42 nieces and nephews, each of them provided for in his will. When the extensions were finished, the route of the main road to Yass was moved to the back of his home so he built a new front, facing what was to become the Hume Highway. More rooms were added on each end as well as a gabled entrance with four large pillars.

Hume also established a large vineyard and orchard at Cooma, an Aboriginal word for 'one' or 'first', and records show Hume talked a lot about his home wines. His orchard was quite extensive and one day he let a group of troopers replenish their food stocks while on the way to quell the Chinese goldfields riots. The troopers became so drunk and disorderly he had to call the police to get them out.

When Hume died in 1873, the property was passed to a nephew but later came up for government auction and in the 1890s became a hospital for consumptive people, called the Nordrach Institute. It was advertised in Sydney newspapers as the ideal country home for people suffering from consumption and promoted the healing powers of the bracing winds.

The institution only lasted five or six years before the house came up for auction again. It was bought by a man named Jack Bourke, who turned it into a successful horse stud. But the buildings fell into disrepair and a Canberra woman bought the house in the 1960s. She, however, didn't have the resources to restore it so she donated it to the National Trust.

Extensive renovations were carried out as an Australian bicentenary project, and the house was opened to the public using voluntary guides from Yass. A Hamilton Hume Foundation comprising mostly local people was set up to raise the explorer's profile. Its patrons were former electronics king Dick Smith and media magnate Lachlan Murdoch.

THE ORIGINAL BRICK STABLES.

Coombing Park

When Thomas Icely wanted more land to add to the grazing empire he built during the 1830s he simply got on a ship to England and asked Lord Bathurst, the colonial secretary. This unusual ploy of going over the head of the colony's resident governor, combined with the fact that he wasn't shy about squatting on any large area of land that took his fancy, made Icely extremely unpopular with the neighbours.

But that didn't concern the convivial host to governors, church leaders, police chiefs, lawyers and other leading figures in the colony. He became the biggest landholder in the Bathurst district in the central west of New South Wales.

Icely was born at Plympton in Devonshire, England, in November 1797. The son of a merchant and ship-owner, he married Charlotte Rothery in 1830 in England, and had four daughters and two sons. From a second marriage to Louisa Bartlett in 1856, he had a daughter and son. He arrived in New South Wales in September 1820, bringing merchandise which he sold profitably. A pastoralist and stock-breeder with a sound general and commercial education, he took up a 2000-acre (810 hectare) grant at Saltram, near Bathurst, and later established Coombing Park Estate, near Carcoar, in 1831.

Icely was a noted breeder of sheep, cattle and horses, including racehorses. He built large stores, a cheese factory and foundry, and mined for copper and gold on his Coombing property. A leading Anglican, he helped build St Paul's at Carcoar. He was also a magistrate, a shareholder of the Bank of Australia, trustee of the Savings Bank of New South Wales and was a member of the New South Wales Legislative Assembly for a total of 21 years up until his death in February 1874.

THE CRAFTED VERANDAH PILLARS.

VICTORIAN-STYLE COOMBING PARK.

THE FRONT VERANDAH.

Icely worked hard for what he got, despite his manipulation of the system to suit his own purposes. He was already a rich man through merchandising and shipping interests when he first looked for new business prospects in the Carcoar district, 40 kilometres from his home at Bathurst.

The first 556 acres (225 hectares) of Coombing land he claimed by squatting was near the junction of the Belubula River and a creek he also named Coombing, which meant 'hollow valley' or 'sheep fold' in his native Devon. He built a cottage and stocked the land with sheep, cattle and horses.

That was the beginning of his empire and from then on he used every means possible to add more land to Coombing. The property eventually comprised almost 210,000 acres (85,050 hectares) and provided work for hundreds of people, including labourers, maids, groomsmen, gardeners, carpenters, overseers, brickmakers, coachmen, boundary riders and shepherds.

Icely ran the estate with the aid of 62 convicts, who gradually built the original homestead and outbuildings between 1838 and 1842.

The village of Carcoar, the second-oldest settlement west of the Blue Mountains, was the administrative centre of the bustling district but for years its population couldn't match that of Coombing. Even police and the Cobb and Co coach line worked from offices on the property.

After taking legal possession of Coombing in 1835, Icely brought out his two brothers-in-law, the Rotherys (*see* Cliefden), to be his neighbours on the adjoining Cliefden property. And, to keep everything in the family, his sister married the only other major landholder, William Lawson jnr, son of the explorer.

Although he had convinced authorities that a detachment of police should be stationed at Coombing, Icely always feared escaped convicts and bushrangers. One night in August 1863, Ben Hall and his gang raided the property and stole Comus II, one of the Icely's best racehorses, and its half-brother, owned by a police sub-inspector who had left it there to rest. A stable hand known as 'Charlie the German' was shot in the raid.

Police Chief Superintendent Edward Morrisset was a guest at Coombing that night. He had spent the day trying to track down Hall and his gang and was reportedly deeply embarrassed about the incident.

Not long after, fearing for his family's safety, Icely left his eldest son in charge and went back to his Sydney home. He never returned to Coombing again.

In 1851 gold had been discovered at Ballarat and hundreds of enthusiastic young men had come to Australia to

THE ENTRANCE HALL.

try their luck. Among them was Freeman Cobb and three other 20-year-old Americans who decided it would be much easier to make their fortune by running an efficient transport system than it would be digging for gold. They had had some experience with Wells Fargo so they imported coaches and in 1853 set up a company running staged services between Melbourne and the Victorian gold fields.

They made their fortune in 18 months and sold out in May 1856 to a Thomas Davies for £16,000. The company changed hands again five years later when it was sold to a consortium led by James Rutherford and Canadian-born William Franklin Whitney for £23,000. They were the ones who built up the company in Australia and later expanded to New Zealand, South Africa and Japan. In 1862, they transferred the company's headquarters from Victoria to Bathurst to follow the goldfields trade. Bathurst then was the only settlement west of the Blue Mountains and an important centre for business and trade.

Before long, Cobb and Co had bought out many of its rivals, expanded into Queensland in 1865 and embarked on a program of diversification, which included founding the Eskbank Iron Works at Lithgow, shipping jarrah from Western Australia to India, operating pastoral enterprises, and becoming involved in the extension of the railway network across New South Wales.

The company was highly successful and had a string of branches and franchises throughout Australia. At its peak, Cobb and Co operated on a network of tracks much longer than those of any other coach system in the world, covering 28,000 miles (44,800 kilometres) a week. Around 6000 of their 30,000 horses were harnessed every day.

But the advent of the motor vehicle and the railway in the early twentieth century as well as the economic effects of World War I resulted in the general decline of the coaching industry and led to the eventual closure of Cobb and Co. Most New South Wales coach lines had ceased operating by 1897 and Cobb and Co's Charleville factory closed in 1920.

The last coach run for Cobb and Co was between Yuleba and Surat in Queensland in August 1924, just over 70 years after the first passenger coach ran out of Melbourne on 30 January 1854.

Cobb and Co, which had extensive pastoral interests as well as its coach line, bought Coombing in 1881 on the recommendation of William Whitney. By 1886, he and James Rutherford were the only partners left in Cobb and Co.

Whitney died in 1894, and several years later Cobb and Co's assets were divided between James Rutherford and William Whitney's estate. The Whitney family company retained Coombing.

In the late 1890s Isabella Whitney knocked down the old Icely home and built the present one on the same site. The large, elegant, single-storey brick villa was designed by G.A. Mansfield. Constructed from sandstone bricks made on the property, it is surrounded by lawns and gardens dotted with evergreen English oaks, English elms, olive trees and weeping willows planted by Thomas Icely. The willows are said to have grown from cuttings that came from Napoleon's grave.

The magnificent 150-year-old stables and shearing sheds built by Thomas Icely still stand.

William Whitney's grandson Ewart King and his wife Audrey ran the property for the Whitney family company for more than 50 years before they both died. Their son Berkeley and daughter-in-law Penny live there now.

At 2400 hectares, Coombing is a much smaller property than when Thomas Icely owned it. Mrs Audrey King always took the view that was probably just as well. She didn't believe in people owning so much land and Coombing was still a big property for the district. It was also just as peaceful and picturesque.

The Ewart Kings moved from their cattle station in south-west Queensland just before the end of World War II to look after Coombing when Isabella Whitney, who had been running it, died at the age of 96. They only meant to stay a few months until the family sorted things out but spent the rest of their life there.

Nothing much has changed. The house and most of the wonderful old furniture is still the same, except for a small kitchen that was added to the verandah for convenience and warmth in winter.

Completely renovated, the sprawling Victorian-style home has six bedrooms, each with its own marble fireplace and view out over the rolling hills. The drawing room, one of the most used in the home, leads to the front verandah and has a northern aspect that catches the winter sun. The

THE SITTING ROOM.

formal dining room has an impressive carved oval cedar setting, matching high cedar bookcases and, like the other rooms, an ornate marble fireplace and wall mirror. A billiard room leads off the front foyer and hallway, separated by heavy Persian curtains.

The original kitchen has been replaced by a smaller, more modern one, and an office and telephone room has also been incorporated.

Although separated from the house and now used as a tool shed, the original Cobb and Co office is still there.

The carved black oak dining settings, sideboards, court cupboards, settles and bookcases were brought from England by Isabella Whitney. They are enhanced by Australian red cedar chairs, settees and tables. The high, solid doors and decorative surrounds are also early Australian cedar.

On the wall in the entrance foyer the Whitney family coat of arms shares pride of place with the gold crown-topped framed photographs of King Edward VII and Queen Alexandra, and George V and Mary. The gold crowns are the sign of an original grant.

The original hanging lights and gas chandeliers throughout the home have been converted to power, but look as impressive as they did when new, more than 100 years ago.

Coombing Park was used as the set in 2004 for the Australian TV mini-series *Jessica*, based on Bryce Courtenay's best selling novel about rouseabout Jessica Bergman who was born to hardship and family cruelty. The film chronicled her struggles to rise above the injustices she faced.

Berkeley King recounted how although Isabella Whitney had lived to a great age and was in the house until 1941, in the last few years of her life she hadn't been able to look after the pastoral empire and it declined.

'After she died in 1944, the family told my father he would have to manage it or they would sell it,' he said. 'So we moved here to live and he took over management.

'Three families lived in the house and we had only a small part and there were rules where we could go and where we couldn't go. Through the years that all changed and eventually we were the only family in the house in the 1950s.

'I left boarding school in 1958 and spent ten years doing my own thing. I came back here in 1966 and was married in 1970 and, after lots of ups and downs in the relationship with my father, we left here in 1978 and didn't come back until 1997.'

Mr King said that on their return they realised the property, which was now 2400 hectares, was again in a bad state of repair. Closer settlement had forced the sale of half the property in 1943.

A year after they returned, their son George King took over the property management and it started to pick up. They introduced new management processes and the pastures began to recover.

George held the position for a couple of years and then became managing director. He now runs only cattle because the Kings are single-minded in having only one enterprise to save on overheads.

Mr King said that after his father died they bought Gobabala at Nevertire and another 1500 acres (607 hectares) adjoining Coombing Park. They run 2500 cows, wean calves to Nevertire and sell to feedlots.

Penny King recounted how she and her husband believed they couldn't live in the house as a family the way it was. There were lots of built-ons around the verandah and they wanted to fix the plumbing, which was desperate, and make a family room.

'After a couple of years there were so many things that needed doing it looked as though it could be our job forever,' she said. 'Things had been added on through the years like butcher shops, milk rooms, paint sheds, dairy and studios.

'We wanted to get the house back to the way it was intended to be lived in and the way it originally looked. We took off all the add-ons and then we decided that this could be more than a lifetime's work and we should start now.

'It took us about fourteen months to renovate. We haven't done everything but it is a lovely house to live in. We pulled down all the add-ons. Because we put so much effort into it, we thought we should take ourselves out of the equation for [our son] George.

'He could look at the house and say it was just an eternal sink for money and would drag down his project of restoring the farm, so we thought it should help itself. We've had some heritage help and there is some more to come.'

Berkeley King said he and his wife considered they were custodians of the house. It was important to the national heritage and they felt a sense of duty to preserve it.

'A lot of the decisions we make are based on how we think it should look 100 years from now,' he said. 'Our sense of duty tells us we should leave it better than we found it.'

Dundullimal

When wealthy merchant John Maughan arrived in Sydney from India in 1827 with £9000 in his pocket, he was keen to buy a piece of good land to run sheep.

His first block was within the Limit of Settlement, just east of Wellington in central western New South Wales, but he believed there were more opportunities farther west where squatters had taken up big parcels and for which yearly land licences were issued in 1836. In 1841 Maughan bought one of these licences from Charles and Dalmahoy Campbell, who had squatted on 8000 hectares they called Dundullimal, a local Aboriginal word meaning 'hailstorm'.

He set about building a homestead from hand-split, hewn and sawn cypress pine on high ground overlooking a bend in the Macquarie River. It had a rustic look from the outside but inside there were glazed French doors, plaster and wall-papered walls and a bell-pull system for calling servants.

In the next few years, Maughan added a store, stables made from local sandstone, a blacksmith shop, shearing shed and woolshed. In 1846, with a couple of neighbours, he selected a site for a courthouse and lock-up and school, and the village of Dubbo grew around them from the property's initial population of twelve.

The property also included one of the few places where the Macquarie River could be crossed by stock being driven from Queensland and northern New South Wales to the Victorian markets. This helped Dubbo become a major stock-selling centre.

The stable complex, a significant reminder of Australia's pastoral heritage, was built in 1848 after John Maughan received more secure tenure to the land. It was extended in 1862 to include meat, store and cart rooms. At the same time, corrugated iron brought from England and carted over the Blue Mountains by dray was put on the roof to cover the ironbark shingles.

Maughan sold Dundullimal in 1858 to neighbours Cornish and Brocklehurst and retired to Darling Point. Cornish sold to Brocklehurst in 1864, who sold to Thomas Baird in 1871. Baird had cattle that were bred on the

DUNDULLIMAL, THE OLDEST SLAB HOME IN AUSTRALIA.

Georgina River in Queensland, fattened on Dundullimal and shown in Melbourne, where one was judged the best ox in Australia.

Baird's daughters sold the property to grandson Peter Palmer in 1954, who gave it to the National Trust in 1986. Until then, few people had realised the property's historic value. Dundullimal homestead, just down the road from Dubbo's Western Plains Zoo, had for 30 years since the 1950s been used as a hay shed and a shelter for sheep. Over the years, white ants had attacked roof timbers and parts had fallen in, weakening the walls, which then collapsed in several places. The homestead had lost its west wing to fire in 1901 and the east wing to floods in 1955. Fortunately, local Dubbo woman Toni Milling asked the National Trust to look at it and they sent out archaeological representatives who realised it was the oldest slab home in Australia. It is also considered the most sophisticated.

In 1988 the National Trust undertook the property's restoration with the help of a bicentenary grant. Restoration took about eight months. The property's best-preserved room, a bedroom, was left as it was so people could see the lath and plaster construction, roof beams and floorboards. The iron covering the original ironbark shingles on the roof is also genuine, in place since 1862.

The bicentenary restoration, which cost around $300,000, began with the stables, which accommodated four horses. The original loft entry is still there. Stored hay was dropped through into the mangers and louvre windows created a fresh airflow.

The blacksmith's shop was the heart of the station. Everything from horseshoes, major repairs and hand-made nails came off the large anvil. The bellows have been restored and the forge reconstructed to bring the shop to working order.

Dundullimal, the convict-built stone stables and the stockyards are good examples of early colonial life on the land. Dundullimal, like many remote properties, had 'strangers' rooms' set aside for travellers who expected a meal and a bed for the night. These are located at the end of the low verandah, made from round cypress pine rafters.

THE BLACKSMITH'S SHOP.

The sitting room has a tented ceiling and wallpaper copied from an 1852 design. An original piece is protected by a perspex cover.

One room contains an original iron bedstead with hand-painted flowers on the posts and a bedspread made by Dubbo National Trust and Embroiderers Guild members. The fireplace and red cedar mantelpiece is the same as others in the house.

The wide breezeway-style hall contributes to the coolness of the house. A large section of original plaster is still in place there.

The hand-hewn pine ceiling beams and pit-saw marks on the ceiling timbers are in contrast to the attractive workmanship on the red cedar doors, windows and architraves.

THE SANDSTONE STABLES.

Errowanbang

When Francis Rawdon Chesney Hopkins dissolved his partnership with Alexander Wilson and sold the homestead block of his Errowanbang property, he built a new house on the eastern side almost next door. Hopkins took the name Errowanbang with him and lived at Carcoar while it was being built. The neighbouring section became Old Errowanbang (*see* Old Errowanbang). The property had first been owned by explorer and army lieutenant William Lawson who, with Gregory Blaxland and William Charles Wentworth, was the first to cross the Blue Mountains in 1813.

Errowanbang is the third house on the property. The two previous ones were destroyed by fire. Parts of the second house — the billiard room and part of the rear wing — are incorporated in the present house, built by Hopkins in 1898.

It followed a format similar to the first house, which was timber rather than brick. Hopkins died after falling down an old mineshaft on the property in July 1916 but Errowanbang stayed in his family's estate until 1976 when Roy Gerathy bought it in a run-down condition.

He and his wife did what they could to carry out necessary repairs but the job was probably too difficult for them in the end. The property fell into disrepair, again because of economic pressures, and in 1999 Mrs Gerathy asked son John, a Sydney lawyer, to become involved with the house. Since then he has restored the property to its original condition.

The main problem was to try to water-proof the house and that meant diverting water, both subterranean and from the roof, away from the improvements. White ants were another big problem, which has now been remedied.

'I suppose what we've really tried to do is give Errowanbang another 100 years of life. That's the sense in what we've done.

What you see is only one little part of it but what you don't see is what costs the money and that's what's in the ground and what's in the roof and what's behind the walls,' John Gerathy explained. 'At this stage the most important thing I can say about Errowanbang is that the house is well protected from water, which is the most essential thing to keep its heritage intact.'

Mr Gerathy has rebuilt all the timber structures of the verandahs and restored some of the old cottages, sheds and stables, which took several years to do. The stables had suffered the same fate as other outbuildings with attacks by white ants and infiltrating water.

Mr Gerathy's previous experience with restorations of heritage buildings has given him an appreciation of old workmanship and methods. He has enjoyed the chance to put his knowledge to good use at Errowanbang. 'I think it's a chance to go back into yesteryear because the trades then were so good, the workmanship was excellent and done in times when people did most of it by hand. They didn't have huge machinery and equipment that actually

produced cut timber and all sorts of quality of the work so we're doing that.'

He has converted parts of the house into ensuites and made other small changes he and his wife Hilda believed to be in keeping with the original character. The colour schemes are original.

Besides the main house, they have also restored the station jackaroos' quarters and that has become two-bedroom accommodation.

They built a small fountain area at the front of the house which sits on top of a large concrete in-ground tank. They don't draw water directly from the tank to the house but feed it to the original well at the back of the house. They reticulate the house water from there.

Mr Gerathy and his wife Hilda had been spending weekends at Errowanbang, near Mandurama in central western New South Wales, while restoring the old homestead, repairing fences, improving the pastures and tending a Murray Grey herd. But Mr Gerathy decided to partly withdraw from the legal practice and slow down his property development, which while not that big a business always had a project underway, such as restoring the Sir Joseph Banks Hotel in Camden. Mr Gerathy would spend around twelve days a month working at his Macquarie Street practice and the rest of the time at historic Errowanbang. Mrs Gerathy helped clear the decks to enable the lifestyle change by selling her optometrist practice at Neutral Bay.

The change in focus has given the couple the scope to work with their stud cattle at Errowanbang, continue their improvements and take some time out with country people. They like spending time with their neighbours by getting

A DECORATIVE ANTIQUE TRUNK.

THE DINING ROOM.

together for a barbecue or wine dinner, a tradition started by Mr Gerathy's father back in the 1970s.

Mr Gerathy began his law career with Lionel Bowen, a former attorney general, who in 1972 left him to run the partnership when he was 26. The firm has been in the same offices at 187 Macquarie Street, since 1967 when Lionel Bowen moved there because he was initially in state parliament, situated just across the road. Mr Bowen is still a consultant in the firm but his daughter Anne is now Mr Gerathy's partner. The firm has stayed a small city practice, which Mr Gerathy pointed out ran against the trend in law, but it worked for them. 'We have five or six lawyers and that gives me the opportunity to now do other things without having to be there all the time,' he said.

STRIPED WALLPAPER IS A FEATURE.

Mr Gerathy has always been involved in property development, building his side of the Bowen and Gerathy practice around commercial property. He was also involved in his father's farming pursuits on weekends at Grose Vale and when his father moved to Errowanbang in 1976. Mr Gerathy began helping his mother to run the property after his father died in the late 1990s. When his mother died, he took over.

THE SITTING ROOM.

ONE OF TWO STAINED-GLASS
INSERTS IN THE FRONT DOOR.

In Sydney, the Gerathys live in the wharf terraces at Woolloomooloo, opposite Finger Wharf. Their back windows face the Mrs Macquarie's Chair section of the Botanic Gardens and the front windows Sydney Harbour.

Hilda Gerathy comes from Norway but has a strong affinity with the country and regularly travelled between Sydney and Errowanbang for four or five years to help with its conservation. 'In Sydney everything is crowded but we can relax here,' she said.

'I used to spend a lot of time in Norway in cabins in the mountains and in one way coming to Errowanbang is like going to the cabins. And there are distinct seasons here so it gives me more feeling of being home than in Sydney. Life is also a much slower pace. You can do it or you don't need to do it. I love Sydney but it's a good change to get away.'

Mr Gerathy said that, while Errowanbang was not a large property, it was large enough at 88 hectares to run a cattle stud operation. In 1972 his father started a Murray Grey stud at Grose Vale and called it Bellgrove and he was involved in that with him.

'He moved the stud to Errowanbang in 1976 because it was too hilly at Grose Vale and the area down there was a bit tighter. He also bred thoroughbreds which we raced with some success although none of us was real gamblers.

'I think the stud started to dwindle out in the late 1980s, early 1990s because there was an economic problem and my father became tired of the Murray Grey bureaucracy, but it was his dream to run a stud here. We're doing that now with a joint venture with the New South Wales Minister for

Primary Industries Ian McDonald, who also lives in a cottage on the property.'

John Gerathy and his wife have worked through the 2.8 hectares of gardens to remove plants and shrubs that had passed their use-by date while trying to re-establish its original state, and make it easy to maintain. Mr Gerathy senior was keen on roses and imported them from England and Ireland and parts of Europe. The huge rose beds are now a feature, with some of them being transplanted to the western side of the house.

The garden also has some very old orange trees which produce fresh juice, year in and year out. A white box has been made a special feature and there's a variety of pines that were planted by the house's builder and original owner Hopkins.

Hopkins liked to travel and he introduced a Japanese bamboo to the garden that nobody else in the area would have had. Mr Gerathy has replanted it near the outbuildings.

THE KITCHEN IS DESIGNED TO BE PRACTICAL.

Fortuna Villa

When gold was officially discovered in October 1851 in the quiet Bendigo Valley at a place called The Rocks, thousands of miners swarmed to the area to seek their fortune. A government camp was established the following year and by 1855 the small bustling shantytown had given way to the township of Sandhurst.

In 1855 an eccentric German, Johann Gottfried Tobias Christopher Ballerstedt, built one of the first quartz crushing mills on the goldfields. By early 1856 he had built an eight-room, double-fronted, two-storey house of red brick with stucco dressings to the window and door openings. He also built a detached kitchen and store between the house and the quartz mill. In 1857, Ballerstedt bought the land from the Crown on which his house and mill stood.

Ballerstedt was born in Russia in 1796 and had fought against Napoleon in the battle of Waterloo as a soldier in Prussian Field Marshal Blücher's victorious army. Together with his son Theodore, Ballerstedt had arrived in Bendigo in the early 1850s, after they had tried their luck in the Californian gold rush of 1849. In 1855, they had begun working an open-cut mine on the Victoria Reef and were laying the foundations for a fortune from a claim that was allegedly bought from a couple of schoolboys who had opened it up successfully.

FORTUNA VILLA, COMPLETED IN 1900.

THE ELABORATE CAST-IRON LACE-WORK INCLUDED THE HOUSE NAME.

BEAUTIFUL STAINED-GLASS PANELS.

Between 1855 and 1861, Ballerstedt and Son made the extraordinary profit of £243,000 and became Australia's first mining magnates. As evidence of their standing in the community, the Ballerstedts hosted a dinner for the governor, Sir Henry Barkly, during his visit to Sandhurst in 1857.

Ballerstedt's house was next to the New Chum line of reef and astride the probable extension of the Nell Gwynne line of reef, with the lower floor actually penetrating the reef. The grey–green stone is still visible at many points around the lower foundations of the mansion.

Between 1858 and 1869, substantial construction work was carried out on the surrounds and to the crushing mill. A lookout tower was built above the detached kitchen; a billiard room and adjoining stables were added adjacent to the store.

The house was accessed from a private road to Alley Street, providing a direct route to Ballerstedt's claims and workings on Victoria Hill. In March 1869 local architects Vahland and Gretzschmann called for tenders for a two-storey addition to the house. This gabled wing to the south added another three rooms and was typical of the architects' romantic classical work, similar in appearance to their treatment of the Echuca Town Hall built in 1867. The house was surrounded by a large masonry and brick wall with an impressive arched gateway leading to the main entrance overlooking the mining operations of the Bendigo goldfields.

In May 1871 Ballerstedt's son Theodore sold the house to George Lansell for £20,000, an extraordinary sum for that time. Lansell was a young Englishman who had come to the goldfields after reports sent to him by his brother Wooten, a ship's officer who had travelled widely.

Born in Margate, Kent, in 1823, George Lansell was the eldest son of Thomas Lansell, a grocer and tallow chandler. When he was fourteen, George left school to help his father in the family business.

George and his brother William landed at Port Adelaide in 1853 and headed for the diggings at Echunga where they prospected unsuccessfully for gold. They returned to Adelaide and fell back on their old trade of tallow merchants.

Later they decided to move to the Victorian goldfields, where news of big finds was now thrilling the colony. The two men went to the Bendigo Valley where they were reunited with their brother Wooten.

Realising that few of the thousands of diggers had made any real fortune, the brothers formed a partnership, setting up a butchery and soap and candle factory at View Point in the heart of the small community of Sandhurst. The business prospered but complaints about the smell from the tallow works forced them to move.

But George Lansell was determined to strike it rich from gold, so he dissolved the partnership with his brother William and invested all his savings into some of the more primitive sorts of quartz mining, losing everything in the process. Later going back into business with William, Lansell bought into various companies in the next few years although few returned him any profit. Then he bought a large interest in the Advance Company, on the Victoria Reef, and after several years it began to pay good dividends. He also bought a substantial interest in the Cinderella Mine on Johnson's line of reef and the returns on it were also good.

These mines were the cornerstone of the George Lansell fortune. He became interested in almost every reef in the district and his sound judgement proved useful in their development. He was appointed director on the boards of 34 mines and his influence over the destiny of Bendigo grew. He never hesitated to spend lots of money in his search for gold.

After buying Ballerstedt's house, Lansell commissioned several architects to draw up plans for more development but nothing came of it. He continued with alterations to the quartz mill in 1871 and the excavation of a dam at the newly named Fortuna Crushing Works.

In 1874 the foundation stone was laid for the construction of a new 30-head stamper battery. On 16 November that year, part of the chimneystack associated with the new crushing battery blew over in a storm, damaging the walls to the tailing treatment works. In the subsequent rebuilding, the height of the walls on the northern side of the tailing treatment works was increased.

In 1875 Vahland and Gretzschmann prepared drawings for a new principal entrance on the western side of the building and a verandah on the eastern side. The elaborate cast-iron lacework for the verandah, supplied by G.C. Scott of Melbourne, included a panel positioned above the original entrance with Lansell's new name for the house, Fortuna Villa, worked into the lacework.

Romantic classical façades were added to the northern elevation of the house and to the southern elevation of the billiard room. Statues were positioned on the parapets and in the garden.

In 1876 Lansell returned to England for the first time and travelled extensively throughout Europe. Following his return to Australia, the work continued with the previously exposed red-brick external walls being cement rendered.

In 1879 construction began on the Pompeii fountain, fashioned after the one in the House of the Great Fountain in Pompeii. Lansell had returned from Italy with lanternslides of the excavations and had decided he wanted one.

The creation in 1880 of the elaborately glazed conservatory on the lower level of the lookout parallels that at Mandeville Hall, Toorak, by Charles Webb in 1878 and at Frederick Sargood's Ripponlea at Elsternwick. Coach-houses adjoining the stables were built and the main access drive to the villa changed to a wide avenue opening from Chum Street.

During this period Lansell also converted the tailing treatment plant into an outdoor swimming pool. Four dams were built and landscaping of the area outside the walled garden surrounding the house began.

The two *Sequoia gigantes* were planted either side of the axis to the front of the house and the driveway from Chum Street was fenced and planted with an avenue of eucalypts. Trees were also planted to screen the poppet heads of Lansell's 222 and Fortuna mines.

THE ELABORATELY GLAZED CONSERVATORY.

His wife, Bedelia Lansell, died childless in September 1880 and Lansell left Sandhurst and the Bendigo goldfields to return to England. His business associate E.I. Dyason was left to manage his interests and live in Fortuna during his absence. Lansell had no intention of returning to Sandhurst, but after remarrying and receiving a petition sent to England and signed by 2628 people asking him to return, he changed his mind.

In 1887 Lansell returned to Sandhurst, later to be called Bendigo, with his new wife and three children. In the next twenty years Fortuna expanded along with the Lansell family. No cost was spared to beautify the building and surrounding gardens.

Beginning in 1888, Lansell added a three-storey extension to the north side of the house, including a master bedroom with adjoining dressing room and the first of the indoor bathrooms and toilets. These rooms adjoined the original billiard room, linking the main house to the stables and crushing battery.

THE DISTINCTIVE CUPOLA.

However, the major feature of the extensions was the picture gallery on the third floor. Measuring 37 feet by 21 feet and 22 feet high (11 metres by 6.5 metres and 7 metres high), this unique room with its curved ceiling, enriched cornices and other embellishments was Lansell's showpiece, displaying his wealth as well as catering for his obsession with the game of billiards — a fully imported billiard table occupied the centre of the gallery. The entire extension was heated by central heating and Fortuna is considered to be the first private residence in the colony so heated.

Lansell continued expanding Fortuna. In 1890 the architect Emil Maurmann

designed an attic bedroom addition, which was built over the original part of the house and adjacent to the great billiard room. This provided bedrooms and sitting rooms for the staff.

Outside, the rose garden was established on the tailing dump to the south of the main lake, the lookout tower on top of the conservatory was relocated to the rose garden and numerous statues were positioned around the garden.

In 1893, the last of the three billiard rooms designed by William Beebe, another local architect, was added to the south of the house at ground level. The upstairs billiard room and picture gallery was converted into a ballroom.

STATUES ON THE PARAPETS.

POMPEII FOUNTAIN DECORATIONS.

Between 1893 and 1895, a new entrance hall replaced the earlier hall and a bay window was added to the first bedroom at the front of the house. In addition, the music room was extended onto the eastern porch, enclosing the earlier open colonnades, and a hipped roof replaced the lookout tower on the conservatory.

In 1900 the whole of the eastern front of the house was extended and by 1904 the intricately decorated plaster arches and metal ceiling had been added to the reception room. A shadehouse was built beside the fountain.

Lansell also had the quartz-crushing battery extended. The addition of a spacious hall to the lower level of the main house, principally a statuary, allowed the music room above it to be further extended.

In remodelling the building, the distinctive cupola and stairwell were introduced, replacing the previous curved stairwell. Above the music room an attic was added, complementing the previous addition of 1890.

In March 1906, George Lansell died at the age of 82 but Fortuna was still to reach its peak. In 1907 Edith Lansell completed the work begun by her husband 36 years before.

In what appeared to be a frenzy of activity, Edith supervised the final additions and alterations to Fortuna, including the conversion of the original billiard room at the north end of the house into an office complete with bay window and dressing rooms. A gymnasium was added above the office with large folding doors opening into the upstairs ballroom and bay windows added to other windows on the western façade along with a full-length balcony with access to both the upstairs gymnasium and ballroom.

Many internal rooms were remodelled at this time with new plaster ceilings or pressed-metal ceilings added. Fine marble bath and basin combinations were installed in the bathrooms adjoining the main bedrooms.

A guest room added in 1900 was used by vice-regal guests when visiting Bendigo. These included Baron Sir Henry Loch, the Marquis of Normandy and the Earl of Hopetoun. Many state govenors and federal governor-generals were also hosted by the Lansell family.

Fortuna Villa was finally complete, and beautifully complemented by extensive landscaping which included 13 acres (5 hectares) of spacious grounds containing five lakes, gazebos, a boatshed and jetties, tennis court and pavilion, garden seats, a small fountain adjacent to the conservatory, new entrance gates, and gravel paths and drives.

The original garden wall had been reduced in height at the front of the house and finished with an iron palisade. Mr Lansell's crest, containing his initials 'GL', can be seen on the chimney, now at floor level but more prestigiously placed before the balcony was built.

Worthy of note are two garden fixtures rarely seen nowadays: a wrought-iron arbour and the summerhouse. There is also a tunnel, which was probably used for storage and the transportation of gold from the bullion room to the coachhouse on the other side of the building.

Fortuna Villa is now owned by the Department of Defence and, for security reasons, no photographs may be taken inside.

Gainsborough

Gallipoli veteran Samuel Frederick Falls, like many other young men, joined the Australian Army in 1914 to do his part in World War I. He landed at Gallipoli with the 2nd Light Horse Regiment in May 1915 and was on active duty there until the regiment was pulled out.

Leaving the Light Horse, he was transferred to France. On 10 July 1916, while he was working in a bomb store at La Boudrelle, a detonator went off and, among other injuries, blew off his left hand. After a long convalescence he was discharged with a pension in late 1917.

Originally from Lismore in northern New South Wales, Falls went to Brisbane to live. In 1938 after buying land in Crescent Road in the elite suburb of Hamilton, he built a Tudor house originally named Lexington. The name was changed to Gainsborough by a later owner.

It was a prime site with views of the Brisbane River to the east and west, but there are no records to show whether Falls lived in the house and it was probably built as an investment. In 1940 he sold it to a Francis and Mary Pfitzenmaier.

Falls bought the property back in 1944 and this time owned it until 1950 when he sold to Moshe and Gerte Hoffman. Susan Gallagher, the present owner, bought the house in 1996 and has carried out extensive restoration.

Ms Gallagher said that before making up her mind to purchase the home she spent many months driving past, looking and checking out the sun and the shade during a couple of seasons. At first she thought the house appeared to be in a lot of shade but that was incorrect; it actually caught the sun for most of the day.

GAINSBOROUGH WAS BUILT BY A GALLIPOLI VETERAN.

'I was able to buy the house in October 1996 and embarked on considerable renovations inside. Structurally it was wonderful with a lot of lead glass and beautiful dark English oak timbers,' she said.

'There are two fireplaces, one in the large lounge room downstairs and one in the main bedroom, which is above the lounge room. We removed the wine-coloured carpet with a leaf pattern and put Tasmanian oak and mahogany wood parquet throughout the ground-floor living area. Without really changing the tradition of the house, we turned it back to an elegant family home.'

The architects, Chambers and Ford, built several other houses in similar style in fashionable Hamilton and Ascot on the north side of Brisbane. It was a popular style during the inter-war years and other architects like Blackburn and Gzell, H.G. Driver, E.P. Trewern, V.H. Frame and Lange Powell also produced Tudor houses.

Brisbane City Council's Heritage Unit noted that the periodical *Steering Wheel and Society and Home* carried an article on the Crescent Road house and pointed out some of its prominent features, like the dormer with wavy-edged weatherboards, the circular-headed entrance, the heavy timbering with intervening rough-cast panels on the ground floor and multi-coloured brick with dressed stonework used sparingly in the external angles. It considered the house to be at the vanguard of new housing styles in Brisbane, which would slowly but surely supersede the weatherboard house to which people were accustomed. Brisbane Council has listed the house on its heritage register.

Ms Gallagher was born in England with an Australian father, and Swiss mother who came from an hotelier family outside Zurich. She was educated in Toowoomba in Queensland and after school spent a year at university before going to London where she studied at a college of fashion. She speaks French, German and English and was offered a buying position in Switzerland by 200-year-old company Ciolina Modehaus. 'I worked in the fashion industry in the better days of trading. The company had top labels and we sold to prominent people like Versace. I travelled to the US and Canada buying furs that were made into coats in Italy by Fendi,' Ms Gallagher said.

'I married a Brisbane barrister and came here in the early 1980s to start a new role as a mother. I have a residence in Switzerland and since 2002 spend a lot of time there and part in Brisbane. After living in Switzerland for nearly eighteen years in the late 1960s and 1970s, I warmed to this European-style home with its architecture.

'I have to say that in Brisbane, its Queensland-type wooden homes built on stilts are much more popular, but we find the people from Melbourne and Sydney relate to the architecture of this home. I am a proud owner and hope that I will have the opportunity to pass it on one day to my son, who is a lawyer at Goldman Sacks in London. I must add that when I bought this home I paid $465,000 and I thought I had paid probably $10,000 or $20,000 too much. Now my rateable land value has increased to $1,000,050.'

In 2003, Ms Gallagher removed a free-standing garage that was built into the side of the hill because she wanted a few modern conveniences rather than having to walk down twenty cement steps to get to the garage. She decided it would be more practical to excavate the small piece of land she had and build a new garage.

She designed a suspended slab that now extends from the back of the kitchen, creating a family room and a large terrace area with views across the city. Under the terrace, the slab provides the roof of a two-and-a-half car garage and a large storage area.

'We have done that without interfering with any of the architecture of the house, and as it is mainly an underground area, people don't really notice anything is different,' Ms Gallagher said.

THE DINING ROOM.

Gamboola Cabonne

LEFT: GAMBOOLA CABONNE, BUILT WITH SPRAYED CONCRETE STUCCO.

BOTTOM LEFT: THE FRONT GARDEN FOUNTAIN.

BOTTOM RIGHT: THE FRONT ENTRANCE PERGOLA.

The Rev. Samuel Marsden, later known in the colony as 'the Flogging Parson', arrived in Sydney on the *William* in March 1794 to be the assistant chaplain in New South Wales. Making his home at Parramatta, he was given a grant of 100 acres (40 hectares) and the use of convict labour.

He showed himself to be an excellent farmer and later, after being given more grants of land, he took an interest in sheep breeding. Although his efforts could not be compared with those of John Macarthur, his experiments were of great use in the early development of the wool industry.

In 1806 Marsden owned around 1400 sheep, out of the 21,400 in the colony, and had nearly 3000 acres (1215 hectares) of land. Some of his land was at Molong in central western New South Wales where his flocks were looked after by his son-in-law Jon Betts.

John Smith managed the properties for Betts but eventually bought the land and, with the original sheep from the Betts–Marsden flock, established his own stud, which he called Gamboola, around 1848. He provided a sound-framed sheep with fine, medium wool, which included the genes from six merinos he imported from England.

John Smith's sons eventually took over his vast empire of properties. Wallace Arabin Smith ended up with Gamboola and his estate was divided between his six children in 1910 when the youngest daughter, Phyllis, turned 21. This was done by taking the total value of the estate and, after an allowance for their mother, dividing it by six. The three elder girls, Dorothy, Marnie and Naomi, each received £10,000, and Phyllis received 770 acres (312 hectares) and the difference in cash. The two boys, Dudley and Kenneth, took Gamboola.

The Amaroo Shire records show that Gamboola at the time of the division comprised 8501 acres (3443 hectares) in the Molong parish and 435 acres (176 hectares) in the parish of Boree Nyrang. Before 1911, Dudley had bought three portions and part of a fourth from his father's estate. This he leased to a Miss Glasson or her brother W.R.

Glasson until 1923 when it was sold to W.R.M. Holt, a cousin of Dudley's. He named it Printhe, said to be a Queensland Aboriginal name for the goanna.

The two boys then divided Gamboola. Kenneth took the eastern block that included the original homestead; Dudley took the western side and, in 1912, built a homestead on it he called Gamboola Cabonne.

The house was built with a sprayed concrete stucco and originally had a terracotta tile roof. Covering 75 squares including the vast verandahs, it had ornate ceilings, lead-light windows, and six fireplaces. The extensive fretwork in the house was typical of the era, and was almost art deco in style in the entry hall and main living room.

Located approximately midway between Gamboola and the township of Molong, the house was close to Molong Creek, and records show that in 1913 a heavy frost burst three main pipes of the water system.

Dudley Smith was a local veterinarian and set up his clinic in the eastern wing of Gamboola Cabonne, but he did not practise there for long. With the outbreak of World War I, he enlisted in the Molong Half Squadron of the Light Horse Brigade and left Australia on the ship *Star of Victoria* in October 1914.

His wife Annette went to Sydney to live with family, and Gamboola Cabonne was managed by Ted Evers, an employee of John Smith. He had also managed Boree Nyrang, another Smith property in the district (*see* Boree Nyrang) before it was sold to Sir Norman Kater in 1900.

Dudley Smith fought with the AIF from the beginning of the Middle East campaigns. He commanded a squadron of the 1st Light Horse through Gallipoli, Egypt, Sinai and Palestine, and returned to Australia in 1919 in charge of a mounted regiment. He had won the Distinguished Service Order and the Victorian Decoration.

Dudley Smith sold Gamboola Cabonne in December 1922 to John Archibald Murray, of Uanda, Torrens Creek, Queensland. He had left the property the previous year to live in Sydney. The *Molong Express* reported in November 1921: 'Lt Colonel D A Smith DSO and Mrs Smith left Molong by car for Coogee where in future they will live.'

Always a keen horseman, Dudley Smith in May 1921 began judging race finishes for the Australian Jockey Club and held that position until he retired in 1948. He told newspapers at the time that the sensational alliance of Phar Lap and jockey Jim Pike stood out in his memory after 27 years of judging race finishes. Dudley Smith died in 1950.

The new owner of Gamboola Cabonne, John Murray, carried out a full restoration of the house. The *Molong Express* in January 1923 reported: 'This property had been allowed to fall into a state of comparative disrepair since Major Smith's departure from the district and prior to entering into occupation Mr Murray decided to have the beautiful home completely renovated.

'This important undertaking was entrusted to the well known firm of C Morrison of 170 William St, Sydney, and a staff of experts under the direction of Mr G Standring came to Molong some weeks ago to carry the work into effect. The result of their activity is to be seen in the splendid way the homestead now presents, both as regards the interior and exterior improvements.

'In addition to structural alterations designed to give added efficiency in house-keeping and home comfort and repairs and renovations to the subsidiary buildings and offices necessary in a modern station homestead, the whole of the walls and ceilings have received attention at the hands of skilled artisans.

'The ceilings throughout have been painted in ivory white and the walls papered in delicate art and tapestry design, some dainty colour effects and contrasts have been obtained. The quality of the work reflects the highest on Mr Standring.

'The homestead has been refurnished throughout by Beard Watson and Co Ltd, Sydney, the high quality of the furniture, floor coverings and general equipment constituting a splendid advertisement for that firm and an illustration of the high standard reached in Australian furniture manufacture.

'The dining room is furnished in oak of Jacobean period, the window drapings of brown cloth trimmed black, with valance, and the floor covered by Axminster carpet of Persian design over inlaid parquetry linoleum. The sitting room is also Jacobean in design with an Axminister rug of brown, toned blue.

'The bedroom is furnished in maple and polished rosewood, sycamore and maple, with artistic window drapings and floor coverings. Altogether the furnishings are in keeping with the beauty of design of the homestead and its natural setting and Mr Murray is to be congratulated alike upon his choice of a residence and his taste in home decoration.'

The Murrays sold to Thomas Pearse Leslie in 1931, who held it until 1956. After that there was a string of owners up until 1999 when present owners Alison and David Trowbridge bought it.

The couple took such a liking to the old 24-room homestead they gave up their professional jobs in Sydney, bought it and moved in. They are still working on the restoration but have no misgivings and have never looked back.

'Coming from the city we had had nothing to do with cattle or growing lucerne or repairing fences or things like that,' Mr Trowbridge said. 'But we have good neighbours who have been kind and helpful to us, and now we are almost seasoned landowners.'

Mr and Mrs Trowbridge grew up in Sydney and lived at Roseville. Mr Trowbridge worked in consulting engineering and Mrs Trowbridge was in IT software support for seventeen years working for various companies.

THE BONES OF THE ORIGINAL GARDEN WERE RETAINED.

They had always had an interest in having a heritage home to renovate as a long-term project and had looked around the Roseville area, but one weekend saw a newspaper magazine advertisement for the historic Gamboola Cabonne. Out of interest they went to have a look.

'As we drove over the hill and saw the house, my wife said, "You're in a lot of trouble, boy," and when we walked in the front door, we agreed it was home,' Mr Trowbridge said. 'So after much contemplation we decided to make the move, because we hadn't planned to do that. It wasn't in the scheme of things at all. We resigned from both our jobs, packed up in Sydney and moved six months later on a wing and a prayer.'

Mrs Trowbridge said telecommuting was a potential option for her but they realised that with the scale of what

they were taking on, they certainly couldn't both dedicate the time to employment as well as restoring the house and running the property.

'Because we had professional backgrounds, we had made the decision that either one of us could get employment in the area and my husband got a job within three weeks with the Department of Primary Industries as an IT manager which left me up the ladder painting,' she said. 'We could have adapted our skill sets to get jobs but drew a straw. One gets to go to work and one gets to stay behind. I think I won.'

The Trowbridges have spent considerable time restoring their home. They have replaced most of the plumbing, put

in insulation and heating and are renovating the main rooms one at a time, changing the colour schemes, opening up the old fireplaces, replacing the hearths, putting up picture rails and lights of the period, together with carrying out lots of detail work such as scraping paint off old decorated door hinges.

Outside they have replaced the guttering and downpipes, and put in new water tanks. The Trowbridges grow lucerne and agist cattle which meant they had to replace lots of fencing, build laneways for cattle movement and carry out revegetation projects on the creek.

Mrs Trowbridge said they moved to Gamboola Cabonne with a ten-year plan so they didn't burn themselves out. The renovations were substantial but their pleasure was in doing as much of the work as they could themselves. 'In our first winter we had lots of pipes burst so we replaced the lines.

There are many unseen events like that. You think you are going to do something quickly and simply but it grows into something bigger than Ben Hur. So we keep a diary on what we have done and how we are progressing.'

A design consultant helped out with the garden because, coming from Sydney, the Trowbridges were not sure what they could plant, and, being on a creek, the house is subject to heavy frosts in the winter. They discovered many of the brick edges and paths in the garden were still there and were just grown over, so they dug them up and put back some of the trees in keeping with the style.

'We wanted a garden in keeping with the era and style of the house. We've kept the bones of the original garden with the stone edgings and bricks around the driveway areas and we've planted hedges and garden beds,' Mrs Trowbridge said. 'Our large yellow box trees are original and the crepe myrtles have been there for some time but it's a spring garden with lots of blossoms in September.'

ONE OF THE MANY ORIGINAL FIREPLACES.

The Giese Home

It's 1974 and Christmas Eve in Darwin. Most of the 48,000 people in the northern city are busy celebrating the festive occasion and the coming holiday break. Several weeks earlier Cyclone Selma had hovered out to sea before changing direction and disappearing. New warnings about Cyclone Tracy are being taken seriously but most people believe it shouldn't interrupt their Christmas.

In late afternoon ominous cloud covers the city, which is now being lashed by heavy rain squalls and fierce wind. By 10pm the wind is causing property damage and by midnight it is obvious the cyclone is going to wreak havoc.

In the next six hours of Christmas Day Tracy destroys three-quarters of Darwin, killing 65 people and injuring 645, 145 of them seriously. Another sixteen are lost at sea. The wind reaches speeds of 217 kilometres per hour before the anemometer blows to pieces. Rainfall overnight tops 255 millimetres. About 70 per cent of homes are wrecked, resulting in a damage bill of $800 million. More than 26,000 people are evacuated, and by New Year's Day only 10,000 remain in the devastated city.

Four out of five homes on Myilly Point built for executive-level public servants in the late 1930s survived the cyclone, although one of them — now known as Burnett House after the architect — was badly damaged, and another was damaged less severely.

The homes are part of the development of Commonwealth Territorial Government and illustrate Darwin's architectural and social history. Used by the public service until the cyclone struck, they were elevated, open, airy and built on big blocks of land.

The architect, Beni Carr Glynn Burnett, was appointed by the federal government in 1937 and was the first to design appropriate housing for public servants in Australia's tropical north. He apparently worked under the guidance of an architect called Henderson in the Department of Works in Canberra.

The houses Burnett designed were to replace older homes in a much more vernacular style with bamboo push-out shutters and big wide verandahs. They were not very strong even though Darwin was prone to cyclones, fortunately not all like Tracy.

The new houses were different. They did not have verandahs all the way around and they had floor-to-ceiling moulded S-shaped louvres made from asbestos. (All the older houses and many public buildings in Darwin incorporated asbestos in their construction somewhere.) The houses had an open living area with bedrooms off to the side. These had batwing doors and in most of the houses the louvres went the full height of the wall so everything could be opened up for cooling. At first there were just the open louvres, but later fly-screens were added, which must have been an absolute delight to the people who lived in the houses before fans came along.

LEFT: THE GIESE HOME SURVIVED CYCLONE TRACY.

BOTTOM LEFT: THE HOUSE IS SURROUNDED BY TROPICAL GARDEN.

BOTTOM RIGHT: THE VIEW TO THE SEA.

THE COMPACT DINING ROOM.

Despite there being a number of designs, with different styles and floorplans, all the houses were basically the same: elevated, cypress pine floors so the white ants couldn't eat them, and the distinctive louvres. They were streets ahead of what other people had.

Harry and Nancy Giese moved to Darwin in 1954 from Canberra when Mr Giese was appointed director of social welfare. It was October and very hot when they arrived.

Mr Giese selected the last house in the Myilly precinct. The director of works lived next door, the director of health lived on the other side and the magistrate lived in the first house, which is now the headquarters of the National Trust.

While her husband died in 2000, Mrs Giese still lives in the same house and remembers sheltering under the kitchen table while Cyclone Tracy banged and crashed around them. The overhang on the roof was damaged by part of a roof that blew off the hospital across the road, but otherwise the house escaped unscathed while the one next door was completely destroyed.

Mrs Giese explained how her son Richard, now a Darwin doctor, closed the louvres on the side the cyclone was coming from and then, after a lull when it changed direction and came back, he closed the louvres on that side and opened them on the other side. That probably stopped the roof from blowing off.

Trees in the garden were blown over and there was no power. The hospital had a generator and they allowed the Gieses to run a line so they had lights two days later. A 1000-gallon (4546-litre) water tank on a concrete block in the backyard disappeared in the cyclone and they later found it on the beach.

The Giese house is open-plan, like all those designed by Burnett, with a large living area and the kitchen and bathroom off to the side. The tops of the partition walls don't

PAINTINGS ADORN THE BEDROOM WALLS.

extend as far as the ceilings and there's little privacy. There are louvres in the inside walls as well.

The house is all fibro and the floor is cypress pine from the Tiwi Islands. The floor was sanded and stained in 1983 and has never been touched since.

There are three bedrooms, two smallish, with the main bedroom located off the living area. The toilet and bathroom are original. A sewing room has been turned into a dining room.

The kitchen has a walk-in pantry. A fuel stove was taken out and replaced by an electric stove, and the louvres let in the sea breeze from Fannie Bay.

Mrs Giese said possums were frequent visitors in the wet season. 'They are quite noisy but not too intrusive. They get in the ceiling, and when they start to breed and fight there is terrible screeching but I've become used to it.'

Much of the garden has been re-planted since the cyclone and the garden is almost a tropical jungle now. 'I have concentrated on colour and flowering trees and shrubs which attract the wildlife,' Mrs Giese explained. 'I have lovely birds and they are all great foragers, raking up the garden which oxygenates the soil. Two white cranes live here and there's black scrub fowls, goannas and frill-necked lizards and a few golden tree snakes. They're not venomous and they don't worry me. As long as you leave them alone they leave you alone.'

THE OPEN LOUVRES.

Mrs Giese has had a busy life in Darwin, which she attributed to being the result of moving there when it was a developing area. She was a founding member of the Northern Territory Arts Council and a federal director of the Arts Council of Australia. She was a member of the music board of the Australia Council and was chairman of the council of the Darwin Community College, the city's first tertiary institution. When it became the Darwin Institute of Technology she was chairman of that council, and then when it became the Northern Territory University, she was deputy chancellor for three years and in 1993 took over as chancellor until 2003 when she retired. For her community work she was awarded an OBE and AO.

National Trust director Elizabeth Close said the Myilly Point homes were once the most stately in Darwin. They are now significant because they are the only four left and have been continuously lived in or used since first built.

'The other significance for them is that Myilly Point is where the bulldozers stopped in the 1980s when Paul Everingham was the Northern Territory administrator,' she said. 'He had a plan to clear all of the land and build a casino. What happened here is that because Mrs Giese and her husband had lived in the house for more than 30 years, they realised it was about to go so began moves to save it and the others. It was a long bitter fight over twelve months with the government and administrator and galvanised the whole community, but eventually the homes were saved.'

The National Trust owns two — Magistrate's House and Burnett House — and a block of land where Tracy destroyed another. They have full heritage listing and are protected by legislation.

Ms Close said they survived the war and the cyclones and she had her fingers crossed they would survive for a long time to come. But she thought it was the luck of the draw they survived Tracy. A lot of the older places were damaged but survived while the newer homes blew apart.

'If we don't watch what else happens around Darwin, we won't have any of the older homes left,' she added. 'There's a few salted around in private hands but a lot were sold and shifted to the back blocks.

'Units seem to be the rationale nowadays built from cement and cement bricks. The cypress pine is hard to source, certainly to build numbers of houses like this. It still has to be found for repair jobs on floors and rafters and that is quite a challenge.'

Government House

LEFT: DARWIN'S GOVERNMENT HOUSE HAS SURVIVED CYCLONES, AIR RAIDS AND WHITE ANTS.

BOTTOM LEFT: THE TROPICAL GARDEN.

BOTTOM RIGHT: THE SIDE VERANDAH.

Government House in Darwin is the Northern Territory's oldest building, surviving three major cyclones, earthquakes, 65 air raids and continuous attacks by white ants. Also known as the Residence, the Residency, and the House of Seven Gables, Government House has been lived in since the central stone room, now the drawing room, was built to form the main section of the first house in 1871. Situated on a hill overlooking the entrance to Darwin Harbour, it has been the home for a succession of residents and administrators and has earned the affection of Darwin's population, coming to be regarded as 'pretty special'.

The eighteenth administrator, His Honour Ted Egan AO, and wife Nerys Evans also think Government House is special. 'It is a beautiful house. It is a very seductive house. It makes people love it. The staff love it and want to do things for the house just as if she was a living person that says, "Come here, love me, work for me and take care of me please because I'm worth it," ' Ms Evans said.

Ted Egan commented it was like the affection sailors had for a ship. 'You think of the house as "she",' he said. ' "She is a grand place" and the level of loyalty and devotion of the staff is something that doesn't just happen. It's self-motivating. The house seems to have established a decorum of its own and everyone fits in or they don't seem to come here. You never hear of a bad employee or someone who didn't love working here. Even the people who work on a temporary basis say, "We would love a fulltime job here." '

Ms Evans agreed. 'Everyone is nostalgic about the house. The major factor is someone has lived here all the time. It's been a residence. It's a working house and is used every day.'

Government House stands on the site 20 metres above Darwin Harbour where the Larrakia people assembled in April 1870 to watch Captain William Bloomfield Douglas, his wife, two sons, five daughters and an Irish maid arrive to become the first government resident. They moved into two huts on the beach while Captain Douglas supervised the construction of the first house.

The central room was built with local porcellanite stone from the cliffs at Fannie Bay and was hand-carved by Chinese, groups of prisoners and tradesmen, with timber bedrooms, bathrooms and pantry opening off it on either side. The kitchen was built from logs and stood on its own a little way from the house. The roof was thatched and the floors made of cypress pine.

Captain Douglas wanted the stone room to double as a courthouse as well as be used for other public purposes such as church services and for some of the first billiard games to be played in Darwin. But while he enjoyed living in the house, so did the white ants, which happily munched through all the timber.

Captain Douglas left in 1873 but not before he wrote to the South Australian government officials in Adelaide, who

THE CREST ON THE FRONT GATE.

A FUNCTION ROOM.

then had responsibility for the Northern Territory, to complain about the damage by the white ants. He also suggested another storey should be added.

The ants continued their path of destruction and turned the house into what the second Northern Territory administrator, George Scott, described as 'a dilapidated barn'. The ants also destroyed the house piano and wine stocks.

The new government secretary and architect John George Knight, who had helped design Parliament House in Melbourne, addressed the problem of the white ants, saying the Residence 'appears to have been built upon a great bed of these destructive pests …' He agreed an upper storey should be added and recommended it be built from stone and cement and the locally grown cypress, which appeared to be termite resistant.

But the timber for the upper storey was imported from the south and within twelve months the white ants had made a feast of it. The damage was so great that locals feared the upper storey would part company with the ground floor in a heavy squall. As a result, it was pulled down in 1877 by the third resident, Irish-born Edward Price, and the construction of a new house was put under the

supervision of Knight and senior surveyor and supervisor of works Gilbert McMinn. They retained the stone central room as the core and built the additions that featured a seven-gabled roof from stone and cypress pine. The cypress was also used for the floor.

McMinn noted that the rooms, although not many, were large and in case any future resident required a greater number of rooms, could be divided by a wooden partition without any alteration being required to doors or windows. Following its completion in 1879, Mr Price reported, 'The new Residence is now complete and is a plain substantial building and its fine appearance from the harbour will I trust have a better effect on our visitors than the old unsightly shanty which was more like a cow shed than the Government Residence.'

The *Northern Territory Times* reported: 'The House of Seven Gables known as the Residence is now finished and though it may not be considered a model of architectural skill, it may claim to be a comfortable house and well suited to the climate. There is no doubt that the squaring of the stone for the Residence by Chinese added to the cost but it has rendered the building more substantial and solid.'

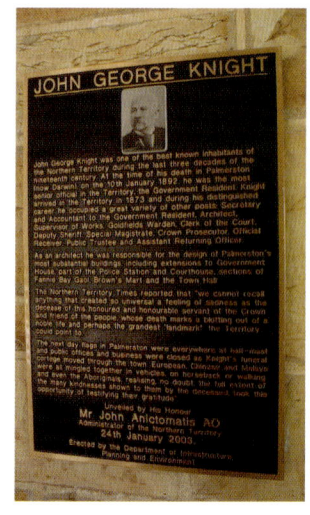

In an unusual twist, architect John Knight became the fifth resident and moved into the house in 1890. He made more changes, including the covering with cement of some of the stone on the outside that had rotted away because of its salt content. He also cleared some of the surrounding overgrown vegetation to open the 180-foot (55-metre) verandah to the sea.

Charles Dashwood replaced Knight as resident in 1892 and he was the first to experience a cyclone in the house. It devastated the town in January 1897, flooding the Residency and blowing away part of the roof and verandah, although the main section escaped serious damage. The flagstaff was ripped from its foundations.

Appointment of the eighth resident, Adelaide solicitor and former member of parliament representing the Northern Territory in the South Australian government, Samuel Mitchell, coincided with the federal government taking control of the Territory in 1911. One of his first jobs was to report on the state of the Residency.

He described it as dilapidated and generally unattractive because of its dark, moist paintwork. He said the roof was leaking again and the lighting so inadequate it was impossible to read at night with the kerosene lamps.

John Gilruth was the next resident and he changed the name of the Residency to Government House and the resident's title to administrator. He also claimed the state of the house was so bad that 'no white woman would live in the quarters …'

The servants' bathrooms and sleeping quarters were rebuilt and the kitchen modernised. More cement had to be put on the exposed stonework.

Darwin people disliked Gilruth's administration so much they marched on Government House and demanded he be sacked in December 1918. The big crowd broke through the

THE DINING ROOM'S ABORIGINAL PAINTINGS.

93

picket fence, damaged latticework on the windows and pulled down the netting around the tennis court. Gilruth packed up and left a few weeks later.

Another government report on the condition of the house in 1925 found it had not been painted since 1918, the gutters were corroded and water spilled everywhere when it rained. It was painted in 1928 and parts of the back and side verandahs were filled in with bamboo lattice and shutters.

Another cyclone hit Darwin in 1937 and again caused widespread damage. Most of the Government House garden was wrecked and a garage destroyed. Repairs were makeshift with some new verandah slats nailed from roof to floor but Hilda Abbott, the wife of administrator Charles Abbott, did her own redecoration that included a new paint job in white, jade green, blue, cream and yellow.

Mrs Abbott also rejuvenated the terraced gardens with coloured stones. A union-run newspaper called the *Northern Standard* described the renovations this way: 'Government House has been changed from an eyesore to a veritable fairy palace at a trifling cost of some thousands of pounds.'

On 19 February 1942, Darwin was attacked in a surprise air raid by Japanese aircraft. The staff at Government House took shelter in an underground room under the administrator's office, which took a direct hit, killing a laundry maid.

After a second raid a few hours later, 243 people had been killed in Darwin and dozens more wounded. An Australian flag flying on Government House attracted the Japanese pilots who riddled it with machine gun bullets. The flag is now in the Canberra War Memorial. Darwin was bombed 64 more times but Government House, although damaged, managed to survive.

In 1950 Darwin was hit by a strong earthquake and Government House was again badly damaged. It was repaired by the then administrator Frank Wise, who also had fluorescent lights installed in the verandahs. Wise considered building a new Government House but scrapped the idea and instead recommended a new roof be put on.

Frederick Chaney in 1970 converted the southern end of the house into a four-room flat to replace the 'lean-to' administrator quarters. He also built a swimming pool in the courtyard.

In 1974, Cyclone Tracy caused the next damage to the long-suffering Government House. It hit Darwin early on Christmas Eve and for the next six hours of Christmas Day destroyed three-quarters of Darwin, killing 65 people and injuring 645 in the process.

The asbestos louvres on three sides of the verandahs probably saved external damage to the main building although

THE QUEEN'S BEDROOM.

A VIEW FROM THE VERANDAH TO THE GARDEN.

He moved the swimming pool to the back of the house and everything looked spic and span for visits by the Queen and Duke of Edinburgh in 1983 and the Prince of Wales in 1988.

Replacing Mr Johnston in 1989 was another Territory man, James Muirhead, and his wife Margaret. Mr Muirhead was a Supreme Court judge and had presided over the controversial Lindy Chamberlain trial.

The Muirheads made the historic house more accessible to the public and, with the National Trust, organised a series of open days so that Territorians could have a closer look. Mr Muirhead also established a committee to advise on the best way to decorate the house so various administrators' tastes did not override the longer term plan.

In February 1991, Mr Muirhead announced his philosophy on the role of Government House: 'We take the view Government House, that unique old building known as The House of Seven Gables, with such an interesting history, belongs to the people of the Territory. It is their house and should be utilised as such. It is to the credit of government of all persuasions that the old place has been repaired and reinstated, not demolished, despite severe damage resulting from both war and cyclone.'

It was during Mr Muirhead's term that Government House was entered on the Register of the National Estate. A few years later it was also recognised under new Northern Territory heritage legislation.

The next administrator in 1993 was former Family Court judge and Northern Territory Chief Justice Keith John Austin Asche, who lived there with his wife Dr Valerie Asche, a prominent microbiologist. During his term, Mr Asche acquired a pair of polished oyster pearl shells with pictures on the inner side painted by a Japanese artist commissioned by John George Knight in 1890. One picture is Knight's own house, made from mud bricks in the 1880s and known locally as the Mud Hut, Mudville on the Sea, or Knight's Folly. The other is the Residency.

The Asches were succeeded by the former Northern Territory under-treasurer Neil Raymond Conn and his wife Lesley. They took an active interest in the history of the house and enhanced its appearance.

Two original doorways between the main rooms — the drawing room and a room called the Prince of Wales Room because he stayed there in 1988 when it was a bedroom — were restored in 1998 to make a substantial function area.

the doors and windows caved in. The roof was loosened and water damaged inside walls, which had to be replaced.

The new administrator's quarters lost their roof and were so badly damaged there was no alternative but to demolish them. New quarters were built in late 1975 along with new garages and a gardener's hut.

When John England took over as administrator in 1976 he put new ceilings in the State Room and the whole house received a new roof, retaining the seven-gables design.

In 1981, his successor, Eric Johnston, built a new kitchen within the old kitchen to retain the external appearance of the building. He also repainted the house, carried out a redecoration and put down new carpet.

John Anictomatis AO was the seventeenth administrator from November 2000 to October 2003. Mr Anictomatis, a long-term Darwin resident and devoted Territorian, and wife Jeanette were active in many community organisations.

The current administrator, Ted Egan took over from Mr Anictomatis. Mr Egan said that when the phone call came he asked, ' "Are you sure you're talking to the right bloke?" The woman on the other end said, "Yes," and I said, "Do you know how old I am?" She said, "Yes."

'So I asked for a couple of days to think about it but I phoned back and said I was happy to accept. It's a marvellous job.'

Mr Egan went to Darwin in 1949 when he was sixteen and lived there until a few years before Cyclone Tracy. Then he went to Canberra in the public service but was still involved with activities in Darwin during those few years.

He left the public service and made a living as a singer for 25 years, tapping out tunes on an empty beer carton he called the 'fosterphone' or 'victorphone', depending on which brand he had just finished, Fosters or VB.

'So I don't bring any great specific experience to the job except that I've lived here. I was a patrol officer and know the Territory well, a historian.

'I have an honorary doctorate at the Northern Territory University because my life work has been in the Territory and the advancement of its people getting on with one another.'

Mr Egan remarked that his wife described the job of administrator at his age as a geriatric fairytale. 'It's a pretty accurate description. It's a very demanding job but it's never stressful. You are just moving among achievers all the time, having a great time really and being spoiled by the staff.'

Mr Egan, sworn in as administrator in November 2003, said there was a lovely nostalgia to the house because everyone in the Northern Territory was aware it had survived three major cyclones with minimal damage each time and 65 air raids, most of which were in the area. 'There was some damage to the house but structurally it retained its integrity and it has just recently been rehabilitated in the past ten years to the level it is now. The stonework has been repaired again and the verandahs tiled.'

Mr Egan, an author and songwriter since 1969, has made 28 albums but does not intend to write a song about Government House. 'I've written hundreds of songs but almost all of them are about people. I might write something about a particular administrator. I haven't got it on the agenda but that would be more likely to happen and I would paint the person into the setting rather than do the setting only,' he said.

He recalled that there had been a lot of music at the house on the terrace in earlier days. However, he didn't think it could be done now because there was always the need for amplification. They used to have string bands playing there before the war and it was pretty well the social hub of Darwin. Ms Evans believed that now the house wouldn't be big enough to hold the number of people who would want to come.

'But we have a foundation ball. There's a Government House foundation to look after everything. The furniture now belongs to the house. We have commissioned six paintings because it's lived in. I really think that is important.'

These paintings, which now hang in the dining room, are called 'Seasons of the Kunwinjku'. They are from Western Arnhem Land and depict the various seasons, starting with *kudgewk*, which is from January to March. By Bruce Nabegeyo, the painting is called 'Djabbo'. During *kudgewk*, it's raining and all the rivers are running and full of fish.

Towards the end of the wet the barramundi go to breed and then the dry season starts in about April–May. People

THE FRONT FAÇADE.

are out hunting again and singing the songs. This season is called *bangkereng* and has been captured by Isaiah Nagurrgurrba in a painting called 'Barramundi'.

June–July is cooler and everyone is on the go, active and hunting. The painting for this season, *yekke*, was done by Lofty Nadjamerrek AO, and is called 'Wakewokken', which means sugarbag.

August–September, the season known as *wrrkeng*, is hot and sticky and everyone is cranky. The bush bees are making honey from the plants and trees. Hunting will continue until the first rains. Done by Thompson Yulidjirri, the painting is called 'Hunting Season'.

Done by Danny Djorlom, the next painting is called 'Djitnuk' and is for the season of *kurrung*, which is October–November. It depicts a spirit with fish hooks on his knees, who steals your catch when you're fishing.

The final season is *kurnumeleng*, December. Then the rain starts, the crocodiles are fat, everything is fat. The painting is done by Gabriel Maralngurra, and is called 'Fauna of Flood Plains'. And so the cycle begins again.

Each painting was done on special paper to approximate bark. The work is done with either grass or hair dipped in a bucket of paint.

'We got all the artists in and filmed them in front of the paintings. I can speak some of the language. As a collection, it will be priceless in about 50 years time but I'm not putting a monetary value on it,' Mr Egan said.

GOVERNMENT HOUSE SEEN FROM THE ROAD.

There are 2033 louvres around the verandah and they are opened every morning and closed at night. If there is a cyclone warning, they are tightened with a special tool. Originally they were bamboo.

The Queen stayed at Government House in 1982 so the main guest suite at the front is now called the Queen's Bedroom. It was refurbished in 1994 with new carpets and curtains and a new buffet reproduced in Queen Anne style.

The drawing room is the central stone hall of the original Residence and the oldest-known European structure in Darwin. It is used for functions in the wet season.

A nineteenth-century bookcase is made from mahogany with a carved pediment at the top and bears the Victorian Crown and Royal Cipher 'VR' (Victoria Regina) on the metal fittings.

The dining room is used for formal lunches and dinners. It has red cedar sideboards, tables and chairs. Extended, the table can sit up to 24 people. The room was redecorated in 1992. A Vienna wall clock made in 1880 from walnut with brass pendulum and weights strikes on the half-hour and hour.

The magnificent gardens cover an area of 1.4 hectares. John George Knight was responsible for establishing a tropical grove with terraced walks in 1878–79. The gardens were re-established in the 1930s by Mrs Hilda Abbott. Extensive landscaping was carried out in the late 1970s and again in the 1980s.

Much of the garden is on sloping ground. Head gardener Dermot Wait said there are about 420 different plants, which provide a fairly diverse range utilising different leaf forms, leaf shapes and flower colour.

The oldest tree on the grounds is a Northern Territory native about 104 years old called Ban Yang. The botanical name is *Ficus virens*. The trees can continue growing for 1000 years. Another significant tree is a *Toona australis*, commonly known as Australian red cedar. The trees are fairly rare in Darwin and Government House has one of the biggest.

A great deal of development is being done, together with the ongoing maintenance. Mr Wait has tried to maintain a tropical theme within a tranquil setting. His dream is to have an oasis of green in what will be in time a concrete jungle because of the massive development in Darwin.

Iandra

Restoring an old home locals call 'the castle' took on a whole new meaning for Margaret Morris when she and her husband bought the historic 57-room Iandra mansion set in rolling wheat country.

They particularly wanted to acknowledge the achievements of the original owner, member of parliament and share-farming pioneer George Greene, but it took several carpenters working fulltime for more than fifteen years, and numerous painters and electricians to help bring the home back to pristine condition. One carpenter spent two years repairing hundreds of broken leadlight windows.

But when the main restoration was finished, all the hard work was clearly worthwhile. 'We were more than pleased with what was done,' Mrs Morris said. 'We could have turned it into a guesthouse or something else but that would have cheapened our aim in life.'

Built from steel-reinforced concrete, the mansion with its turret-like balconies lies a few kilometres from the south-west New South Wales village of Greenethorpe, which was named after Iandra's original owner, George Henry Greene. Greenethorpe in its heyday had two schools, two cafés, two butcher shops and a barber. Now there's only one school, a post office, general store, a one-man police station, hotel, fuel depot and rural supplier, and three churches. The village's Shamrock Hotel, made from mud bricks, is one of the oldest in the district and is still thriving.

Iandra is the second homestead built on the property. The first home, named Mt Oriel, was built in 1880 from bricks fired on the 13,000-hectare property Mr Greene bought in 1878. In 1908 he converted the single-storey house to the present two-storey reinforced-concrete building using the same foundations.

During this time he also developed the village of Greenthorpe. Many of the farm's employees lived in primitive houses, some with bag walls and bark roofs. Mr Greene gave the job of providing better residences for them to building contractor W.T. Millard, of Young, and the contract provided for four-room cottages with corrugated iron walls, lined with Baltic pine. Each was to cost £120 and would have a toilet and 1000-gallon (4546-litre) water tank.

The school, post office and hall were included in the plan but Mr Greene vigorously opposed a hotel. However, after one lost hearing, a hotel licence was eventually granted in 1911 to a John Gavin.

An English architect was engaged to plan the new Iandra home but Mrs Greene did most of the design. She wanted to ensure she could enjoy the views of the rolling country-side and the distant Weddin Mountains.

The rebuilding work began in August 1908 and the original Mt Oriel home was left largely intact, being incorporated in the new building. The total cost amounted to around £63,000, a huge sum back then.

A large staff of servants looked after the home while seven gardeners were employed who were also responsible for tending the orchards, lawns and hedges on the grounds.

IANDRA'S GOTHIC CHURCH.

At the same time Mr Greene built the elaborate reinforced concrete stables, a water tower with silo underneath, a filtration plant, sheds, and 40 houses for share-farmers.

The property also had its own Gothic church, school, store, post office, blacksmith shop, staff quarters and a shearing shed. Today, the shearing shed has also been faithfully restored by the Morrises.

No doubt Mr Greene enjoyed the good life because Iandra had all the modern luxuries way before its time. Electricity was supplied by a steam-driven generator, hot and cold running water was available, and servants could be called by bells installed in every room.

Mr Greene began growing William Farrer's Federation wheat in the 1880s, which yielded 37 bushells an acre while its nearest competitor returned 29 bushells. He also introduced a share-farming system in 1893 which was so successful it attracted hundreds of people eager to have a look how it worked, including an agricultural Commission of Inquiry from Scotland.

Around 350 men were employed on the property, not counting the 61 share-farmers, contractors and carriers. The share-farmers eventually bought their own piece of land and Iandra now comprises around 1150 hectares. Crops like canola, triticale and oats are still grown.

Mr Greene became a prominent breeder of shire horses, experimented successfully with superphosphate and was the first farmer to demonstrate the reaper binder and, in 1910, the Massey Harris reaper thresher, now known as a header. He also ran sheep, and at one time the property carried more than 19,000.

In addition, Mr Greene organised the layout for the village of Greenethorpe and used his influence to get a rail line built there from the next small town of Koorawatha.

THE LARGE ENTRANCE HALL.

THE DINING ROOM AND ITS FEATURE TIMBERWORK.

By the early 1900s, Mr Greene was sending more than 100,000 bags of wheat to the siding at Greenethorpe, the biggest yield to come from one property. One harvest of 10,000 tonnes involved more than 600 people, 23 carting teams, 700 horses and nine steam chaff cutters, resources never before seen on that scale in New South Wales.

Mr Greene died in 1911 and the property was subdivided and sold privately between 1914 and 1927. Iandra farm manager Leonard I'Anson, who had arrived there in 1906 after a six-week wagon trip from South Australia, bought the homestead block and adjoining 2300 acres (932 hectares) in 1927. He had been one of the share-farmers before becoming farm manager in 1912.

Alfred I'Anson ran the property until 1956 when he sold the homestead and some of the surrounding land to the Methodist Church for use as a home for under-privileged and first-offender boys. Another family member, Keith I'Anson, lived 5 kilometres away until the mid-1980s.

Mr and Mrs Morris, who had a farm at Rylstone, first found out about Iandra when they began taking boys from the home for weekends. One weekend in late 1974 they had to drive the boys back to Iandra.

A SUNNY NOOK.

THE SITTING ROOM.

'We came to the front and I saw this great concrete house and thought, "How do they ever clean it?" ' Mrs Morris said. 'My husband had sold his structural steel company in Sydney and we didn't want to invest the money back there so when he heard Iandra was for sale, he was interested.

'We knew it was cropping country and ideal for fat lambs and wool so we bought it in 1975 and were faced with the mammoth restoration task. The front door was covered with corrugated iron, the billiard room windows were smashed and the house generally was in a poor state.

'The carpenter asked where he should begin work,' Mrs Morris continued. 'We told him the flagpole. He said, "Why?" We said if we start on the ground we might never get the work finished but the flagpole is a sign the job is over so if we start there, we can stop any time we want. It was more than fifteen years later working fulltime before the job was finished but my husband wanted everything to be authentic.'

Iandra, designed by an unknown English architect and built by Edward G. Stone, is a distinctive example of the federation Romanesque architectural style with Tudor influences that reflect its feudal-like role in the history of the area. It is an excellent example of reinforced-concrete construction, rendered on the outside to resemble sandstone.

At the back, two-storey wings form a courtyard, which has a well as its central feature. A square tower with slit windows has an octagonal turret on top and is complemented by tall medieval chimneys.

A crenellated parapet runs down one side and the roof is clad with asbestos cement shingles. The guttering and ridge capping is copper.

Large areas of timber wall panelling are present inside. The stairway and foyer panels are oak and the dining room Queensland blackbean.

Mrs Morris said the house was cold in winter because there was no heating, and very hot upstairs in summer. Sometimes she slept in the office where it was cooler.

Maintaining Iandra is never-ending and the job is made particularly difficult because of hard-to-get-to areas such as the windows on the top storey. Mrs Morris said the windows need work done to them but access for a builder and painter requires the use of a cherry picker, an enclosed platform on the top of a crane-like arm mounted on the back of a truck and designed to lift people high in the air. And then the tradespeople have to be co-ordinated so they can be there at the same time.

Some upgrading of the electrical wiring is also on the agenda and that's another difficult job because the wires have been hidden inside the thick walls, a modern concept unheard of elsewhere when the home was built.

Mrs Morris said stories that Iandra was designed so Mr Greene could entertain royalty don't appear to be true, although a governor-general, Lord Northcote, once stayed there in 1908.

'The share-farming was such a success people were coming from overseas to have a look and we think Mr Greene just needed a big home so he could put them up for a few weeks. They were also people used to a high lifestyle.'

The garden features 100-year-old Moreton Bay fig trees, planted by Mr Greene as a canopy for a circular front drive that never eventuated, along with an orange tree and honeysuckle. There are many roses, some original pines, lots of natives, agapanthus and lilac.

Citrus and fruit trees provide Mrs Morris with all the ingredients to make jam, and pepper trees line the road boundary. A well fed by run-off from the roof and two bores supply water for the garden. Tennis and croquet courts at the front of the house have been abandoned.

THE UPSTAIRS VERANDAHS.

Lal Lal

Archibald Fisken was only eleven when he landed in Victoria from Scotland with his parents and uncle and aunt in the 1830s. His father, also Archibald, brought with them a prefabricated iron house and 40 casks of oatmeal.

Archibald senior built the house at the top of Lonsdale Street in Melbourne and, intending to keep an historical record, wrote in his diary about seeing Governor Charles La Trobe riding past. He also wrote about Aborigines holding a corroboree under a big tree on the Yarra River, but they were about the only entries.

Young Archibald's uncle, Peter Inglis, didn't stay in Melbourne. He settled on a property he called Ingliston at Ballan on the Werribee River, north-west of Melbourne, and the boy went there to live. He was mentored and tutored on the property.

Inglis put Archibald in charge of the property when he was nineteen. It was a huge run that stretched all the way to Ballarat, with what would become the Lal Lal property forming part of it.

In his thirties, Archibald married Charlotte McNamara, sixteen, from Sydney. The wedding was held in Melbourne and his friends at a buck's party the night before had a drunken foot race down the cobblestones in Collins Street.

Archibald by now was a competent farmer and his uncle gave him Lal Lal on the proviso he would never put his name on a promissory note. So Archibald took his new wife there and they lived in a small stone house on a lower section of the property.

He built granite stables in 1858 to house Akbar, his top thoroughbred. The story goes that on this horse Archibald outrode the bushranger Captain Moonlite. Moonlite led an incredible double life as a clergyman by day and a bushranger by night. He was arrested in 1872 for a bank robbery at Egerton, near Ballarat, and sent to Ballarat Gaol but escaped (see Borambola).

Archibald and Charlotte had a son they called Archibald James and he too worked on the property when he was old enough. He married May Wanliss. Her forbears had apparently come to Australia with the Fiskens in the 1830s.

Archibald James and May built the present Lal Lal homestead in 1911. The old stone house was difficult to live in: it was small, there had been lots of additions and they wanted something more fitting.

The new homestead overlooked a magnificent lake that Archibald had dammed on the Lal Lal Creek in 1847 to supply water for the farm. (Lal Lal is an Aboriginal word for water.) It originally had a timber retaining wall but that was swept away in a flood in the 1860s. Granite quarried on the property was used to build a new one.

Archibald James and May had one child and they called him Archibald Clyde Wanliss Fisken. He married Elspeth Cameron from Tasmania and they had four children: Archibald John, Cynthia, Topsy and Virginia.

Archibald Clyde, educated at Geelong Grammar School, went to England and joined the Royal Artillery in World War I. He was awarded the Military Cross for bravery in France.

In 1934, he was elected the federal member for Ballarat and served one term. He was chairman of the Australian Meat Board for ten years and also served on Buninyong Shire Council. He died in 1970.

THE TOOL SHED.

LEFT: THE EDWARDIAN-STYLE LAL LAL HOMESTEAD.

BOTTOM LEFT: ROSES SURROUND THE VERANDAHS.

BOTTOM RIGHT: THE LAKE ON LAL LAL CREEK.

His son, Archibald John, also went to school in Geelong and it was there that he met Patricia Falkiner of the Riverina sheep-breeding family. When her father joined the navy in World War II, she went to live at Boonoke North, the property owned by her grandfather Otway Falkiner. There she had a governess and then attended a subsidised school on the property with about fifteen other children from neighbouring stations. However, the school burnt down and she went to Wagga Wagga for a few months before attending Hermitage Grammar at Geelong.

Archibald Clyde Fisken's daughter Topsy was also at the school and through her Patricia Falkiner met Archibald John. They were married in Melbourne in 1950 but went to Lal Lal to live, where they had four children.

Patricia Fisken now lives in the homestead. She said that for the first eighteen months she and her husband lived in the shearers' quarters. 'That was character building, especially in the middle of winter when you could scrape the condensation off the rug on the bed. My eldest son Archibald David Clyde was born there.

'Eventually we built another house on the property and moved into that. David now lives there. My other son Geoff, who manages the property, lives in a house he and his wife Suzie built. I have two daughters, Rena, and Anita, who lives in western Australia.'

The Lal Lal homestead is Edwardian double brick and faces the south, which is unusual because it misses the winter sun. The brickwork in the home is magnificent with no sign of wear or cracks.

THE SITTING ROOM.

The sixteen-room house has a bedroom wing and a service wing that are about equal size. There were four bedrooms when they had servants and Mrs Fisken's husband Archibald John slept out on the south verandah. However, because there is no staff now, Mrs Fisken has done some alterations. The kitchen was dark and inconvenient so she put in windows facing the lake. It had large glass panels in the roof but they were painted over and covered by green Holland blinds. The paint and the blinds came off!

'We knocked a door through the wall where the servery was between the kitchen and the dining room so you can walk through. The adjoining scullery was stripped out and we put in another big timber-framed window. The three main rooms are really good. The drawing room overlooks the lake and Elspeth, my mother-in-law, put in a big picture window when she lived here. I put glass panels in the doors between the sitting room and drawing room.'

These main rooms all have red cedar ceilings 13 feet (4 metres) high.

The dining room furniture is original. The large mahogany table seats fourteen and the sideboards have legs carved like lions. A large painting that almost fills an entire wall was done by a Polish artist from Gdansk and was bought specially for the room by Archibald James.

The house has two long hallways, six pantries and three bathrooms. The staff wing has been turned into an area for children to play.

The rambling gardens are the result of a succession of dedicated Fiskens. Much of the

THE DINING ROOM AND ITS MAHOGANY FURNITURE.

104

LOOKING THROUGH TO THE SITTING ROOM.

garden structure was established around 1911 when the homestead was built and it hadn't changed a great deal until Pat Fisken took over.

Her mother-in-law had been a keen gardener and she inherited some of her ideas by planting mostly evergreen shrubs in order to make the garden easier to look after. Mrs Fisken has also converted the surface of a tennis court from grass to sand, again for easier maintenance. Novel garden pieces include a metal dog and dragonfly and granite sculptures.

One of the features of the garden are the mature trees, like the magnificent redwood, weeping elms, maples and palms that were planted more than 100 years ago. They make a good backdrop. There are also lots of roses, *Philadelphus* and rhododendrons.

ONE OF THE HALLWAYS

Before he died, Mrs Fisken's husband Archibald John had wanted the garden to join the lake, which is a good distance from the house. She decided to create that effect by building a low stone ha-ha wall to the lake's edge.

Traditionally granite had been quarried from the property to create the network of paths and stone walls used in the garden and Mrs Fisken is still doing that. She is creating new areas whenever she can, although her sons believe she should be making the gardens smaller rather than bigger.

The Fiskens run cattle and 13,000 sheep, and grow hay to feed their cattle in winter and to sell, as well as other crops. The property covers almost 5000 acres (2025 hectares).

A 100-YEAR-OLD PALM TREE IN THE GARDEN.

Luxulyan

Courtney Hawke arrived from Cornwall in the late 1880s and went to work on an orchard called Roseteague on the slopes of Mount Canobolas, an extinct volcano near Orange in central New South Wales. His employer, John Hicks, had come to the colony in 1854 and, after working for three years with George Hawke, of Pendarves at Byng, had bought a block of timbered land at Canobolas in 1858.

Hicks cleared just over 1 hectare and planted it with cherries, apples, peaches, pears, plums and grapes. His son, Joseph Solomon Hicks, took over Roseteague in 1875 and planted another 5 hectares as well as 4 hectares on a nearby property called Braehead. He also replanted the original orchard and by 1900 had 29 hectares of fruit trees.

By then Courtney Hawke had learnt the ropes and saved enough money to buy just over 18 hectares of undeveloped land from Joseph Hicks in 1899. He married local girl Maryanne Favell and they moved into a slab hut on the property he called Luxulyan.

Using six draught horses he cleared the land of trees and rocks and planted table grapes. That turned out to be a disaster because he couldn't get them to the Sydney markets fast enough. Making wine was out because he was a strict Methodist. However, the cherries, apples, pears and plums he grew were a big success. He worked hard on the orchard and, with a handful of other pioneers, helped to make Orange the main fruit-growing district in New South Wales.

Hawke had two daughters, Beatrice and Sissy, and two sons, Wenford Courtney and Harold. The youngest daughter, Beatrice, died while having her third child. Sissy, who had been in Europe, came home via the United States in 1939 after World War II began but died from an infection.

By 1910, Courtney Hawke could afford a new house and he commissioned Orange architect William Lamrock to design one. The federation cottage is double brick with bluestone foundations and was built for £800.

Drawing on the Cornish tradition of hedging, Hawke bordered the house and the orchard with rows of pines to give protection from the wind. The generations since have taken out most of the hedges except a 5-metre manicured wall of dark green that's now a feature of the gardens.

Courtney Hawke had a billiard table and piano for the family's use and he and his wife liked entertaining guests, a tradition the Hawke family has vigorously continued. In 1917 the governor-general, Sir Ronald Munro-Ferguson,

THE REMNANTS OF THE HEDGE.

had lunch at Luxulyan and he and his party and domestic staff posed for photos on the front verandah.

Sheds for the sulkies were made from ripple iron. When the family moved to cars, the sheds were extended. While they are still there today, old stables have been pulled down.

Harold Hawke worked on the orchard with his father and later, in 1936, married Marjorie Ainslie, the daughter of William Arthur Ainslie, a jeweller and optician. They had a son, Courtney Robert, named after his grandfather. Harold bought the property from his father in 1945, and after Courtney Hawke retired and moved into Orange, Harold took up residence in the house. Harold's brother Wenford bought a property at Oberon but later went to Sydney.

LEFT: LUXULYAN, AN EARLY 1900S FEDERATION COTTAGE.

BOTTOM LEFT: THE FRONT VERANDAH.

BOTTOM RIGHT: THE SIDE ENTRANCE.

THE SITTING ROOM.

Courtney the younger married Helen Smith, known as Fem, and they moved into a small cottage on Luxulyan. In 1972 they bought a property next door called Mousehole which had an old 1880s weatherboard cottage with a wattle and daub interior. They lived there until 1979 when Courtney's father Harold retired and moved into Orange. Courtney and Fem sold Mousehole and took over Luxulyan.

Originally the house had gas lighting and then a generator. In the 1950s the electricity was connected and rooms like the bathroom were modernised.

Courtney and Fem have made a number of changes but the house has remained much the same. It originally slept a family of four children and had four bedrooms. Now it has three bedrooms but they are all large and have marble fireplaces.

A cement-floor dairy was inside the house but it has been taken out. 'We knocked down several walls to lighten up the house and we added a new kitchen because we are both keen cooks,' Courtney Hawke said.

'We moved the kitchen into the old laundry area and the old kitchen area is now the dining room, which has a long timber table for dinner parties. My father filled in the back verandah and put in a huge fireplace but we pulled that out and put the verandah back to what it used to be.'

In the early 1980s, after they were hit by drought several seasons in a row, Courtney and Fem made the decision to sell the orchard and keep the house. The fruit trees were also old. Now they have just the 0.8 hectares that the house and gardens sit on and instead of growing fruit they have a business in Orange.

THE MAIN BEDROOM.

LOOKING ALONG THE FRONT
VERANDAH.

THE WATER TANK CELLAR.

Because of their love of food and wine, the Hawkes planted a small vineyard of 200 vines of Italian sangiovese grapes in their backyard. They get up to 200 bottles of wine each vintage for their own use. The wine is called Hill of Hoist because the clothesline shares the area with the vines. An old brick water tank was converted into a perfect cellar.

The garden and fern house initially established by the senior Courtney Hawke in 1910 has been changed enormously. The hedges around the house were part of the original planting but have been trimmed down to let in more light. Harold Hawke put in a vegetable garden at the back of the courtyard hedge and replaced the tennis court that was there with a South African couch bowling green.

When Courtney and Fem took over, they pulled out more hedges and took half the bowling green for a swimming pool for their young daughters, Coco, Georgie and Simone. On their thirtieth wedding anniversary, the swimming pool was taken out and replaced with a formal rose garden.

The garden is designed to be low maintenance and there are lots of trees: olives, *Pinus pinea*, linden and plane. Agapanthus fill each side of the front steps.

A terrace at the bottom of the garden is paved with two weeping elms underplanted with bulbs, lilies, lavenders, bay trees, mint and thyme for fragrance. A large albertine rose hangs off the fence.

There are two dirt wells in the garden that go down about 30 metres. They are still used.

A VIEW OF THE GARDENS.

Mena

James Dalton arrived in Orange in central New South Wales in 1849 and built a store of slabs with a bark roof. He helped to clear the surrounding land of stumps and with the help of another man dug a drain from the store to the main channel, then called Blackman's Swamp Creek.

While James Dalton was working on the clearing and drainage, he closed the store, re-opening it only when a customer came along. The deals that took place were often on a bartering system. There was only one other store in the town at the time. It was owned by John Arkins, who was also the postmaster and clerk of petty sessions.

James' brother, Thomas Dalton, joined him in a partnership in 1858 and they established the firm of Dalton Bros. Gold had been discovered at Ophir, near Orange, in 1851 and the town was growing at a fast rate.

In 1861 James Dalton built the first flour mill. His brother Thomas did not believe the venture would be profitable and had no share in it but its success was clearly demonstrated when flour from the mill won a string of prizes around the globe, beating the world's leading manufacturers. Dalton Bros thrived and in the 1870s the store was the biggest in the country, dealing in a wide range of

MENA, A DALTON-FAMILY HOME.

goods including food, clothing and wool. The building was continually remodelled until it had a street frontage of more than 60 metres and boasted 20 plate-glass windows.

The brothers also established warehouses, stores and an importing agency in Sydney, and held Gulgo, Milbey and Bygoloree stations in the Lachlan district until the partnership was dissolved. In 1928, the stores were sold. Since that time the Orange store has operated as Western Stores, Farmers, Grace Bros and now Myer.

The Daltons were one of the colony's richest and most influential Catholic families. Thomas Dalton, who was member for Orange for nine years, mayor of Orange in 1877–78 and a Papal Knight Bachelor, died in 1901. James Dalton, who was mayor of Orange in 1869–70, bought land he named Duntryleague after his birthplace Doon-tri-liag in County Limerick, Ireland. In 1876 he built a mansion befitting his standing and influence in the community, and lived there until his death in April 1919.

By 1935 the big home had been unoccupied for about six years. So Duntryleague estate — with its 73 hectares, magnificent mansion, stables and gatekeeper's cottage — was bought by the Orange Golf Club for £12,000. It is still the home of golf in Orange.

James Dalton's son, Thomas Garrett Dalton, was also involved in the Orange community and was mayor from 1903 to 1905. He also managed the family business. James Dalton built Thomas Garrett a house in Kite Street,

Orange, around the same time as he built Duntryleague. Named Killarney, it, like other homes the Daltons built in Orange and district, is an excellent example of historic architecture.

Kangaroobie was another Dalton home between Orange and Molong. It fell into disrepair and until new owners took over was becoming increasingly derelict. Locals say that cattle could walk in the back door and out the front. The new owners have restored the house and its surrounding gardens, and have brought new life to this part of the Dalton family legacy.

When Thomas Garrett Dalton died, Killarney was sold, became a private hospital and was renamed Mena. It was sold again in the 1940s and was turned into residential flats.

Since then Mena has had a string of owners, each of them undertaking some conservation work on the house. The present owner, commercial photographer Scott Gilbank, bought the house in 2004 and decided to restore it as close as possible to original.

Timber verandahs on the sides were pulled down and the tiled front verandah was extended to replace them. Matching the hand-cut tiles used when the house was built was difficult but Mr Gilbank eventually sourced the 35 square metres needed in France.

Moulds were taken from the pillar posts at the front and new ones cast for the sides. The timber floors inside were polished and stained and Mr Gilbank had new furniture made in Indonesia to suit the period. Fortunately, all the cedar joinery and stained glass windows were original and in good condition.

The house was repainted inside and out and the garden was rejuvenated.

Mena has five bedrooms, four formal rooms, a sitting room, two bathrooms and an office. There are twelve fireplaces. A gardener's cottage, stables and a garage are at the back.

Mr Gilbank believes all the work has been well worthwhile. He feels he is really only a caretaker, a temporary custodian, of a house that belongs to the community.

THE FRONT GARDEN.

Merribee

Merribee homestead was built to impress, clearly intended to show that a highly successful man lived there. And William Wilson Killen was a successful man. Born in County Antrim, Ireland, in 1860, he came to Australia with his parents and younger brother Edward in 1876 and worked on his father's property Carnerney near Jerilderie in southern New South Wales.

From there his father sent him to manage Elsinora, a property of more than 250,000 acres (101,250 hectares) of unstocked, unimproved and waterless country 160 miles (256 kilometres) beyond Bourke and the Paroo River in western New South Wales. The nearest railway station was 250 miles (400 kilometres) away.

He spent seven years there before leaving his brother Edward to take over. During this time he had stocked the property with 70,000 sheep in a highly successful venture.

Mr Killen managed Pirillie on the Warrego River for Goldsborough Mort and Co for three years and in 1893 leased Bull Plain Estate, near Corowa, with R.E. Young. He bought 16,000 acres (6480 hectares) of that property in 1903 and sold it in several lots in 1908 so he could buy Merribee at Binya, near present-day Griffith in the Riverina.

Merribee, owned by Godfrey McKinnon, was originally called North Gogeldrie, but Mr Killen changed the name because he apparently liked the name of the Victorian town of Werribee, changing the first letter to avoid any confusion between the two. The property then comprised 33,000 acres (13,365 hectares).

In 1891, Mr Killen had married Marion Young, the daughter of Charles Young, who was the member for Kyneton in the Victorian government for nearly twenty years. When they bought Merribee, the plan was to build an impressive new 25-room, three-storey homestead with a tower, to replace the small house already there. Interestingly, although Mr Killen was a Presbyterian who didn't drink or smoke, the homestead included a fully enclosed underground cellar.

Mr Killen brought out two stonemasons from Northern Ireland to dress the sandstone, which was quarried on nearby Mt Binya. Around 40 other tradesmen were employed for the two years it took to complete.

He had already planted an orchard and shade trees on the slope of a gentle hill near the proposed site before construction began.

By 1917, Mr Killen had acquired a total of 1.1 million acres (445,500 hectares) of land in New South Wales and, although a dedicated businessman, still found the time to

THE FRONT ENTRANCE.

become actively involved in community affairs. He was a member of Yanco Shire Council, the Narrandera Pastures Protection Board, New South Wales' Graziers Association, Stock Owners Association and the Farmers and Settlers Association. He was also elected to the federal parliament, holding the seat of Riverina from 1922 until his retirement in 1931. At 6 feet 5 inches (196 centimetres), he was the tallest man in parliament.

Management of Merribee went to his son Harold Charles Killen. Another son, William Bertram Sydney Killen, managed properties in the Narrabri district and a third, Edward

LEFT: MERRIBEE WAS BUILT TO IMPRESS.

BOTTOM LEFT: THE STABLES' WALL.

BOTTOM RIGHT: THE FIRE-WATCH TOWER.

Cecil Lyle Killen, managed Warrawidgee station west of Griffith. Mr Killen had one daughter, Marion Alice.

After his wife's death in 1926, Mr Killen married Myra Dean of Bellevue Hill in Sydney. He died in 1939 at his seaside residence in Manly, but Merribee stayed in the family's hands until 1948.

There were a number of owners after the Killens. Real estate company L J Hooker owned it in 1963 but sold off 10,000 acres (4000 hectares) divided into three blocks for closer settlement. Roy and Dawn Butcher, of Leeton, won one of the blocks.

The Butchers sold their block to Col and Les Irvin in 1976 and bought the homestead block, which then comprised 3300 acres (1336 hectares). The National Trust listed the homestead on the register in 1977.

In 1978 Warner Bros looked at Merribee with the idea of filming Colleen McCullough's *The Thorn Birds* there. Directors and script writers flew to Merribee and hinted Robert Redford was interested in the lead role. But the estimated $17 million cost of making the movie in Australia was considered too high and the television series was made in America.

The Butcher family sold Merribee in 1980 to a West Australian family and since then it has changed hands numerous times, sitting idle for some time. The present owners are Rachelle and Paul Pearsall.

Few young families are prepared to buy and restore a three-storey homestead finished around 1912 and in need of lots of loving care, but that's what the Pearsalls did. The property had gradually been cut up by the succession of owners and when the Pearsalls bought it just before Christmas in 2004, Merribee comprised only 360 acres (145 hectares).

In 1995, the Pearsalls had bought a small farm at Young in southern New South Wales and lived there with their children Alanna, Katia and Joel for nine years. Mr Pearsall is a grain trader and worked as a manager before establishing his own grain storage and trading business with facilities at Carrathool and Benerembah.

In late 2003 they decided it was probably a good idea to move to Griffith to be closer to the business. Mrs Pearsall's family also lived there on an orange orchard at Lake Wyangan. They had looked at buying the Merribee homestead about five years earlier but decided then that it probably wasn't right for them.

When they moved to Griffith they intended to build a new home but Merribee came on the market again so they decided to put in a tender and were successful.

'We bought only the homestead block of 360 acres [145 hectares] so there is no arable land because we are on a ridge. Other people own the property around us. So we have bought the house,' Mrs Pearsall said.

THE SPACIOUS DINING ROOM.

'But she is a lovely old thing and it is quite amazing how many people have either been here or know about it. We met an elderly man at Barellan one day and he said, "I haven't seen you before, are you new in the district?" and I said yes and introduced myself.

'He said, "Where are you?" and I said, "At Merribee homestead," and he said, "I remember coming in and watching movies there in 1954." So there is a lot of history and association and we just enjoy living in it and over the years we will do the garden and the house as we can. It is very liveable now but we will enhance what we have.'

'We bought the property with the intention to make it our family home and that comes with challenges,' Mrs Pearsall commented. 'There is a lot of work to do but we will prioritise and enjoy what we are doing because we don't want it to be stressful.

AN UPSTAIRS BEDROOM.

'We hope we will add to the life of the house and fill it with laughter and friends in the next five, ten or twenty years or how long it takes. But at least someone is here to maintain the house and ensure she survives for another 100 years.'

'We would like to restore the house to its former grandeur, including putting up some wallpaper, doing more painting, replacing picture rails that were removed, replacing light fittings and some decorative work that encompasses the late Victorian–early Edwardian era, like researching the colours and the fabrics,' she added. 'But because we are a young family we will incorporate our own sense of comfort to bring the house alive again. We will do that over a number of years.'

Victorian and early Edwardian and federation in its design and about 115 squares in total area, Merribee homestead has a grand entrance foyer with a Victorian arch, cedar staircase and joinery, cypress floorboards felled and milled on the property, and ornate pressed-metal ceilings on the ground floor.

The ceilings in the five bedrooms on the first floor are timber beaming, which was introduced in the early 1900s and part of the Edwardian era. There are marble fireplaces — white, grey and a brown terracotta colour. The marble fireplaces were traditionally installed in the show rooms: the dining room or smoking rooms and drawing rooms. Fireplaces in other rooms are timber with cast-iron inserts.

The design is traditional; a central hallway runs from front to back with the rooms leading off on both sides. The third floor, or attic level, is a large room with windows on three sides. It has been used as a venue for various functions, including a children's fancy dress ball, and as a movie theatre. At one end a staircase leads up to the tower where a fire-watch used to be kept up in summer.

From the tower a door opens on to what has been dubbed the 'widow's walk'. It originally covered most of the roof.

Through the years restoration work has

THE ENTRANCE HALLWAY.

CERAMIC TABLE SETTING.

been done by different owners and the kitchen and bathrooms have been updated.

The timber verandah and fretwork is again Edwardian. The wide verandah runs along three sides of two of the house storeys and offers excellent shade.

The balustrading, finials and bargeboards are timber but pressed-metal lining has been used on the outside of the tower as well as the gabled area at the front. The doors have brass touch-plates and handles.

There are servants' quarters at the back as well as separate workmen's quarters. The outbuildings include the old stone stables and a garage, which are original.

Mrs Pearsall said their plans for the property also include the restoration of the garden, which had been left to its own devices.

'We will restore some of the lawn and grass areas. We will plant trees and garden beds, perhaps a fountain and put in a new driveway. We will use some of the natural stone from the property and use it in retaining walls and fenced areas in the garden.

'There is so much stone in the area, it is almost a travesty not to use it. A simple elegant garden we can enjoy with friends and family.'

Merrilla

LEFT: THE STONE, GEORGIAN-STYLE HOMESTEAD OF MERRILLA.

BOTTOM LEFT: THE FRONT VERANDAH.

BOTTOM RIGHT: THE COURTYARD.

In May 1823 Brigade-Major John Ovens, Captain Mark Currie RN, an ex-convict named John Wild and a small group of Aborigines set out on horseback from the Moss Vale area to explore the then unknown country south of Lake Weerawa, now called Lake George. A few days later they passed Limestone Plains, now Canberra, and came upon a stretch of land they named Isabella Plains after the daughter of Governor Thomas Makdougall Brisbane.

In early June they discovered what is now the Monaro Plains and set up camp, where they were met by a group of Aborigines. The Ovens and Currie party, the first white people the Aborigines had seen, managed to discover from them that the area was called Maneroo or Monaroo.

Currie was impressed by the great expanse of rolling hills and downs, much of the rich grassland having no trees. So too was the government, which gave Captain Currie a 2000-acre (810-hectare) grant on the Wollondilly River as a reward for discovering the region.

Currie later acquired an additional 700 acres (284 hectares) from Robert Fopp, a neighbour on the western boundary of his land, and this initial holding formed the original Merrilla station. Currie never visited the land he held and leased it to James Chisholm who eventually bought the freehold of the 2700 acres (1094 hectares) in 1839.

James Chisholm became a member of the New South Wales Legislative Council, serving for a total of 27 years until his death in June 1888. He was a successful pastoralist and had settled in the Goulburn district when he was young. He acquired extensive property, including squatting interests. He held East Bland Plains, Kenu, Myali, Mount McPherson, Gledswood near Narellan, and Kippilaw near Goulburn and just down the road from Merrilla. Kippilaw was gained through marriage.

In 1866, Chisholm gave the Merrilla land to one of his nine sons, William Alexander Chisholm, who had married Jane Seton Kinghorne in 1858; and his family held it until 1984. Jane Chisholm died in 1875, aged 47, and William

Chisholm married again to Alice Isobel Morphy in 1877. Alice, concerned for the welfare of her son Bertram, who was serving as a Light Horseman on Gallipoli, sailed for Egypt in mid-1915. Bertram was wounded in action about this time but he later returned to his regiment.

Seeing the lack of facilities for troops in Cairo, Mrs Chisholm opened a canteen nearby at Heliopolis. It was so well received that she opened another at Port Said. Later, with two like-minded women, Verania McPhillamy and a Miss Rout, she established a popular canteen at the Suez

PART OF THE ORIGINAL COTTAGES.

Canal crossing at Kantara. This was developed to include dormitories and dining rooms and eventually had the capacity to handle thousands of men.

Mrs Chisholm's canteens became a cherished institution in the Middle East. Soldiers flocked there in their spare time or when on leave. For a small price they found care, comfort, food, and the luxury of showers. Most of all they were provided with a small touch of home.

Throughout the war Mrs Chisholm put a lot of her own money into the canteens. Any profits were used to provide amenities on the troopships carrying the men home after the war.

She also later helped fund the establishment of the Returned Soldiers' Club in Goulburn. For her war work she was appointed a Dame of the British Empire in 1920.

Older than 60 when the war ended, Dame Alice remained active and soon put her energies into ex-servicemen's welfare, the Country Women's Association and the RSPCA. Later she lived quietly in retirement, dying in 1954 at the age of 97. She is buried in the small Kippilaw cemetery, a few kilometres down the road from Merrilla. Most of the other members of the Chisholm family are also buried there.

William Alexander Chisholm died in October 1902, aged 70.

Originally there were three separate stone cottages, all believed to have been built by James Chisholm before 1858. In the 1860s the cottages were joined together to form the Merrilla homestead.

In 1937 the first-built cottage was demolished and its stone used to build the Georgian-style two-storey addition designed by Bertram Chisholm for his brother Maxwell, who was then living at Merrilla. The second cottage is now the main entrance wing with double front doors and two windows either side facing south-east down the valley across the lawns, garden and swimming pool to the river.

The rubble stone used in the early cottages was quarried on the property. The hand-cut timber, original timber joinery, shingle roofing, hand-made nails and the cellar are still a part of the house, even though the homestead has been extensively renovated by successive owners.

The first renovations by then owner Michael Darling, who bought Merrilla from the Chisholm family in 1984, were done under the guidance of heritage architect Howard Tanner and landscape architects Michael Bligh and Jenny Churchill. The brief was to combine history and present lifestyle needs to preserve Merrilla's original architecture and character, and they did that well.

The homestead forms a traditional U, with three sides and a courtyard in the centre. The wide formal entrance hall is flanked by the drawing room on one side and a study or library on the other. Folding doors mean each can be separated from the other or from the hall that leads to the formal vault-ceiling dining room, which opens onto the central courtyard.

Dado panelling and original window detailing enhance the drawing room and library. There are also two small inscriptions etched in a pane in the drawing room window

by William Chisholm's daughters Edith and Alice when they became engaged.

There are three bedrooms on the ground floor and two bathrooms. The front bedroom has bay windows and all three have open fireplaces. The laundry is original and opens on to a back bush-timber shingle verandah.

Present owners are Malcolm and Eileen Webster, who have a home at Whale Beach but always wanted to live on a property in the country with lots of history. They saw Merrilla in 2002 and bought it.

The Websters, who have clothing shops in Sydney, also carried out extensive renovations. The large French country-style kitchen is new along with an Aga stove, the limestone

THE VAULT-CEILING DINING ROOM.

THE STUDY/LIBRARY OFF THE ENTRANCE HALL.

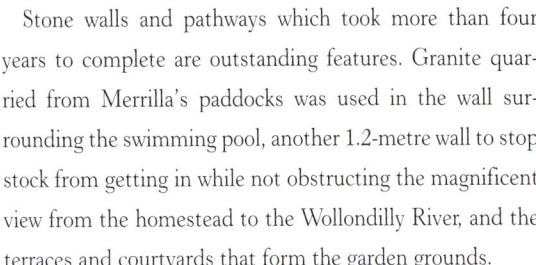

The refurbished drawing
room.

paved floor, and the addition of an office at one end and a casual family dining room.

Upstairs the layout was altered to fit in an ensuite and dressing room for the main bedroom. The dressing room was formed from several cupboards. A second bathroom was added as the three upstairs bedrooms had shared one bathroom.

New damp proofing was put down and new carpet laid, and the house was painted in colours chosen by the Websters.

Mrs Webster said the house was in good condition when they bought it but it looked tired. 'We put in French doors in the dining room. There were sliding glass doors that didn't suit,' she said. 'It was originally a billiards room but we put in wood panelling and made it into a dining room opening on to the central courtyard.'

The courtyard is paved in slate from a nearby quarry and is protected from the weather by a high stone wall. There is a pergola, ornamental pond with fountain and concealed lights in the iris beds.

Merrilla, an Aboriginal name meaning 'place of rest' or 'running water over stone', has extensive gardens, partly resurrected from the original ones by the landscape architects. They were designed to fit in with a guest lodge, swimming pool and cabana.

Prior to the Websters, the Darling family had wanted the nucleus of the old garden preserved while fitting in with the new extensions and the complete cluster of Merrilla buildings. The job took seven years to complete and the transformation continues under the Websters as trees mature.

Stone walls and pathways which took more than four years to complete are outstanding features. Granite quarried from Merrilla's paddocks was used in the wall surrounding the swimming pool, another 1.2-metre wall to stop stock from getting in while not obstructing the magnificent view from the homestead to the Wollondilly River, and the terraces and courtyards that form the garden grounds.

Old beds were re-primed, new ones prepared and extensive drainage and irrigation and new lawns put in. A small ornamental lake was built at the entrance, while towards the river a windmill is a reminder of the rural setting.

A large pergola and terrace was built on the north-eastern corner in the style of renowned landscape architect Edna Walling. It is almost a secret garden in itself and is entered from a long path.

Several rare trees have been made into features. According to Aboriginal legend, bunya pines when planted in pairs bring good luck. The pair at Merrilla is more than 140 years old.

Scots and Stone pines have been pruned to increase their lifespan while new ones have been added to ensure the trees will always be part of Merrilla. English elms, lindens, spreading photinias, myrtle and hedges of *Viburnum tinus* and japonica were also part of the original garden.

Agapanthus and iris line the drive and large herbaceous borders frame the lawns. The kitchen garden includes olives, figs, walnuts, almonds and asparagus. Peony and lilies form an exotic pocket in a corner below the library window. The gardens are topped off with rose and lavender hedges and a white picket fence around the garden.

The grounds include a tennis court, swimming pool and shadehouse.

The guest lodge.

Merryville

George Merryman selected the wrong victim when he picked the pocket of a military reservist and stole an easy identifiable coin late one night in 1809 in the markets area of London. The 29-year-old was sentenced to seven years transportation and was shipped to the colony, arriving in Sydney on 2 October 1811, on the 501-ton convict vessel *Admiral Gambier*. The ship carried 197 male convicts and a detachment from the 73rd Regiment as guard. It was under the command of Master Ed Sindrey.

In February 1813, Merryman married Mary Smith, also a convict who had arrived in Sydney on the *Minstral* four months earlier. It's likely Merryman had known her back in London.

The pair worked in a factory at Parramatta and in 1814 had a daughter Esther, who died a year later. Another daughter, Mary Anne, was born the same year. After Merryman received his certificate of freedom, a son, James, was born in 1817. Another son, George, was born in 1820.

In 1821, George Merryman took up a life at sea and left his family to fend for itself. He returned several times only to renew his certificate of freedom but vanished, presumed dead, while whaling in 1828.

Merryman's wife Mary had died in 1825. Three years earlier, her son James had been adopted by a Joseph Raphael, friend of the family and a wheeler-dealer who also owned a Sydney grocery shop. Raphael later became the guardian of

MERRYVILLE, DESIGNED FOR LIVING IN STYLE.

Mary Anne Merryman. James became a successful ship-owner and publican and later the mayor of Sydney. A street is named after him at Miller's Point.

George jnr had been put in an orphanage and it was four years before his sister Mary Anne, pretending to be married, could get him released into her care. He was then twelve years old but later went to live with another family friend Joseph Levy, who was the baker at Berrima.

George married Charlotte Garner in 1844 at Sutton Forest. She was thirteen and pregnant at the time and was the daughter of convict James Garner, who was transported to Sydney in 1823.

George and Charlotte's first son James was born in 1845 and their second, George the third, in 1847. For some reason about this time, the 'y' in Merryman was changed to an 'i', so the family name became Merriman.

James Garner in the 1850s had a hotel at Yass, and George and Charlotte moved there to live where they had two more children, John and Johanna. But in 1859 Charlotte took up with a German university graduate while husband George had followed his father's example of leaving home and abandoning his family. He was later killed in a mining accident at Kiandra.

In 1865, young George the third became the first of the Merrimans to get into the fine wool industry, which was going through good times. He founded the Ravensworth stud at Yass, initially called Dam Creek, and later added to his property.

THE DOUBLE-BRICK SHEARING SHED.

His brother James had been caught stealing sheep. He spent six weeks in the Yass lock-up but later received a two-year jail sentence for a second offence.

AN OUTDOOR TOILET.

George III married Mary Ann Dowling, and their daughters Charlotte (who died the same year) and Susannah, and three sons, George W., Walter and Ernest, were born at Ravensworth. By now, fine wool grown on the property had earned them a big reputation and the stud sheep were winning a host of prizes.

When George Merriman III died in 1915, Ravensworth, its stud and flock of sheep were divided between his three sons. His daughter also received land.

Walter Merriman in 1903 had set up his own small stud that he called Merryville, which was part of the original Ravensworth, and his ambition was to breed champion stud sheep. His brother George W. had earlier branched out on his own and was breeding sheep on his adjacent Vale View property. But he and his son Frank were killed in a car crash in 1937 on the Hume Highway. Ernest was looking after Ravensworth.

Walter married Kate Sleeman in 1908. She was the daughter of a mining engineer who had worked in America, and a Cornish mother. They had six children: Daisy, Ree, Ronald, Sylvia, Hazel and Bruce.

Bruce joined the navy in 1944 against his father's wishes but was discharged before he could sail overseas and was sent home to take over the essential task of running Merryville. He believed his father, who had friends in high places, had intervened.

Bruce later married Peggy Smith, whom he met at the Sydney Sheep Show in 1947, and they went to Merryville to live. Kate Merriman left in 1949 and went to Sydney, where she had a flat at Bondi and later Vaucluse. She often returned to Merryville but enjoyed being with her new Sydney friends, including actor Chips Rafferty and radio star Jack Davey.

Walter was knighted in 1954 for outstanding services to the sheep industry. He established a merino sheep dynasty and the genetics he developed have had an influence on 70 per cent of the world's fine-wool sheep. By then Merryville covered nearly 24,000 acres (9720 hectares) and ran 30,000 sheep. It was always busy with staff, including secretaries, cooks, jackeroos, family members and their children, gardeners and shearers.

Sir Walter died in 1972 and Bruce Merriman took over as managing director of the family business, which now had a string of family shareholders.

But times in the 1970s were tough and family members, particularly the daughters, wanted to cash in their assets. They were not getting any dividends and wanted their share.

Bruce Merriman knew he could take the sheep to Beverley — the property bought by Walter in 1921 at Boorowa where the Merryville Stud is now based — and sell Merryville, which would make most of the family happy. The auction was held in November 1978 and Merryville, then 1995 hectares, was knocked down to Robert Clark for $985,000.

Since then the property has been carved up into small blocks for housing and what's known in the bush as 'Pitt Street farmers' — mainly solicitors, doctors and other professional people who want to get away from their city lifestyles and be farmers on a couple of acres on weekends.

Rob Clark still owns Merryville, which is now only 184 hectares, but since 1996 has leased it long-term to Brendan and Rowena Abbey. They live in the homestead and buy, fatten and breed cattle which they sell to a national supermarket chain. They also run some sheep.

Merryville is still a magnificent house designed for living in style. Walter Merriman dug the porphyry bluestone used

THE HUGE DINING ROOM.

in its construction from a quarry on the property. The stone was the same as that which was used to build his father's house on Ravensworth.

The first Merryville house Walter built in 1905 had only eight rooms and the family lived there until 1935 when the present 23-room homestead was architect-designed and built around it. It was meant to be impressive enough to match the standing of the family in the community.

The tiled-roof house is still mostly as original as the day it was built. The kitchen is unchanged except for the old wood-fired stove having been replaced.

There are ten bedrooms — including staff quarters at the back with their own bathrooms — a large dining room, large formal sitting room, billiard room and two offices. The dining room has seven exposed timber beams on the high ceiling, original picture rails and wallpaper.

The floorboards are timber and the doors and architraves are maple. There are three open fireplaces while an old boiler provides central heating to the rest of the house. It circulates hot water and Ms Abbey commented that, although it took about a day to warm up, the house then stayed warm.

The Abbeys still use the billiard room, which also doubled as a trophy room. Billiards was another of Sir Walter's passions and his cue bag still hangs from the wall. Sir Walter had regular sessions at the table and

THE DINING ROOM CREDENZA.

THIS IMPRESSIVE PIECE STANDS IN THE BILLIARD ROOM.

EXPOSED TIMBER BEAMS ARE A FEATURE OF THE DINING ROOM.

would play visitors until he was ready to retire for the night. Drinking was banned in the billiard room.

A huge walk-in safe next to the billiard room is a reminder of the times when wool was king and the money was rolling in. The office and secretarial rooms were in this end of the house.

A bluestone-paved circular driveway leads from bluestone entrance gates to the impressive double-car portico at the front of the house. The paved driveway is new and was added by the Clarks.

At the back of the house is a meat house built from bluestone. There is also a bluestone kennel big enough for fifteen dogs.

As the Abbeys run some sheep on the property, the historic double-brick shearing shed built by Sir Walter in 1916 is still in use. There are shearers' quarters and a small cottage as well as sheep and cattle yards.

Brendan Abbey's family has been friends with the Merrimans for a long time and Ms Abbey said it was good moving into a house they once owned that was full of history. 'It's a lovely old place to live in. It is large with plenty of room for guests and for entertaining and, although it gets cold in winter, it is cool in summer.

'There is an enormous oval-shaped garden, including 230 rose bushes, that takes a lot of work to look after but it is

rewarding and we spend a lot of time in summer sitting on the long verandah drinking the occasional red wine with a steak and salad.'

The roses were Sir Walter's pride and joy. He spent hours tending them and took great satisfaction in winning prizes at the Yass flower show year after year.

Large trees, shrubs and banks of cypress pines protect the house from wind and weather. The other trees are mostly European, including golden elm. There used to be a large orchard with about 60 apple and pear trees but it has been replaced. A vegetable garden has also gone.

The Abbeys, only the third family to live in the historic home on Dog Trap Road, use Merryville as a working farm.

'My husband has been involved in feedlots and cattle for years so we spend a lot of time travelling but this is home base now, which is good, because I had spent too much time on the road,' said Ms Abbey.

While life at Yass was a different pace to that in Sydney, it was still busy. As Ms Abbey remarked, 'I enjoyed Sydney, I loved my time there but I was happy to get back to the country. I always envisaged I would end up back in the bush and as it happened I ended up with a cattle bloke in a magnificent old house.

'I grew up on a cattle property in the Hunter Valley so it was something like returning to the fold. I do the business books here, although my husband is the brains. I'm the back-up.'

Ms Abbey was a corporate banker in Sydney for years. She set up the treasury and risk management section for Optus Vision, was corporate treasurer for oil exploration company Ampolex, and was also director of syndications at ANZ investment bank.

'When we first moved to Merryville I was still working in Sydney so I commuted for four and a half years. I came up late Fridays and went back on Mondays, which was about a three-hour drive down the Hume Highway.

'But I got tired of being on the road and not being here with my husband. I was also getting exhausted working long hours in Sydney so I could get the time off on weekends. So I gave away the Sydney job but I am on the board of Country Energy and go back there for board meetings.

'I have also been elected to Yass Valley Council. I wanted to put something back into the community because I still have a business brain and I look at council as a $25 million business, which some councillors didn't seem to do.'

Monte Cristo

LEFT: MONTE CRISTO HAS BEEN
RESTORED TO ITS FORMER GLORY.

BOTTOM LEFT: THE CAST-IRON
RAILINGS.

BOTTOM RIGHT: THE GARDEN
ROTUNDA.

When Reg Ryan first saw Monte Cristo in 1955, he knew that one day he would own it. But the magnificent Georgian-style home, perched on a hill overlooking the south-western New South Wales town of Junee, on sale for £8000 was so far beyond his financial means, it seemed an impossible dream.

The young tailor, who had a business in neighbouring Wagga Wagga, thought he became the new owner four years later when the price had been dropped to £2000 because the property had fallen into disrepair. He put down £1000 and, after arranging further finance, moved in with his wife and baby daughter.

However, there was a slip-up with the contract and three months later the Ryans were evicted and had to move back to Wagga. From there they moved to Wyong on the central coast to run a mixed business.

Monte Cristo was put back on the market by the estate of the original owners but there were no takers and it again sat idle, a victim of vandals and thieves. A caretaker named Jack Simpson was appointed to look after the house but he was unable to stop the deterioration.

The movie *Psycho* was screened in Junee in 1960 and, after seeing it three times, one of the local youths went to the house and shot Mr Simpson. After that vandals wreaked havoc on the home because nobody would take on the job of looking after it.

But Mr Ryan believed he was meant to be Monte Cristo's guardian and the protector of a piece of Australian history that was in danger of being lost, so he sold his Wyong business and returned to Wagga. He was devastated to find Monte Cristo was almost gutted but he still bought it for £1000 and moved in for a second time.

'It was really just a shell. Doors and windows were torn off, the lead flashing stripped from the roof, all the mantelpieces pulled out and the cast-iron railing and frieze torn down and smashed. Why I still wanted it, I don't know,' he said.

THE FRONT VERANDAH.

'But we moved in. The day we took over there were no doors or windows, no water, no electricity and no furniture and we had three little girls and my wife Olive was five months pregnant. She didn't want to come.'

The family shovelled dirt and rubbish from the dining room so it could be used and nailed canvas over the doors and windows. Apart from no water or electricity, there was also no sewerage or phone.

They made the ground floor habitable first by connecting the electricity to one room, glazed the windows and cleared the rubbish out of an underground tank for a water supply. Second-hand doors were bought from other old buildings and fitted.

It was eighteen months before anything was done to the upper floor, where possums and bats had made a home. The

windows were glazed to make the house secure and when that was done the Ryans set about the formidable task of full restoration, which to some extent is still going on.

Monte Cristo was built by Christopher William Crawley, a pioneer grazier with two blocks of land totalling 520 acres (210 hectares), who later became a Junee publican and storekeeper. There was no town there then and Crawley in 1876 built a slab and pise hut on a hill to the west of the present Junee.

Taking out a £250 mortgage on his cattle, he upgraded to a two-room brick cottage with a hipped roof and later added two more brick rooms under a skillion roof, and a front and back verandah. He built a laundry on the southern side, also with a skillion roof, a row of sheds on the northern side to house his horses and equipment, and dug an underground water tank, which he lined with bricks. A farm worker named Morris moved into the original hut.

Mr Crawley was an astute man and when the government decided to build the southern railway line between his two properties, he saw a rare opportunity to make money, so he built a hotel on his land adjacent to the site of the proposed railway station. The Junee Hotel is there now.

Mr Crawley also bought up more land and, by 1883, five years after the railway arrived, he owned most of the land on which the town now sits. A new settlement called Junee

Junction began to develop around his hotel and store. The settlement was renamed Loftus in 1883 after the then governor of New South Wales but was gazetted in 1885 as Junee in accordance with local usage.

The town soon became one of the state's most important railway centres and it benefited from the consequent need for accommodation and railway repair facilities. Local government was established in 1886 and a courthouse was built in 1890.

In the meantime, Mr Crawley was making lots of money and in 1884 began to build a new mansion from bricks baked on his property. The old home behind the new house became the kitchen and servants' quarters. He named the new house Monte Cristo.

Mr Crawley also built a brick dairy, two brick stables for his racehorses and a large building behind the main house for a ballroom. In 1902 the house was lit by carbide gas. He also set up a nine-hole golf course and put in a tennis court.

In 1910, after a fire in the kitchen, the roof of the cottage was raised a metre, and a bathroom with verandah was added to Monte Cristo. Mr Crawley died the same year, aged 69, from a carbuncle on his neck that became infected from his starched collars. His wife Elizabeth survived a

further 23 years before she died in 1933, aged 92, from heart failure caused by a burst appendix.

The Crawleys had seven children: Helen Ann (Lillian), Lydia Blanche, Florence Agnes, Angela Christina, Mervyn Marmaduke, Aubrey Clarence and Alphonse Hilary. All the girls were taught music and painting, and Lillian in particular became an accomplished pianist who in 1895 composed a piece of music for a ball at Government House.

Mervyn, nicknamed the Queensland Pioneer, owned extensive pastoral holdings in the state while Aubrey, who played the violin, became a doctor. Alphonse, also a fine pianist, was a solicitor and practised for 62 years, a record for a solicitor in Australia.

Mrs Crawley usually wore black lace dresses, lace cap and a cape with a stand-up beaded collar in Queen Victoria style.

THE WITHDRAWING ROOM.

THE SITTING ROOM.

She ruled the house and servants with an iron hand and drove around in her own phaeton pulled by her pony Gecho.

The last member of the Crawley family lived in Monte Cristo until 1948. The household furniture and farming equipment was auctioned and a caretaker employed to look after the house until it was sold, but the asking price of £8000 frightened off buyers until Mr Ryan offered Alphonse Crawley £2000 in 1959. That was the deal that went sour and it was 1963 before the Ryans moved back in for good.

The house is built in Georgian style but has Victorian flourishes such as floral cast-iron lace and decorative plasterwork. The elaborate treatment of both front windows on the ground floor, with triple arches capped by a decoration of incised and moulded plaster, is typical of the taste of the 1880s.

The sandstock bricks were baked on the property under the watchful eye of Mr Crawley and were laid on a large dry-stone rubble foundation. The downstairs walls are four bricks thick and two bricks thick upstairs. The floors are all 1½-inch (3.8-centimetre) cypress pine, locally milled.

Monte Cristo is simple in its layout. Rooms open off a central hallway that runs the length of the house. The downstairs ceilings are lath and plaster with wide elaborately moulded plaster cornices. The staircase is in the hall just behind an archway.

The ceilings upstairs are cypress pine with timber cornices. The doors, architraves and skirtings are redwood. The doorknobs are china and glass and the touch-plates and keyhole covers are a variety of designs.

The cast-iron balustrade and frieze work design is 'Australian ferns' by Victorian firm Monteath and Son. The firm registered the design in 1884 and it was originally painted in natural colours.

Because the house had been gutted by vandals, the original décor was lost. But the Ryans took great care with the choice of wall- and ceiling papers and, although modern, they are as close as possible in design and colour to the original papers of the period.

The painting of the cornices and woodwork has been carefully copied from the original, although there have been some colour changes where necessary. Fitted carpets similar to the ones now used at Monte Cristo were available during

the period but would not have been used as extensively. Linoleum was generally considered the best floor covering for bedrooms.

The curtains have been chosen to match the Victorian designs as closely as possible and some are hung on heavy wooden rods with wooden rings. Others are fitted behind gilded brass pelmets which were originally used in the house.

The Ryans made no attempt to use similar furniture to that sold by the Crawleys at auction in 1952. But they did choose Victorian furniture representative of the period up to

THE BREAKFAST ROOM AT THE FOOT OF THE STAIRS.

the 1880s, which they have collected from all over Australia and some from overseas.

The sitting room or parlour, the first room from the front entrance, was the Crawley family's living room and once housed a walnut Ronisch piano. The Ryans have furnished it with a walnut seven-piece parlour suite from the early and mid-Victorian periods. The room also features a wonderful collection of Mary Gregory glass.

The dining room lies across the hall and is used when the family is home. The furniture is made from Australian cedar and mahogany. A large bronze and ormolu gasolier with cut-glass prisms hangs from the ceiling. The house was originally lit by oil lamps but a carbide gas plant was installed in 1902. All except one of the original lights were destroyed.

The breakfast room is at the foot of the stairs. The breakfast table and chairs and a pair of bookcases are made from mahogany while a chiffonier is cedar made in 1830.

The original upstairs boys' bedroom has a walnut suite made in Sheffield in 1860 by Mercer and Son. The girls' bedroom across the hall is furnished in satinwood of the 1840s, including a half-tester bed, dressing table, chest of drawers, wardrobe and music table. The mantelpiece clock was made around 1803. Along the hall the walnut settee dates back to 1690.

ONE OF THE BEAUTIFULLY FURNISHED BEDROOMS.

The drawing, or withdrawing, room, features ebonised furniture of the 1860s because Queen Victoria was mourning the death of Prince Albert. She had all her furniture ebonised and the British Empire followed.

Across the hall is the main bedroom. The mahogany four-poster bed was brought to Australia in 1805 by an early pioneering family, the Waites. When Mr Ryan bought the bed at a sale, it had been lying in a backyard for years rotting away. Fortunately, he was able to restore it.

Off the balcony is a small bedroom originally used as a box room where trunks and luggage were stored. It was made into a chapel room for Mrs Crawley, as she apparently only left the house twice after her husband's death.

The original cottage, which became the kitchen and

servants' quarters, survives behind the main house. Other buildings include the original dairy, located across from the cottage; the coach-house and stables, which house an excellent collection of horse-drawn vehicles; and a blacksmith shop and workshop.

Mr Ryan rebuilt the ballroom on the original site; it had been demolished in the war years when building materials were scarce. The Ryans still hold functions in the room, including a period costume ball every year.

Mr Ryan to some extent has mirrored original owner Christopher Crawley. Mr Crawley built the first hotel, called The Railway, and general store in the town. When the hotel, now called the Junee Hotel, came up for sale in 1986, Mr Ryan bought it and was the owner up until 1989 after carrying out quite considerable restoration work.

Monte Cristo is recognised as one of the most haunted houses in Australia. Mr Ryan boasts of having ten resident ghosts and all have been seen at different times. Cameras play up by switching on and off.

'I haven't seen a ghost but have had experiences with them. My wife doesn't like being in the house on her own,' Mr Ryan says. 'Olive has had hands on her shoulders, her name being called and was shaken vigorously in bed. You hear them walking around at night, down the stairs.

'Visitors can get a shortness of breath, headaches and asthma attacks. But we have never felt threatened.'

Reg Ryan was born in Wagga Wagga. His father was a baker but got flour on the lungs and had to give up the profession. Then he took a job with the railway as a fettler so at one stage Mr Ryan lived in tents by the line. There was one for his parents, one for him and his brother, and one for the kitchen. After a move to Broken Hill, the family lived in a rough hut made from flattened 4-gallon kerosene tins and hessian walls. 'Now we live in a house I've refused $10 million for, so that's not a bad step up the ladder,' Mr Ryan comments.

'I'm a tailor by trade and I still do a bit. When the ball comes up I might make a few dresses for friends but that's all I do nowadays. My wife was a seamstress and came to work for me in Wagga and that's how we met.

'The conservation of Monte Cristo, which means Mount of Christ, has taken 42 years and I'm still not finished. But it has all been worth the effort.'

Mt Boninyong

When Andrew Scott arrived in Melbourne from Scotland in 1838, he paid the highly inflated price of £48 for a horse he named Flora, and then rode inland looking for a block of land on which to settle. He left his wife Celia, and their children — Robert, Andrew, Martha and Thomas — in Melbourne while he was away.

In Melbourne people had advised him not to go north of the divide because he had a wife and children and could find himself in danger from hostile Aborigines. He found the land he wanted in the Victorian central highlands near present-day Ballarat and squatted on 16,000 acres (6480 hectares) of heavily timbered volcanic soil.

The area was originally known as Scott's Marsh because part of the land was wet and boggy, but when the creeks were cleared about 1889, it became known as Scotsburn.

Celia Scott was the first white woman in the district and in 1840 it was reported that she rode across the dry bed of Lake Burrumbeet.

Scott called his property Mt Boninyong, which is a local Aboriginal word meaning 'big mountain'. The nearby former volcano is now called Mt Buninyong while the small village down the road is Buninyong.

The Scotts lived in a tent made from a ship's sail for nine months while they built their first house from wattle and daub. They made additions as the family grew.

Andrew Scott had broken his trusty horse Flora to the harness and plough and she became quite legendary, doing lots of work on the property and living to a ripe old age. He had also paid £60 for a second horse, the same amount that he paid for the passage of the family's two servants from Scotland.

THE GRAND HOUSE OF MT BONINYONG.

When bad economic times hit and banks foreclosed on settlers, the Scotts were also targeted. Celia Scott was allowed to keep her wedding rings but all her other jewellery was forfeited. Fortunately, they were allowed to keep Flora and a cow for each member of the family. Andrew Scott put Flora to work sowing a paddock of potatoes and they were rewarded with a massive crop that got them out of financial trouble.

But Flora also had a mind of her own. Once, Scott rode her to Warracknabeal in the Wimmera, but lost her after she wandered off one night. Some time later, they found her on the way back to Mt Boninyong with a foal at foot. She was heading home in her own time.

THE DINING ROOM.

THE SITTING ROOM.

Andrew Scott died in April 1853 and the property was divided between his two eldest sons, Robert and Andrew. Robert kept Mt Boninyong and Andrew's share became known as Yuulong.

Robert, his wife Sarah and his mother Celia lived in the old Mt Boninyong home until he decided it was time for something grander. In 1883 he demolished the old house and the new one was built in 1884 on the same site. Thus, the thriving garden we see today pre-dates the main house by about 40 years. Interestingly, the pioneer Scotts brought some of the plants with them from Scotland.

The architect for the new building was Reed Henderson and Smart of Melbourne. The house was identical, brick for brick, to one designed by the same architect that became a kindergarten training college in Kew.

Robert and his second wife Lorna were the first generation of the Scott family to live in the new house, together with their four children (two from Robert's first marriage).

The present owners, Celia Burnham and her husband Graeme, continue the family line, as Celia's father, Robert John, was Robert's

son from his second marriage, and took over the house next together with his wife Mary. They had three daughters.

'I am the youngest; [then there's] my sister Susie, who lives in Melbourne, [and] is a part owner with us; and Sally, who lives in Mt Gambier,' Celia explained. 'We have three daughters: Sarah, who lives in Tasmania; Emma, who lives at Hamilton; and Lisa, who lives in Melbourne.'

Celia said the house had never been altered in any way. It stands as it was built in 1884 and the same family still lives in it.

It is Scottish Baronial in style. The front is solid brick and the back is double brick. Mt Boninyong has 25 rooms, including eight bedrooms, a large drawing room, dining room, library, and what was a schoolroom. There are also servants' quarters.

The house still has its original slate roof, with 16-foot (4.9-metre) ceilings downstairs and 14-foot (4.3-metre) ceilings upstairs.

Graeme Burnham grew up in Moulamein in southern New South Wales and has been on the land all his life. He and Celia lived on a property on the Hay Plains that was reasonably remote before taking over Mt Boninyong from Celia's parents.

'We came back because we wanted to educate our girls and I had some capital that allowed us to set things up for our family. Each generation has had to buy the previous generation out, or the siblings, so generations have worked hard and have valued the place,' Mr Burnham said.

The Burnhams run sheep and shorthorn cattle and grow crops. Mr Burnham also works off-farm as a consultant.

The Scott family has taken daily rainfall measurements for the Weather Bureau since 1856, with the result that Mt Boninyong has a more complete weather record than Sydney, Melbourne or Hobart. In fact, rainfall measurement has become something of an institution for Celia's family, the legacy of her great-great-grandfather Andrew Scott who sent his first rainfall report to the colonial meteorologist in 1856, only two years after the Victorian Meteorological Office was established. Celia Burnham took over the reins in 1984, and each day at 9am a family member checks the rain gauge in the garden behind the homestead and records the reading in the rain register.

As Celia commented, 'My father used to do it, and it's just continued. It's something that's always been done. It's no arduous task. It's part of life at Mt Boninyong.'

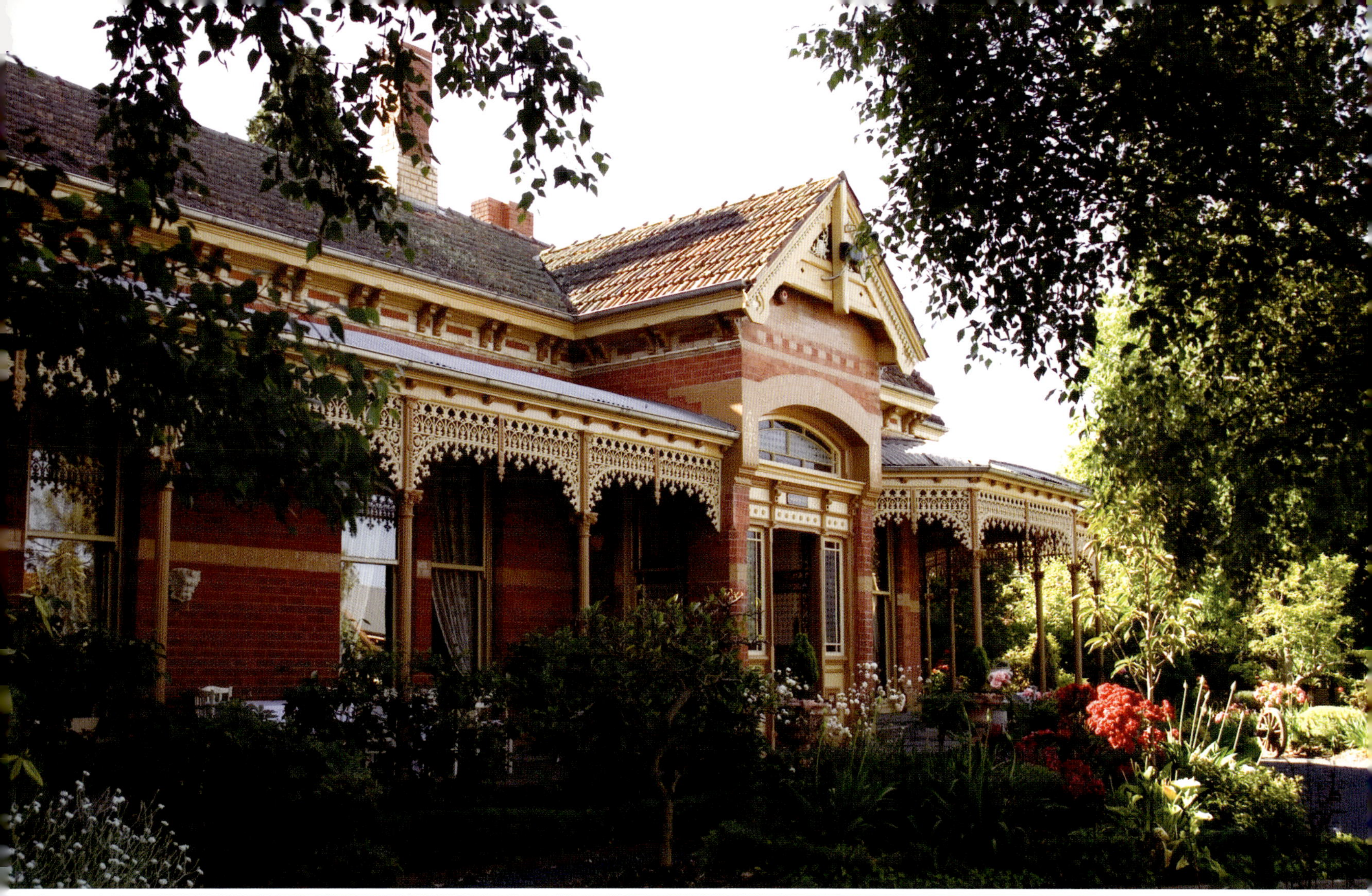

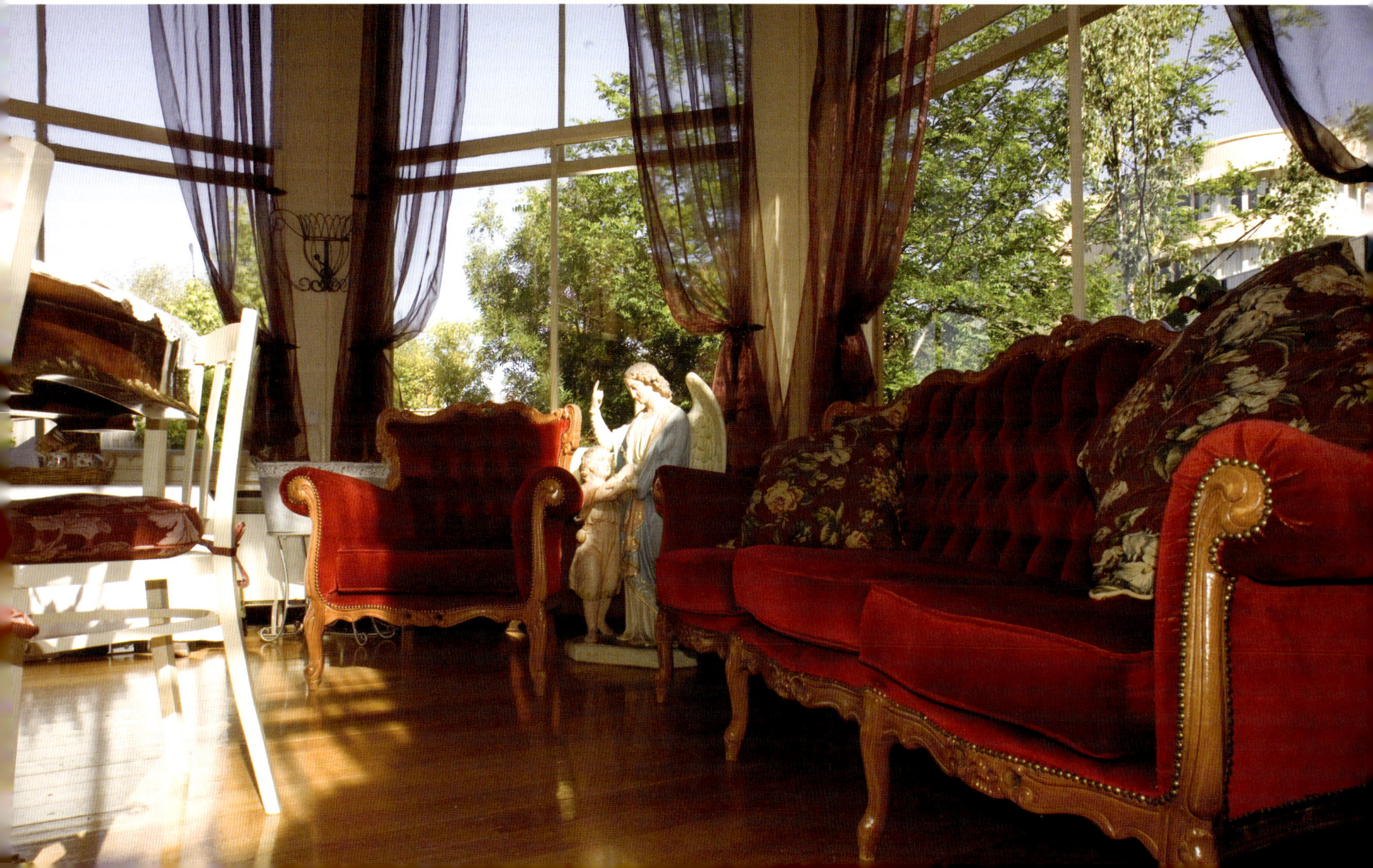

Nieder Weisel

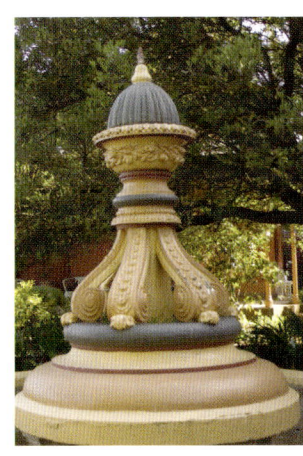

When Irishman Edward Stephens built his new home in the mid-1880s in the Victorian town of Ballarat, it had a mirror image underground where he and his wife Sophie lived in the summer to escape the heat. The bluestone-walled 'summerhouse' had front entry steps leading up to the garden, two formal rooms, and four small rooms.

Mr Stephens, a legal manager for a number of Ballarat mining companies, came from Dublin and the triple-brick house built for him in Webster Street became known as the most prestigious address in Ballarat's most fashionable area. It was undoubtedly one of the first houses in Australia with an underground section. Underground houses are common now in the hot opal mining towns of White Cliffs and Coober Pedy.

Mr Stephens lived in the house for about five years and in 1893 sold to John Heinz, who owned the town's ice works and also had a butcher shop. Mr Heinz and his wife Sophie moved in with their eight children and named the house Nieder Weisel after their village in Germany.

Because he had a large family and needed more room, Mr Heinz built a second level on the two wings at the back. This allowed each child to have a room of their own.

Mr Heinz was elected to the local council in 1894 and was mayor of Ballarat in 1899 and 1900. He died in June 1907. Some of his descendants continue to live in Ballarat.

Mrs Heinz sold the house in 1919 to the Red Cross to be used as a place where returned wounded soldiers from the war could be rested and looked after. Governor-General Sir Ronald C. Munro-Ferguson chose the house as the first in Victoria to be used for this purpose. However, when the servicemen arrived in Ballarat, they refused to move in because the house had a German name. As the governor-general and his wife held the title Count and Countess of Novar, and because Lady Munro-Ferguson was the first president of the Red Cross, the house was renamed Novar in their honour.

In 1922 it was converted to a private hospital, still managed by the Red Cross and registered with the Public Health Department. The returned servicemen had complained Ballarat was too cold for them, in stark contrast to Mr Stephens who thought it too hot, and had moved to other premises at Bendigo.

Hospitals at the time had large numbers of patients suffering from polio and diphtheria and there was a need to keep newborn babies away from them, so Novar became a midwife nursing hospital. The first baby born there was named Novar Mossman, and Ballarat's 2005 mayor, David Vendy, was also born there.

Later, hospitals had a problem with tuberculosis and again there was a need to isolate adult patients so Novar became a general nursing hospital with a TB chalet at the back. Doctors also did minor operations there.

In 1956 the Mental Health Authority took over the house and it was used for psychiatric services. Patients were often seen relaxing in the sun in the front gardens.

In about 1988 St John of God Hospital bought the house to be used by its private nursing group, but it sat vacant for thirteen years. The plans to redevelop the property never eventuated. The gardens were asphalted so they could be used as a car park and the local fire brigade often used the underground summerhouse for torch-light training in breathing equipment for new recruits.

In 2001 Greg and Samantha McIntosh made an offer to buy Novar. The house had not been on the market but the owners agreed to sell.

'About thirteen possums lived here when we came. Our children were spoiled because we had just finished eight years of renovations to the house down the road and when we moved here they were devastated. Five layers of carpet and possums,' Mrs McIntosh recalled.

'The second day we were here some kids from the neighbourhood knocked on the front door and said they were afraid they might lose their playground, which was the asphalt and concrete yard. They said 109 Webster Street was ideal for their skateboarding and rollerskating.'

It turned out the children did indeed lose their playground.

'Four and a half years of digging not only gave us a few muscles but enabled us to get the gardens back to normal. We've scavenged roses, camellias, rhododendrons and 30-year-old weeping elms and it looks a treat,' commented Mrs McIntosh.

One of the first things the McIntoshes did was to rename the 30-room house Nieder Weisel. They have also named main rooms after the people connected with the house through the years. The reading room, the first off the entrance hall, has been called the Stephens Room after the original owner. Used to greet guests, it is the most formal

THE BALLROOM WAS ORIGINALLY THE COACH-HOUSE.

and grandest room in the house. The wall width is about the size of a bluestone block. The room is painted a deep plum, a colour found by the McIntoshes when they scratched back all the layers of paint. There are seven different colours in the cornice, ranging from honeysuckle and deep claret to Egyptian red and shank green. The paints were all specially mixed and colour matched. The colours are the same in the open fireplace.

The doors have six deep indentations shaped like cricket bats. The bats are finished with the twisted detailing of the roots of a walnut tree and there are seven different layers of paint finish.

The reading room has five ceiling roses and large bay windows stretching almost from the ceiling to floor. They can be used as doors to get to the verandah.

The floors throughout are tallow with narrow boards and the ceilings are 18 feet (5.5 metres) high. There are original glass bricks in the passageways, which create a runway effect at night.

A special feature of the dining room is a Belgian marble fireplace.

The ballroom was originally the coach-house. The horse and carts would drive in, drop off the goods for the servants and go back out. The Heinz family bricked the two wings together and turned it into a ballroom.

The McIntoshes have done about 80 per cent of the restoration work themselves. They would love to restore the underground summerhouse next.

THE MAIN BEDROOM.

THE DINING ROOM AND ITS BELGIAN MARBLE FIREPLACE.

'Every room on the ground level is mirrored below, every window, the openings and fireplaces. Parts of the original details, the paint and woodgrain finish on timberwork are still there to be seen,' Mrs McIntosh said.

'We will be guided by the work we have done upstairs. Things like the brass window lifters, servants' bells and the gas lamp holders, we've been able to copy the originals.'

Mrs McIntosh said the house was designed by a clever architect from C. J. James and Co. William Barrows was the builder. Rooms were positioned to receive the sun wherever it was at that time of day. The result is a house with no central passageways and an unpredictable layout. The front door is at the side of the house.

As Mrs McIntosh explained, 'The rooms are positioned to receive the sun wherever it is at that time of the day. The rooms you use in the morning receive the morning sun, the rooms you use in the middle of the day receive the middle of the day sun through glass in the ceiling, and the same goes for the evenings. It works well and controls the heat.'

Old Errowanbang

Explorer and army lieutenant William Lawson, who with Gregory Blaxland and William Charles Wentworth was the first to cross the Blue Mountains in 1813, was a major landowner at Prospect, west of Sydney. He was given the 500-acre (203-hectare) grant for faithful service to the colony and ran a successful farm he called Veteran Hall.

A qualified surveyor, Lawson had paid £300 for his commission in the New South Wales Corps and arrived in the colony from England as an ensign in 1800. Sent to serve at Norfolk Island, he didn't return to Sydney until 1806 where he was promoted to lieutenant and later made aide-de-camp to Major George Johnston.

Johnston had taken control of the colony after the overthrow of Governor Captain William Bligh — the same Bligh whose crew several years earlier had mutinied in the Pacific on his ship, the *Bounty*. Bligh threatened the New South

Wales Corps with the loss of its monopoly and its officers arrested him in the so-called Rum Rebellion.

In 1807, Lawson went to the new settlement of Coal River, now Newcastle, and became commandant. He was sent back to England in 1809 as a witness in the Bligh rebellion trial but returned to Sydney in 1811 and joined Governor Lachlan Macquarie's Veteran Corps, formed out of the New South Wales Corps by those members who wanted to settle in the colony.

Lawson, who had picked up the nickname Old Ironbark, retired to his Prospect grant a year or so later and it was from there he joined Blaxland and Wentworth to cross the mountains in 1813.

Governor Macquarie appointed him commandant of the new settlement of Bathurst in 1819 and he took 100 cattle with him to occupy Macquarie's first grant west of the

OLD ERROWANBANG, BUILT BY EXPLORER WILLIAM LAWSON.

mountains, just south of the Fish River. Later, in 1822, in another first, he discovered coal west of the mountains at Hartley Vale.

Lawson spent much of his time exploring the Bathurst district before he resigned as commandant in 1824 and returned to Prospect, managing his properties through his son William. He was member for Cumberland in the first partly elected Legislative Council from 1843 to 1848 and died in 1850. Lawson in the Blue Mountains was named after him.

It's interesting to note most of the Veteran Hall property was resumed for the construction of Sydney's Prospect Reservoir and Lawson's home was occupied for a few years by the headworks engineer. It was then offered to the federal government as a home for returned invalid soldiers but the offer was refused. Falling into disrepair, it was demolished in 1929.

Lawson, with the help of his son William jnr, became one of the largest landowners in the colony, acquiring around 155,000 acres (62,775 hectares) and running 84,800 sheep, 14,750 cattle and 100 horses.

William jnr was among the first native-born whites to cross the mountains to go sheep farming and the first to receive a land grant, which was just east of Rockley. He was an excellent horseman and won the Governor's Cup on

Spring Gun at the initial Australian Jockey Club meeting held at Parramatta. He became a magistrate in 1836 at Bathurst and sat on the bench there until he left the district in 1852.

William jnr helped his father establish eleven sheep stations. One of these was Errowanbang, between Mandurama and Carcoar, which was one of the first areas to be settled after Governor Darling opened up the land for grazing west of the Macquarie River in 1823.

William snr built the original Errowanbang homestead in 1827 with the help of convict labour. The bricks were made by hand on the property, packed together with cow hair and mud.

He used stringy bark shingles on the roof; and the doors, architraves and mantelpieces were cedar. All the other timber for ceilings and floors was pit-sawn in a cellar at the side of the house. The cellar was later used to lock up the convicts at night.

The original woolshed was built around the same time. It was the first in the district and was a massive structure of bush timber, 120 feet long by 40 feet wide (37 metres by 12 metres) with a very high gable. Strong winds demolished it around 1967.

In 1832 William Lawson jnr married Caroline Icely, sister of Thomas Icely of nearby Coombing Park, and they had ten children. As well as managing Errowanbang, he looked after church and school estates in the district. When the church and school estates were resumed about 1835, he acquired some of the land and Errowanbang then comprised more than 100,000 acres (40,500 hectares).

After the death of his father, William Lawson jnr sold Errowanbang to a Mr Lomax and moved to his father's property Veteran Hall, at Prospect, where he died in 1861.

Little is known about Lomax. He apparently built

THE MASSIVE TIMBER WOOLSHED WAS BUILT TO LAST.

a large kitchen and dining room on the side for cooking and preparing meals for the farm workers because the property had a large staff at the time. In later years the kitchen was demolished.

A partnership of Francis Rawdon Chesney Hopkins and Alexander Wilson bought Errowanbang around 1886. Hopkins was born near Bombay in 1848 and was the son of a British navy captain.

Still young, he went to Ireland to live with his uncle General Rawdon Chesney, a British soldier and explorer. General Chesney's survey of a route for the Suez Canal in 1829 proved the feasibility of building it.

At the age of sixteen he came to Australia to live with another uncle, Sir Samuel Wilson, a pastoralist in Victoria, from whom he learnt the ropes. When he was 30 he managed Peracoota station in the Riverina district, where he married Sarah Jane Kennedy.

In the meantime he had entered into partnerships with Robertson and Wagner, the owners of Peracoota, and had interests with them in other properties in Queensland. Leaving Peracoota at the age of 38, he sold his Queensland interests and went into partnership with Alexander Wilson to buy Errowanbang.

Wilson was the managing director of Australian Estates at the time and with Hopkins also had interests in gold and copper mining at Blayney. Hopkins later had interests in the Wire Gully gold mine and was a founding member of the Pastoralists Union in New South Wales. He also worked tirelessly for the Rabbit and Pastures Protection Boards, serving for many years as chairman and director of the Carcoar branch.

As well as running Errowanbang, Hopkins was a keen writer, creating a number of plays that were successful in Australia, Canada and the United States. He also wrote verse and a number of books.

Hopkins and Wilson built a huge shearing shed on Errowanbang that is still used. Built on four levels it is probably unique in Australia and, with 40 stands, was the biggest in the region.

Designed by an architect named Watt and built at a cost of £5000, the shed is supported by massive stone piers, and the sawn cypress pine timber work inside shows an unusually high standard of craftsmanship.

About 5 tons of nails and bolts were used in the construction of the shed, which could hold 3000 sheep. Hopkins had

an ambition to shear 100,000 sheep in one season and reached an impressive 90,000 in pursuit of his goal.

Before 1900 the partnership was dissolved, leaving Hopkins as the sole owner. The property was then divided, with Hopkins taking the eastern side of the property while the western side, which had the homestead, was sold. He took the name Errowanbang with him and built another homestead almost next door (see Errowanbang).

Hopkins died after falling down an old mineshaft on the property in July 1916. He was trying to make the partly timber-covered shaft safe, having lost a number of sheep that had fallen in.

Now called Old Errowanbang to avoid confusion, the original holding was next owned by a Charles Hebden. He ran a thoroughbred horse stud as well as sheep and cattle. One of his horses won the Sydney Cup in 1902.

Hebden built a water race system on the property with one branch going to the shearing shed to power the shearing equipment, although this never eventuated. But the water was used to fill dams and supply the homestead. Other races went to the mines at Junction Reefs.

Around 1909 Hebden sold about 9000 acres (3645 hectares) of the rougher country and a few years later sold another 9000 acres (3645 hectares) to his nephew Richard Officer, who named it Panuara. When Hebden died in 1915, with the property then known as Errowanbang Ltd, Richard Officer took over management.

He and his wife renovated the homestead, adding a new wing for a classroom, a room for a governess, an office and a dressing room. Bathrooms were added and the ceilings in the original section were replaced.

Officer employed domestic staff at the homestead and a string of station hands. The water race continued to silt up and eventually rabbit holes caused so many problems it was abandoned.

THE SITTING ROOM FIREPLACE.

After Officer died in 1930, his brother Ernie managed the property for a short time, followed by a Bill McKay and then a Ted Holland. The property was resumed by the government and opened up for soldier settlement in 1952.

The present owner of Old Errowanbang, Kath Harries, described how her husband John drew the property in the soldiers' settlement ballot in February 1952. There were 1337 people in the ballot for eleven blocks, which ranged from 764 to 943 acres (309 to 382 hectares) of the 8973 acres (3634 hectares) of Old Errowanbang put up by the War Service Lands Settlement Board.

Mr Harries drew number one block, which included the homestead, so they inherited 22 rooms of an old, very dilapidated house and a woolshed. He spent years making

THE SHEARING SHED WOOL
CHUTE.

improvements, replacing floors, joists and all the doors, making the front door himself.

There was an office, a bathroom, three bedrooms and a long hallway. About five rooms were in poor condition. The house was re-plastered because it was bubbling and coming away in all the rooms. Mr Harries tore off all the plaster, encrusted with layers and layers of paint and old wallpaper, and started again.

The Harries have owned Old Errowanbang longer than

anyone else. They initially had no electricity, but when families began moving into the district and a school opened, it was connected. Phones were restricted to neighbour Bill Crossing, Hopkins at the newer Errowanbang homestead, and the Harries. It was a three-phone party line and everyone listened in to the conversations.

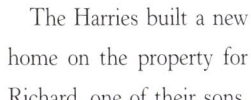

THE WOOLSHED'S SHEEP DIP.

The Harries built a new home on the property for Richard, one of their sons, but he and wife Jan left to manage another property for a few years and so they moved into the new place instead. Their other son, David, lived in the old home for a while but it was empty some of the time.

'When Richard and Jan came back, John had always liked the old home so we said, "Right, they can have all the convenience of the new one and we'll come back here," and that's what we did,' Mrs Harries said. 'John has since died but I'm still here more than 50 years later.'

Richard and Jan Harries run the Old Errowanbang property now with some help from sons Jack and Kelly. They have about 3000 sheep, some of them on another property, and 200 cattle. They also breed stock horses.

Jan Harries said they still use the old woolshed when they shear in October and early November every year. They also use it for drafting and drenching and it has an indoor dip, although she said it needed a football team to run.

The historic shed has numerous signatures on the walls with dates, and shearers have also climbed on to the roof and signed their names in the lead.

Most of the cypress pine timber in the shed came from Canowindra and was milled on site, Jan Harries explained. 'Building the shed must have been a mammoth job because there were no forklifts or cranes in those days and it was all man power, with probably blocks and tackles to get those huge beams up. And the brick piers underneath that hold up the roof are just massive. Everywhere the wool goes or anywhere you walk with the wool the timber has been planed. They were tradesmen who built the shed.'

A Paddington Terrace

Trendy Paddington is one of Sydney's hippest suburbs, a mecca for shoppers and diners. It is probably the only totally intact Victorian suburb in the world and is also the only suburb in Australia to have a National Trust heritage classification. Terrace houses predominate: rows and rows of them with their distinctive iron lace.

The suburb was named by Robert Cooper, one of three partners in the original land grant. He was transported to New South Wales for smuggling silk between France and England but, five years after arriving in Sydney in 1813, he received a pardon.

By the early 1820s when he had become a successful entrepreneur and gin distiller, he built a Georgian estate at the top of the ridgeline with views of the whole area and called it Paddington after a borough in London. He named his house Juniper Hall and it is now Paddington's oldest home.

The grand two-storey Georgian house with wide cast-iron balconies at the front and back had been hidden from view for 63 years behind a row of shops in Oxford Street. It was brought back to life by the National Trust in 1988 as an Australian bicentenary project.

Paddington's first homes were built around the Regency-style Victoria Barracks, a major army base built by convicts between 1841 and 1846. However, in the late nineteenth century, terraces shot up everywhere to cater for Sydney's growing working population and an emerging middle class. On a hillside overlooking Sydney Harbour, Paddington was built out in two periods: 1870 to 1885 and 1900 to 1929. Its Victorian appeal is obvious.

The suburb was originally the home of migrants mostly from England, Scotland, Wales and Ireland and, after World War II, from Italy, Greece and Yugoslavia. Paddington still has a high level of foreign ancestry with only 25 per cent of people in the 2001 census saying their parents were born in Australia. In comparison, 67 per cent said their parents were born in north-west European nations like England and Ireland.

Seventy per cent of people in Paddington live in a typical Victorian terrace house with most of the remaining residents living in apartments.

When Paddington was developing, it wasn't long before the terrace houses occupied almost every piece of available land, eventually resulting in the area becoming an overpopulated slum. The unfashionable nature of the suburb continued until the mid-1960s when an amazing transformation began to take place.

The New South Wales Housing Commission had begun a slum-clearance program and was replacing inner-Sydney terraces — mainly in Redfern, Surry Hills and Waterloo — with single-, two- and three-storey blocks of apartments. But Paddington residents wanted no part of that. They banded together and fought long and hard to retain the nineteenth-century suburb's terraces and its character. They were able to stop the government bulldozers and Paddington now is an excellent example of unplanned restoration. Its real estate prices demonstrate how sought-after properties are here, with the average price of a single terrace house more than $1.2 million.

The old boot repair and linen shops have given way to designer fashion outlets and boutiques, trendy pubs and restaurants, coffee shops and art houses. A Paddington section of Oxford Street — the oldest highway, dating from 1803 and linking the old signal station on South Head through Bondi Junction to Old Sydney Town — is often referred to as the Cappuccino Strip.

THE FRAMED ORIGINAL DEEDS OF THE HOUSE.

LEFT & BOTTOM LEFT: THE EARLY 1900s PADDINGTON TERRACE.

BOTTOM RIGHT: THE ELABORATE WINDOW DECORATIONS.

THE DINING ROOM.

South of Oxford Street is the Moore Park precinct, which includes the famous Sydney Cricket Ground and Aussie Stadium, two of Sydney's great sporting venues; Fox Studios, where Nicole Kidman filmed *Moulin Rouge*, is not far away. Since 1973 a thriving bohemian market is held every Saturday in Paddington Public School.

The suburb is a high-wealth area with 40 per cent of families earning more than $2000 a week. A stroll through the narrow winding streets shows any number of Mercedes, BMWs and Volvos parked at the front of homes.

Fashion designer Kara Hanna and photographer husband Ben Shirley own a typical terrace in Underwood Street, a street that dates back to the late 1880s making it one of the oldest in Paddington. It was named after First Fleeter James Underwood who, with Robert Cooper and Francis Forbes, was granted 100 hectares of land extending from the present Oxford Street to Rushcutters Bay.

The partners had a range of different interests, with Cooper among other things involved in making gin at the Sydney Distillery. But the partners had their differences and the estate was split up.

Records show the first transfer of the Hanna–Shirley terrace was in December 1915 from the Permanent Trustee Company of New South Wales to property agent Robert Sutherland and his wife Annie. They sold it to an Eliza Pringle five days later.

In February 1917 the terrace was sold to Edith Holman, and in December 1924 she sold it to a Margaret Boardman, the wife of commercial traveller Aubrey Boardman. There has been a string of owners since then with the Hanna–Shirleys buying it in 1998 from the estate of two women who had lived there for five years in the 1980s. Rumour has it one of the women was murdered by her male friend, believed to have been a police officer.

'Ben, my then boyfriend, wanted to get into the Sydney property market. We loved terrace houses and we loved Paddington and its restaurants, bars and the shopping,' Ms

THE SMALL BACK GARDEN.

Hanna said. 'We love the old-style terrace houses, the beautiful high ceilings, the wall scrolls and the high skirting boards.

'We haven't done any structural changes but we have worked hard on restoring the house ourselves. We have repainted and made it comfortable for our lifestyle and baby son Max.'

The Hanna–Shirley terrace is medium size with a width of about 6 metres. It has two bedrooms upstairs with a third converted into a bathroom. The huge attic roof leaves more than enough space for another bedroom to be added and the family is considering this.

The front entrance opens into a hallway leading to the small but functional kitchen and family room area at the back of the house, which has been added. Two living area rooms are off the hallway at the front.

There is a small suntrap courtyard, about 1.5 metres by 3 metres, accessed through double doors off the living area. It has no roof but becomes part of the living area when the doors are opened and is used when the family is entertaining. The steep and narrow staircase is original. The terrace is solid and there is no noise from neighbours even though

The entrance hall.

it is joined. However, the other terraces in the same row each have their own layout rather than being a mirror image.

Kara Hanna noted that, although small, the house is very liveable. They have a tiny backyard with roller-door entrance to a lane, which gives them access for their car although there is no room for a garage.

A small sitting room off the dining room.

Raby

LEFT: RABY, SEEN FROM THE SIDE.

BOTTOM LEFT: THE FRONT DOOR
AND ITS PLAQUE.

BOTTOM RIGHT: THE L-SHAPE OF
THE HOUSE CAN CLEARLY BE SEEN.

Built for the Nevill dynasty, the great fortress of Raby Castle in County Durham, England, dates back nearly 1000 years. King Cnut owned the estate in the early eleventh century and could have built the first castle. The present castle was begun by John, the third Baron Nevill, in about 1360.

The Nevills were the most powerful family in the north, renowned warriors whose goal was the Crown itself. At Raby they built a stronghold of towers and walls as a symbol of their power and ambition.

The castle had the grandest medieval kitchen in England, a garrison room with walls 20 feet (6 metres) thick and a Baron's Hall where 700 knights gathered in 1569 to plot the rising of the north in support of Mary, Queen of Scots — a doomed plan that would bring about the fall of the House of Nevill.

After its failure, the castle and its lands were forfeited to the Crown until 1626 when Sir Henry Vane the Elder, member of parliament and important member of Charles I's household, bought Raby Castle and Barnard Castle and its estate for £18,000. The Vane family — as Earls of Darlington, Dukes of Cleveland and Lords Barnard — has owned it ever since, and Raby Castle is now home of the eleventh Lord Barnard.

But how a property in western New South Wales came to be named Raby is something of a mystery.

One of its previous owners, the Australian Estates Company Ltd, claims that William Henry Vane, the third Earl of Darlington and made the first Duke of Cleveland in 1833 for his political services, introduced the Durham breed of shorthorn cattle at Raby Castle. The story goes that somewhere along the line Simeon Lord was associated with the castle and the cattle before he came to Australia in the late 1700s.

Lord's descendants became involved in the pastoral industry and his grandson Francis Lord

bought land on the Macquarie River in western New South Wales, 16 kilometres north-west of present-day Warren. He named it Raby, the Australian Estates Company said, presumably because of his grandfather's earlier English association with the Durham castle.

But Simeon Lord came to Australia as a convict in 1791. Convicted of stealing cloth in England, by 1806 he was trading in timber, sealskin, wheat and coal and had become very wealthy. In partnership with James Underwood and Henry Kable, he even went into the shipping business and at one stage transported convicts in a ship called *Sydney Cove*. A friend of Governor Macquarie, Lord also founded a woollen mill in 1815.

Lord was the most successful of the emancipist merchants. He owned a large house at Sydney Cove and was immensely litigious with his business affairs, taking up a large percentage of the early appeals to the Privy Council. The records of the council show that his opponents may have had good grounds for arguing that he used the council as a means of warding off his creditors rather than in a genuine attempt to test the legality of judgments against him.

In 1823 the government resumed some of his land in Macquarie Place, Sydney, and compensated him partly in

THE SHEARING SHED.

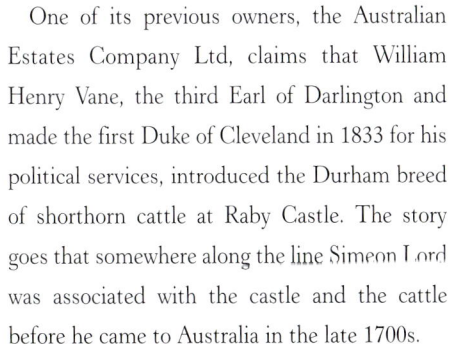

cash and partly in land. Some of the land was taken up at Orange but Lord never lived there.

His grandson, Francis Lord, no doubt benefiting from his grandfather's wealth, built the Raby homestead in 1888 but in 1896 sold out to N.A. Gatenby, who founded a merino stud two years later.

The Australian Estates Company Ltd bought Raby in 1927 and traded as New South Wales Pastoral Company until the CSR company took over in 1975.

Prominent Sydney Holden dealers John and Trish Muir bought Raby in 1982 and carried out extensive renovations to the house. They now run sheep and cattle on the property, which covers 21,065 acres (8531 hectares).

The Muirs live in Sydney but regularly visit Raby, which is managed for them by Ashley and Angela Bell, who live in the refurbished homestead. The Muirs live in one of the homestead's wings and have their own lounge and dining rooms for privacy. Entrances to all other sections of the house are off the verandahs, which run all the way around.

Raby is mainly pise construction and sits in large well-laid-out gardens on the banks of Crooked Creek. The Muirs demolished separate jackaroos' quarters 50 metres from the house and at the same time added a trophy room/lounge on the western side in keeping with the original design.

Raby was built in the shape of an L attached to the bottom of a T. It has a visitors' wing on the southern side,

entered from one of the verandahs that surround the house.

Visitors to Raby have included Prince Phillip, the Duke of Edinburgh, who was there for three days with Lord Rupert Nevill enjoying some bird watching in October 1973. The duke slept in the main room of the homestead. Brick stables were built for his visit. A London lord mayor, Sir Denys Lowson, and Alfred Hayes of the New York Reserve Bank have also stayed there.

The homestead has ten bedrooms; three of them and a bathroom are located in one of the wings. The main living

THE NEW TROPHY ROOM AND LOUNGE.

THE NEW DINING AREA.

PART OF THE NEW LOUNGE.

THE MAIN HALLWAY.

area includes a kitchen and dining room, lounge room and three bedrooms. The main bedroom is huge. The old cook's cottage is a separate building and has two more bedrooms and a kitchen.

The large dining room still has its original furniture, which includes a twelve-seat cedar dining table, matching side table and a glass China cabinet that was a prize for winning the grand champion ram at the Sydney Sheep Show in 1965. A brass mirror hangs over the fireplace.

The large kitchen has been renovated.

The wallpaper throughout the house has been replaced and the rooms have been repainted in the old colours. The ceilings throughout are 4.2 metres high.

Since 1995, when the Bells became managers after Ashley Bell had been overseer, any repairs needed have been done straight away. The Bells have also enlarged the gardens and built a new garden fence.

Jacarandas surround the house along with plane trees and ficus. The driveways are lined with roses and there is a huge area of lawn, all watered from Crooked Creek that runs past the homestead and never dries up. The Bells' youngest son Scott is the chief lawn mower.

The courtyard is surrounded by orange blossom murraya, which is also planted around the meat house and tank. The small orchard has orange, lemon, grapefruit and mandarin trees. There's a tennis court but it needs work, while a cement swimming pool put in years ago has been filled in. A field near the house was once used for polocrosse but now

NEWS CLIPPINGS ON THE STUD'S SUCCESS.

lucerne is grown there to feed racehorses owned by the Muirs. Some cotton is also grown.

Staff at Raby includes a station hand, jillaroo and jackeroo, and three casuals. When it's shearing season, twenty extra staff including cooks and rouseabouts are employed.

The modernised ram sheds are located at the bend of the Crooked Creek billabong. Ashley Bell said the property was one of the lucky places. In addition to Crooked Creek, there's the Macquarie River on the eastern boundary and Duck Creek channel on the south-west, which also have permanent water all year round.

Raby sells sheep all over New South Wales and Queensland, and the rams bring an average price of $4500 to $5000. The stud also does well at shows, winning champion and grand champion ribbons. Apart from around 12,000 sheep, the property also runs 450 Hereford breeding cows and 150 Angus. The Bells use horses for most of their cattle work because that keeps the stock quieter and easier to handle.

Raby grows its own grain and several thousand acres of oats a year, and makes all its own hay. There are twelve silo storages.

FAMOUS RABY MERINOS.

Rose Bay Cottage

Rose Bay Cottage, one of only two remaining single-storey houses designed by colonial architect John Verge, was 'hidden' for 25 years under a false fibro façade and believed demolished until it was 'rediscovered' in 1975. The 1834 stone and brick house was badly rundown, had doors bricked up, temporary walls put in, was a haven for termites, and had a roof full of leaks. But that did not stop Peter Bracher from buying it in late 1993 and beginning a full restoration in keeping with stringent guidelines set out in a state government conservation plan that comprised three detailed volumes.

Rose Bay Cottage in Salisbury Road, Rose Bay, is one of the most important examples of colonial architecture to survive on the harbour and sits between its contemporaries Elizabeth Bay House and Vaucluse House. The first cottage was built around 1834 for James Holt, who was a partner with emancipists Solomon Levey and Daniel Cooper in a wool, seal and timber business.

It was built on 80 acres (32 hectares) of land originally owned by Captain John Piper, who was the colony's Collector of Customs. Piper had amassed an estate of about 1100 acres (445 hectares) near his home, Henrietta Villa, but he got into financial difficulties following an audit of his accounts by Governor Darling.

Levey and Cooper lent Piper the money to get out of trouble but he couldn't make the repayments and was forced to sell his estate. At the auction, Levey and Cooper bought the 1100 acres (445 hectares), which now makes up the Sydney suburbs of Point Piper, Double Bay, Woollahra, Bellevue Hill and Rose Bay.

Levey and Cooper acquired more land, most of which remained in the Cooper family ownership until 1900. Levey returned to England in 1826 and later financed the establishment of the first British colony in Western Australia.

Cooper's cousin, James Holt, came to Australia in 1826 and went to work in the seal, wool and timber firm. In 1831 Cooper went back to England and Holt was made manager of the firm's Australian affairs. Levey died in 1833 and the following year Cooper made Holt a partner. He also became a director of the Bank of New South Wales and a member of the Sydney council. In 1834 Holt commissioned John Verge, the colony's most stylish architect, to build a house at Rose Bay.

The original cottage forms the north wing of the present house and was built in the Georgian style with John Verge's colonial influences. It was not joined with the east wing, which was probably the kitchen and servants' quarters.

THE CIRCULAR STAIRS WERE MOVED TO THE COURTYARD.

LEFT: THE ORIGINAL FRONT OF ROSE BAY COTTAGE.

THE LION GUARDING THE ENTRANCE.

The formal dining room used for special occasions.

The main entrance was on the western façade and the formal reception rooms faced north to Rose Bay. Bush surrounded the house and the nearest neighbours were the few houses on the harbour foreshore.

Holt added a room at the south-western end soon after the house was finished. It is now the present kitchen. Around 1840 another two rooms and a corridor were built on.

Daniel Cooper's nephew and namesake arrived in Sydney in 1843 and in the same year Levey's estate was settled after a long wrangle. Daniel Cooper snr acquired all of his former partner's land.

Holt returned to England in 1845 and Daniel Cooper jnr lived in the house for the next three years until it was leased in 1848 for seven years to bookseller and publisher William Moffit. During this time it was used as a hotel.

A ballroom was added to the southern end of the west wing with two attic bedrooms on top. A second storey was added to the east wing as well as other extensions.

After Moffitt's lease expired in 1855, Daniel Cooper jnr and his wife Elizabeth moved back into the house. He had been left most of his uncle's estate after his death in 1853. They established beautiful gardens with fountains and a pavilion. However, all that remains now is the base of one of the fountains.

In 1857, Conrad Martens painted a watercolour of the house that he called 'The Cottage at Rose Bay'. A copy of the painting hangs in the main hall of the house and the original is in the National Gallery in Canberra.

By 1856 Cooper had become the speaker of the first Legislative Assembly and decided to build a much grander house at Point Piper that he would call Woollahra House.

One of the sitting rooms.

ANOTHER OF THE SITTING ROOMS.

Leah Abrahams bought the house in 1912 and it stayed in her family's ownership until 1985. The Abrahams carried out extensive alterations to turn the house into twelve flats.

A second storey was built over the original John Verge cottage as well as a two-storey extension to the west. The verandah columns were replaced by brick columns and balustrades about 1920.

The fanlights were covered over and three of the six French doors were bricked in. A number of smaller extensions were added and the circular stair was moved from the west verandah to the courtyard to serve as a fire escape.

The house was then called Ritz Flats and by 1950 people believed the original Rose Bay Cottage had been demolished. But under the later façade it was surprisingly complete.

The house was re-discovered in 1975 and had a permanent conservation order put on it. The New South Wales Government Department of Environment and Planning bought the house in 1985 to save it from demolition. There was no legislation at the time to protect historic homes and Rose Bay Cottage was a rare example of Verge's work and one of only two of his single-storey houses remaining in Sydney.

The government later decided to sell subject to stringent guidelines set down in a conservation plan that required the work to be completed within two years or the property would be forfeited. The guidelines took up three detailed volumes and were prepared by conservation architects Clive Lucas and Partners. The only original documents still available were accounts from John Verge.

But although the government did all that work, it didn't carry out any maintenance and the house was almost derelict and full of white ants, which had eaten their way through most of the timber. The house had been occupied by people who rented flats and as they left the government sealed up each flat. By the time Peter Bracher looked at the house there was only one person left, an old alcoholic who was supposed to be some sort of caretaker. The rest of the place was a shambles.

The government made several attempts to sell the house but these were unsuccessful because of the guidelines. There were concerns that after it was sold there could be a convenient fire because it was an excellent piece of land for development. There was talk the property could become a library or be put to some other public use because there were no kitchens or bathrooms, but the government had no real idea how it could be used.

But construction only went ahead in 1883 and by then Cooper was back in England and never lived in the house. He was knighted in 1857.

The Rose Bay house was let on a number of short tenancies. Pastoralist, and later a member of the Legislative Assembly, Walter Lamb, was first and then it went to brothers John Charles and Edward Henry Lloyd.

In 1866 the house was leased to Sir John Hay, after whom the town of Hay was named. A member of parliament, he held many government positions, including secretary of land and works, and speaker and president of the Legislative Council. In 1892 a Mrs Rosa Rougier lived there and she bought the house and grounds of about 7 acres (2.8 hectares) in 1900 after Daniel Cooper died.

Mrs Rougier added a second storey on the west wing, enclosed the south verandah and built a windowed enclosure on the west side of the courtyard. She also put up a cast-iron circular stair connecting the lower and upper west verandahs.

For an unknown period of time, the house was used as the Canonby Girls' School run by a Kate Allenby, but Mrs Rougier subdivided the grounds and sold the house in 1911 to barrister Louis Bosker Haigh and Grace Ann Friedericks.

The subdivision had a number of consequences. The house lost its views of Rose Bay and its entrance from New South Head Road. Salisbury Road was run through to New South Head Road, destroying the summerhouse and tennis court. The front of the house is now at the back and the old kitchen wing faces the street.

Buying it was risky. Nobody would take it on, especially if they planned any change like installing a bathroom or a kitchen so it could be lived in, because that had to be approved by the government. Peter Bracher looked at the contract and thought if he wanted to put in a kitchen and the authorities sat on the application for ten weeks, the clock would be running and the property could end up being forfeited.

'I talked to the government and said I could never sign the contract the way it was but if we could agree on a price and it was taken off the market for six months, I would bring in my architect to work out what we needed to do to the house that was consistent with the conservation plan,' Mr Bracher said.

'The architect worked on it with me but it was terribly difficult. You couldn't walk through the house. You had to go outside and come back in twelve times because of the flats, and you were lost because you didn't know what part of the house you were in.

'But we worked out what we wanted to do and put that to the conservation branch of the New South Wales government and it agreed so we signed on the dotted line and went to it.'

The earliest part of the house is the east wing, which was built in the 1820s. An addition in 1833–34 is what Peter Bracher calls 'the cottage', followed by the lower part of the west wing. The upstairs section was built around 1890.

The house is stone up to the verandah level and brick from there. The east wing is built from stone but added to with brick in 1840.

The roof is slate. The builders reused what they could but most was in poor condition and they had to buy new slate, which was expensive. They bought some second hand that had come from houses being demolished.

There was almost as much work removing as rebuilding. Three or four flats upstairs had to be taken out and what was left repaired. But despite the terrible condition the house was in, it remains one of the more complete historic houses in the country because fortunately the people who owned it early on kept everything.

Mr Bracher did the restoration as an owner–builder, putting together a professional team with his partner Jo's brother-in-law, builder Peter Harris, who was keen to take on the job. The team included several English builders who had grown up working on old houses in England.

'They began in one corner and just kept on going until they finished. The architect came once a week and they worked out things as they went. They had detailed specifications but there were so many discoveries along the way they didn't know how it was going to turn out.

'We didn't even know whether we would want to live in the house because it mightn't work. It might be too big for us. But as we opened up the rooms, which had been divided into two- and three-room flats, we saw how great the rooms were,' Mr Bracher said.

A RELAXED LOUNGE AREA.

THE DINING AREA AND INFORMAL KITCHEN.

of the flats. The roof of the east wing had been raised at some time and it was lowered back to the original height.

'After two years, the work was not quite finished but we moved in. We still had work to do in the east wing but the government was happy we had complied and signed off on the job,' Mr Bracher said.

The architect Alan Croker won top awards for the conservation work, including the Royal Institute of Architects Greenway Award for conservation in New South Wales and the major national award from the Institute of Architects.

The approach to conservation of old homes has changed over time. Back in the 1970s people tended to leave the outside structure and make the inside surfaces look like new, but Mr Bracher's idea was to carefully put the house back together by repairing rather than rebuilding, being very gentle, so they would eliminate the inappropriate later work, leaving the house just as if it had been lived in for the past 150 years.

Where there were layers and layers of paint, they didn't sandblast it off. They scraped anything loose and painted over. They kept it as original as possible.

Mr Bracher has left remnants of its history around the house. Small pieces of old wallpaper remain in convenient corners. The wall to the laundry which was stained and had peeling paint was left as a remnant. About 1840, under Cooper's ownership, all the walls had been done in oak. The back of a door was painted so they left that. The paint schemes are mostly as they were in the 1830s, based on paint scrapes discovered under half a dozen layers of wallpaper and then as many layers of paint. The cornices in the dining room were from the second paint scheme in the 1840s and they were left as they were.

The house has fifteen rooms plus the east wing set up as a two-bedroom town house. It is now set up as five bedrooms with another used as a dressing room adjacent to the main bedroom. There are three large reception areas at the front and the informal kitchen that Mr Bracher and his partner use. The original kitchen in the east wing is separate.

The formal dining room is only used for large family Christmas dinners or other special occasions.

The other houses of architect John Verge that survive in Sydney include Tempe House, which is now owned by the Catholic Church, remnants of a Verge dwelling at SCEGGS School in Darlinghurst, Elizabeth Bay House, Craigmore and Lyndhurst.

'Doors that were removed after walls were filled in for the flats were reused upstairs. Some had been cut down and we put them back together.

'All the window shutters were missing but we found parts of them in the cellar so we knew what each one looked like. The architect, by a careful series of measurements, worked out which ones went where and we used those bits to make new ones that were needed.'

Sections of the floor were replaced. In one room concrete had been poured on the boards to make a bathroom for one

Rose Lindsay Cottage

When Norman Lindsay's second wife Rose wanted her own cottage so she could be more independent of her controversial artist husband's influence, she asked her daughter Jane to design one. Sandstone quarried from the nearby bush by local stonemason Mick Stratton was to be used to build the cottage on land just across the road from the family home, now the Lindsay gallery and studio at Faulconbridge, in the New South Wales Blue Mountains.

Jane Lindsay had used her father's old etching studio as a nucleus for her own house on land next door. The studio was made of local sandstone so that was the obvious material for additions.

Mick Stratton, who had been building chimneys in the district, found a big virgin rock to start his quarry and lumps of stone were transported to the old studio for him to begin the foundations. He chipped and chiselled for weeks, giving each rough block special attention. If the stone had interesting coloured grain, he treated it with special care, matching or contrasting it with the next. Sometimes he lined up a whole course on the ground before he set it into the wall.

Ms Lindsay said Rose was interested in her house. And envious. She kept asking when Mick would be finished so he could start cutting stone for her. However, Jane Lindsay replied she wasn't sure when he would be free. Her house was built but the project had taken hold of Mick and he was making flagged paths and terraces.

Rose Lindsay eventually lured him away and he began to build her house on land further up the hill. Ms Lindsay wrote in her book, *Portrait of Pa*, that her father was suspicious. 'He kept asking me in private, "What is your Ma going to do with that mansion she is building?" but I couldn't give him an answer.

'Although I had designed it to her specifications and knew it was to contain a large living room, dining room and three bedrooms as well as a wide verandah with more Grecian pillars, I really had no idea of her future plans. She just repeated she had always wanted a little place of her own.'

When the stonework was finished, the walls built up to roof height, the verandah flagged and the pillars cast, Rose Lindsay lost interest and the project came to a standstill in 1954. The stone shell stayed that way for around eighteen years until the Lee family bought the land, finished the interior and added a second storey to the existing stonework.

The next owners were Annette and Danny Wotherspoon, who bought the cottage at auction in the 1990s and carried out extensive renovations. Danny Wotherspoon was originally from Lismore and his wife was from Sydney. They lived in a flat in the Sydney suburb of Eastwood but both were keen to leave the city. The Blue Mountains seemed a good option. He was education officer at Taronga Zoo and had a choice of places he could go on transfer to, so he went to Western Sydney, teaching at Colyton High School between St Marys and Mt Druitt.

Annette Wotherspoon, who worked in a library in Sydney, said they thought about building but that was beyond their means. They also looked at the etching studio at the Norman Lindsay Gallery, which was on land with a separate title, and which was for sale at the same time as the cottage. However, it had a coffee shop attached and as they weren't too keen on that they settled on the cottage.

NORMAN LINDSAY'S HOUSE, NOW A GALLERY.

LEFT: THE SANDSTONE ROSE LINDSAY COTTAGE.

BOTTOM LEFT: ONE OF NORMAN LINDSAY'S SCULPTURES.

BOTTOM RIGHT: THE COLUMNS ON NORMAN LINDSAY'S HOUSE.

155

Above: Lindsay's studio.

Below: The Rose Lindsay Cottage sitting room.

After they moved in, the Wotherspoons spent several months deciding how to renovate Rose Lindsay Cottage. They relocated a couple of doorways and separated the open-plan kitchen and dining room.

Mrs Wotherspoon wanted an Australian native wild flowers theme but because the cottage hadn't been finished until 1971, she and her husband didn't have a period to work from for decorating. 'Because it was a bush block, we wanted something that was different so we had an idea of bringing the bush inside,' she said.

'We engaged professional people to do the fabrics and rugs with wildflowers and the interior design. The rugs have waratahs, grevilleas and other flowers from the protea family and we gave each room a wildflower name — Grevillea, Banksia, Treetops — and each a different colour scheme.

'We put in decorative vents and new cornices and skirting boards and each Christmas did a project like replacing

THE ORIGINAL STOVE.

the stairs. We rebuilt the carport and added self-contained accommodation upstairs which we called the loft.'

The cottage garden is almost 1 hectare and includes a great deal of natural bush, including eucalypts, banksia, mountain devils and geebungs. There are sandstone walls and lots of lawn. Paths meander through the garden and the couple put in a frog pond and fountain. Huge swings are from the set of the 1994 movie *Sirens*, which was filmed at the Lindsay home. It starred Hugh Grant as an Anglican priest who visits a notorious artist, loosely based on Lindsay, because of the church's concern about a blasphemous painting done by the artist, played by Sam Neill. Elle Macpherson, Portia de Rossi and Kate Fischer played the artist's models.

Norman Lindsay and Rose bought their 42-acre (17-hectare) bush property for £500 in 1913 from a Francis Foy, who had built the original cottage in 1900 as a halfway house. The cottage was badly in need of repairs but Lindsay added his own distinctive imprint in the improvements through the years.

Lindsay, born in 1879 at Creswick in Victoria, was a prolific artist, sculptor, writer, cartoonist and modeller and was widely regarded as one of Australia's greatest. His nudes caused huge controversy and he spent considerable time defending his right to paint them.

In 1940 irate protestors Lindsay described as 'wowsers' burnt some of the sixteen crates of paintings Rose had taken to the United States for safe keeping because of the war. They had found the paintings on a train.

A childhood sickness forced Lindsay to be inactive so he spent a great deal of time drawing. One of ten children, he and his brother Lionel moved to Melbourne to work on a local magazine.

In 1901 the pair joined the staff of the *Sydney Bulletin*, a weekly newspaper and magazine. They drew caricatures, cartoons and illustrations, and Norman's association with the magazine lasted more than 50 years.

Rose Soady began modelling for Lindsay in 1902 before she became his second wife, his most recognisable model, his business manager and the printer of his etchings.

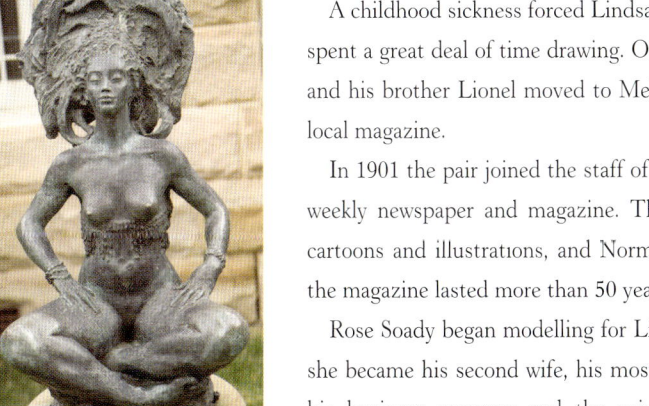

Lindsay went to London in 1909 and was joined by Rose, who replaced his wife Katie, who had left him.

Lindsay returned to Melbourne the following year after having 100 drawings published in a limited-edition book. He moved to Faulconbridge in 1912 and lived there until he died in 1969.

He created cement statues, carved and decorated the furniture, and did lots of drawing. One of his pen drawings, 'The Crucified Venus', caused a stir and was removed from a Melbourne art show. However, the Society of Artists' president threatened to remove all the paintings unless Lindsay's was put back, which it was.

Lindsay began to do oils and watercolours, etchings, writing and building models of ships. His first novel, called *A Curate in Bohemia*, based on his experiences in Melbourne, was a big success. He followed that in 1918 with his much-loved children's book, *The Magic Pudding*, which is now an Australian classic. Other books followed and Lindsay became a popular figure.

Norman Lindsay turned the original cottage into an antipodean Olympus. He added columns to the verandah and a Roman courtyard. The grounds were embellished with a bush swimming pool, fountains and sculptures of nymphs, satyrs and sirens, which reflected his passion for the Mediterranean.

Lindsay also built the etching studio where he worked for more than twenty years. It is now owned by the New South Wales National Trust and has been returned to the original Lindsay estate, which Lindsay bequeathed to the Trust.

Lindsay's pen drawings, etchings, watercolours and oil paintings are well represented in the cottage.

A ROOM IN THE GALLERY.

South Hill

In 1866, the Roman Catholic Church bought the property known as South Hill, just out of Goulburn in the southern highlands of New South Wales, as a possible site for a proposed college to be known as St Patrick's. However, the church found the site unacceptable for a school because a meatworks had been established close by on adjoining land.

So the church sold the land in 1869 for £350 to a J.C. Dalgleish, who had apparently been leasing it from the church to run his cattle. The same year New South Wales Railways also bought some of the land to build a railway line to the south, water tanks for the locomotives and two weirs — all of which are still there.

Dalgleish made a handy profit when he sold it the following year to Goulburn Meat Preserving Company for £900. The company held it for two years before selling it at auction in 1872 to local merchant Thomas Bull for £1040.

Continuing the run of short-term owners, Bull sold in 1875 for £3800 to a Mr Roberts but in the meantime had built a major part of the South Hill homestead.

Roberts sold to Isaac Shepherd in 1877 for £3600. Shepherd added a ballroom and stranger's room and then sold in 1893 to the Chisholm family for £4500. It stayed in trust for Alice Chisholm (*see* Merrilla) until 1917 when the family trust sold to Joseph Collett, a local butcher, for £1800.

He held it until 1926 when he sold to the Roman Catholic Bishop of Goulburn, Dr Barry, for £3750. Bishop Barry intended to farm South Hill to provide produce for the numerous Catholic institutions in Goulburn and put it in the care of the Sisters of Our Lady of Mercy. They changed the name to Marian Hill.

The Sisters employed men to work the property but the venture would have failed without the help of Bungendore farmer Frank Leahy who, locals said, 'hated priests but loved nuns ...' He turned the property into an efficient farm, adding numerous outbuildings and a manager's residence.

The Sisters had big plans to modify the homestead but these never went ahead. Instead they took down the original iron lace verandahs and replaced them with a wider concrete version with heavy brick piers. Over the years, the Sisters dwindled in numbers and the farm became neglected, so the church sold it in 1969 to the Naughton family. They stayed there until 1987 when they sold to a New South Wales company called Old Inns, which planned to use the house for backpacker accommodation.

A VIEW FROM THE HOUSE.

That did not eventuate, however, and the house stood empty for two years. In 1989 Ian and Elizabeth Lipscomb looked at the house for a friend who was interested in buying, but found they were attracted to it themselves.

With their son Michael, his wife Margie and their daughter Gabbie they decided to buy. The younger Lipscombs would live in the old cottage built in the 1930s, and Ian and Elizabeth would live in the twenty-room homestead.

'We weren't quite sure then what we would do with it, which was a silly way to start,' Elizabeth Lipscomb said. 'The house had been empty for two years and was supposed to become a place for backpackers to stay because the owner had bought the Towers property on the other side of the

LEFT: SOUTH HILL AND ITS ADDITIONS.

BOTTOM LEFT: THE BRICK COACH-HOUSE AND ITS OWL HOLE.

BOTTOM RIGHT: THE STRANGER'S ROOM.

river and he was running that as a restaurant. His idea was to have backpackers here and have a flying fox across the river so they could have their meals at the Towers, but the building had become shabby. Fortunately the structure of the house is very sound but it was a big job to get rid of the dampness and to repair the floorboards and ceilings.'

Mr Lipscomb was the parish priest at Batemans Bay so they were able to begin renovations before they moved in. But when they arrived, they discovered bats had got into the ceilings and flew around the house every night.

Although they had limited financial resources to carry out the restoration, the family worked out a budget and was able to achieve most of their goals. They put in two new bathrooms and a new kitchen that was practical yet still free of stainless steel and modern European appliances.

'We did a lot of painting and other repairs. We glassed in the verandahs because we found the wind from the south blew everything away,' Mrs Lipscomb added.

The architect is unknown, if there was one. Elizabeth Lipscomb thinks the house just grew like Topsy. It began with the kitchen at the back, which was the first cottage built, probably in the early 1860s. Then came the coach-house and stables. Thomas Bull built the four main rooms of the larger part of the house. He obviously had servants

because he had bell pulls in all of the eight rooms. The house is brick with cedar joinery. The fireplaces are also all cedar except one in the ballroom, which is marble. The floors throughout are pine and the roof is corrugated iron. The three front rooms have wonderful ceiling roses.

The house can be entered through the front door, the ballroom, the kitchen and a door through the courtyard. Every main bedroom upstairs has four doors, one on each wall, and a chimney or a window. This has made the house difficult to furnish. The curved servants' staircase at the back has been rebuilt along with a light conservatory over part of the courtyard.

The coach-house is brick with an iron roof and an owl hole in one of the gables. The 1860s slab stables are probably the most significant building in the cluster because of their construction.

The 27-door fowl house has heritage status. Mrs Lipscomb applied for a heritage grant of $2000 to replace the guttering, which was letting in water and damaging the foundations. Goulburn City Council decided it could not make a grant without seeing the fowl house, so councillors looked and proclaimed the sheds a five-star hen house. Although people made a great deal of fun of this, the Lipscombs got the grant and the sheds were heritage listed.

Nobody has ever challenged whether they are the only heritage-listed chook sheds in Australia.

The dairy is now used as a studio by Margie Lipscomb, who is an artist.

Today, the property covers 80 acres (32.5 hectares) and carries 250 sheep. As the previous owners bred horses and owned trotters, there was no shearing shed so the Lipscombs have built a small one.

THE DINING ROOM.

CREEPER SOFTENS THE FAÇADE.

Like many historic homes, South Hill apparently is home to ghosts. While Mrs Lipscomb has never seen them, there have been several reported manifestations of a big ginger cat, which is apparently brought to the edge of the bed by a smiling lady.

'It looks just like ours,' Mrs Lipscomb explained. 'She puts the cat on the bed, smiles at you, then she picks it up and vanishes. We've had two manifestations of that by visitors who have stayed in the house.

'We've also had three manifestations of a horse galloping around the house, which is apparently the ghost of a young man who was told to go away and stop visiting the daughter because he was not acceptable. Three [manifestations] is enough to say there's a ghost of some kind there. It also taps on the window of one of the bedrooms.'

Mrs Lipscomb noted there was also a story about a nun who died in the house and now walked around. She was seen by the previous owners but nobody else has seen her.

'We lit candles for the spirits of the house on the stairwell and there doesn't seem to be anything bad here. I had some sleepless nights but when I began lighting the candles, I was okay. We were telling the ghosts, the nun particularly, that if she wanted to stay she had to behave.'

Springfield

William Faithfull, a member of the second detachment of the New South Wales Corps, arrived in Australia in 1792 on a ship called the *Pitt*. He spent seven years as a private and when he left the army in 1799 he was granted 25 acres (10 hectares) of land at Petersham Hill.

Probably more importantly, Faithfull became farm manager for the influential Captain Joseph Foveaux after receiving more land at Petersham and establishing himself as a successful farmer. When Captain Foveaux left the colony in 1801, he left Faithfull half his flock of sheep, his bible and a gold watch.

In 1804 William Faithfull married Susanna Pitt, who came to Australia with her mother Mary, three sisters and three brothers. Their first child, William, was born in 1806 and two years later they received a grant of 1000 acres (400 hectares) on the recommendation of Lord Nelson, whose sister had married Mary Pitt's cousin.

William Faithfull wasn't keen on the land, which later became the Sydney suburb of Burwood, because he thought it was unproductive, so he sold part of it and swapped the rest for another block at Minto. But then he settled on a property he bought near Richmond and later sold the Minto land.

When his son William Pitt Faithfull (the Pitt added to the name to distinguish him from his father) was 22, he applied in 1827 for a land grant on the Goulburn Plains. He had the necessary credentials because he was native born, was the son of a prominent landowner and had worked as an overseer for four years on his aunt's property in the Illawarra district.

The government had just introduced a new policy, which included the granting of 640 acres (259 hectares) in a designated area for every £500 of capital the applicant had. The maximum grant was 2560 acres (1037 hectares or 4 square miles), if the applicant had £2000.

William Pitt Faithfull was interviewed by the Land Board, produced evidence to show he had £2232 in capital, and was eventually granted 1280 acres (518 hectares) with the promise of more land later. He was given permission to take up the land on 31 December 1827, but discovered a Captain Terence Murray had been squatting on it for nearly twelve months. He had built several huts and had begun to clear and plough some of the land to plant a crop.

Murray claimed he had been given rights to the land but checks by William Pitt Faithfull with the surveyor general's office showed Murray's letter of selection had only been lodged eight days earlier. The colonial secretary asked Murray to give the land up, which he did. After losing another block six months later, Murray finally settled on a property on the Limestone Plains, which he called Yarralumla (*see* Yarralumla).

The Goulburn land was known by its native name of Coorangangennoe, but because that was difficult to pronounce, it was called Mount Pitt and then changed to its present name of Springfield.

In 1830 William Pitt Faithfull applied for the additional 1280 acres (518 hectares) he had missed out on, but after fronting the Land Board again, his application was refused. So he bought 610 acres (247 hectares) from his neighbour and applied for a second time in 1837, when he was again refused on the grounds that he was not a British immigrant under the terms of the grants — even though his application had been successful the first time.

A VIEW OF THE BACK, SHOWING THE ORIGINAL SECTION.

He had been running sheep on Springfield from the beginning but had also established an orchard and was doing well supplying mounted police and gangs of convict road builders with meat and stores. But after he lost a flock of sheep being taken south by his younger brother George when they were attacked by hostile Aborigines, he decided in 1838 to turn Springfield into a merino stud.

William Pitt Faithfull had built a hut at the present front gate near a spring, but when it dried up he moved closer to the river and built a more substantial house. It was a colonial cottage, a long low building with a verandah along both sides. It had one large living room, which they called the church room because they had services there once a month, and a separate kitchen. This cottage now forms the south-west wing of the homestead.

In January 1844, he married Mary Deane, who ran a private school in Sydney, and she was joined on the property by her mother, brother, sister and nephew, so he needed more accommodation. In December 1845 he contracted Goulburn carpenter and joiner Thomas Snape to help him build additions.

These were modest and comprised a two-storey Georgian stone building with hipped roof, two large bedrooms, a

dressing room and a verandah. The only access was an outside staircase to a landing on the first floor. The ground floor was a working area.

The building was incorporated into more additions later but is still recognisable. The steps remain although the verandah has gone.

In 1855 William Pitt Faithfull signed an agreement with an Abraham Ferney to make 150,000 bricks for 30 shillings a thousand; and almost three years later, in November 1857, he contracted a James Thompson to do the bricklaying for a new house at Springfield. This house had two storeys with a large square tower over the front door providing a third storey. It had an impressive entrance hall leading to a drawing room and a dining room entered from a smaller hall at the foot of the stairs.

There was a church room beyond the dining room and a smoking room and storeroom. The kitchen and other service areas were housed in a separate building at the back.

The new section joined the existing building built in 1845, which still had its access from the outside stairs. The design apparently came out of J.C. Loudon's book *The Suburban Gardener and Villa Companion* and was in the style of an Italian villa. Books like this were frequently used as

THE FORMAL DINING ROOM.

The drawing room with its white marble fireplace.

references because it was one of the few ways people could copy English designs.

By this time Springfield was self-sufficient and resembled a small village. It had stables, a stone woolshed and a large weatherboard flourmill. The mill comprised huge gear wheels with ironbark cogs turned by four horses, and is still standing today.

There was no shortage of excitement in those days. On 6 February 1865, William Pitt Faithfull's two oldest sons — Percy, 21, and George, nineteen — were taking two of the youngest — Monty, seventeen, and Reginald, fifteen — to Goulburn to put them on the Cobb and Co coach to go back to school at Parramatta. Ben Hall's bushranging gang had been operating on the Goulburn road all that morning. It was only 10am but by then they had held up two coaches and a bullock driver.

When they saw the boys come out the front gate in their drag, Hall galloped up, fired over their heads and yelled, 'Look out.' One of the boys cracked his whip and, in the vernacular, more or less told Hall where to go.

Hall joined gang members John Dunn and Johnny Gilbert and the three rode back to the boys, firing. The boys pulled up and Percy and George returned fire with a rifle and pistol they had, using the drag as cover while the younger boys held the four horses. But one of the horses was wounded and they bolted, leaving the boys without protection.

The boys managed to get back through the fence and began to retreat, with Percy managing to keep the bushrangers at bay with his rifle because it had a longer range than the bushrangers' pistols.

One of Gilbert's shots accidentally hit his own horse in the head as it reared and it fell, pinning him underneath. This gave the boys the opportunity to pull back further. They fought this retreating battle for only a few minutes but more than 90 shots were fired.

Percy stood his ground while the others made it to safety back in the homestead. He fired his last bullet at Gilbert and ran, with Ben Hall pursuing him almost to the house. Hall had one of the boys' handkerchiefs when he was shot a few months later at Forbes. The governor decided to award the Faithfull boys a specially struck gold medal for bravery and gallant resistance but it took twelve years to arrive.

All four boys went on to university. Percy became a barrister, George a surveyor, Monty a solicitor and Reginald lived at Brewarranna station near Wagga Wagga. They never went back to Springfield.

Another son, Robert, was a doctor as well as director of the Bank of New South Wales, the Perpetual Trustee Company and Colonial Sugar Refining Company. There were three daughters: Florence, Constance and Frances.

William Pitt Faithfull achieved a great deal after establishing Springfield in 1827. Besides having a highly successful business, he served on the Legislative Council as the member for Argyle from 1846 to 1848 and again from 1856 to 1861. He also started a school at Springfield that had nineteen pupils and a teacher, with most of the children belonging to property workers.

However, he was getting on and by 1871 wanted to take a less active role in running the show. Only the youngest son, Lucian, then sixteen, was interested in taking over. After spending a month or so at Mudgee with sheep judge Richard Cox, Lucian first took over management of the Springfield stud flock and eventually the whole property.

William Pitt Faithfull's wife Mary died in December 1889 and was buried in the family vault on the property. By now the sheep industry was going through troubled times but Lucian was able to cope and Springfield rode out the storm.

It was also time for one of William Pitt Faithfull's rare indulgences. He ordered a carriage to be built for his daughter Florence by Brewsters of New York. It cost US$1943 landed in Australia. In 1895, Lucian married Ethel Joplin, the daughter of a Goulburn bank manager, and they used the carriage for their honeymoon.

Lucian had intended to build a house on a hill about a mile from the homestead and a few years earlier had planted pine trees there. He called it Pinea but his father was in failing health so, rather than live so far away, he built a bluestone house called the Cottage near the woolshed and that's where he and Ethel lived.

William Pitt Faithfull died at Springfield on 24 April 1896. He was buried in the vault with his wife Mary.

Lucian, now 41, took over and was determined to build on his father's success. Prudent with his finances, he continued to live in the Cottage while sister Florence lived alone in the main house.

Lucian and Ethel had three daughters: Hazel, Florence (later known as Bobbie) and Valerie. He was anxious to have a son but that was not to be.

He improved the breed of his sheep and the quality of the wool. He had promised his wife that if he ever received one shilling and sixpence a pound for it, he would take the family

to England for a holiday. He achieved that price in 1900 and the following year kept his promise and they went to England for several months.

Lucian bred draught horses as a hobby and was a keen trotting enthusiast. He was also interested in horse racing and for many years was president of the Terranna Picnic Race Club, which held a two-day meeting every January.

In his sixties, Lucian began to wonder who would take over Springfield since he did not have a son. Of his three daughters, Florence (Bobbie) seemed the most suited but at twenty she was more interested in the social life of Goulburn and Sydney. Lucian had tried to match her with the boy next door, Irwin Maple-Brown, who lived with his family on Gundary Plains, but Bobbie showed no interest. However, after a visit to Cucumgilliga, a property Irwin was managing near Cowra, she changed her tune when she saw him in a more mature light.

They were married in Goulburn in 1923 and lived at Cucumgilliga for two years, where their son James was born, before moving to Fonthill, a property only a stone's throw from Springfield. Their daughter Diana was born there a few years later in 1928.

In the meantime back at Springfield the wealthy Faithfulls still had no mains electricity. Lucian had installed a generator at the Cottage around 1920 so they had electric lights but water had to be heated by a wood fire. The front section of the main house was lit by gas made in a carbide plant and the rest by kerosene lamps.

THE ENTRANCE HALL.

This bedroom still has its original wallpaper.

The kitchen was still a separate building at the back of the house and did not have running water. Meals were cooked there and carried on trays to the house. The phone was outside the house in a small cubicle on the back verandah, and the bedrooms added by William Pitt in 1845 could still only be accessed by the outside stairs.

By 1935 there were 125 people on the property, including the children going to the new brick school Lucian built, but his health was failing and he could do little. He died in 1942 aged 87 and Springfield lost the Faithfull name. The property was left to his daughter Bobbie Maple-Brown.

A comfy corner.

She and her husband Irwin initially stayed at Fonthill because that was their home. Besides, Irwin had become a prominent grazier in his own right and a Harry Dunn was managing Springfield.

Irwin Maple-Brown had volunteered for reserve service with the Light Horse in 1939 and later became a full-time soldier, joining the 7th Armoured Division. Other men at Fonthill also joined up and, with the Maple-Brown's son Jim at boarding school, Bobbie effectively ran the property.

Jim left school in 1941 and returned to Fonthill to help his mother. Because she had the difficult job of running the property, she had decided to stay there after her father Lucian died.

Irwin's health was not all that good and he left the army after he was given the job of guarding an airfield and realised there was no prospect of him being sent overseas on active service. Soon after he returned in 1943 son Jim joined the Royal Australian Air Force as a trainee pilot.

Bobbie and Irwin moved from Fonthill to Springfield in 1944 to live in the Cottage, with Florence Faithfull, Lucian's sister, still in the main house. Nothing much had changed since Bobbie left in 1923, with electricity still coming from the petrol generator.

Jim Maple-Brown married Pamela Calder in 1947 and they moved into the home Lucian had built in the late 1890s at Pinea for the property manager W.A. Harris. Two years later Florence Faithfull died, aged 98. She was the last of William Pitt's daughters.

Bobbie and Irwin continued to live in the Cottage and wondered what to do with the main house. Virtually no improvements had been made to it in the past 50 years, but wool was bringing a good price and the Maple-Browns, like other growers, were making a good income.

Bobbie and Irwin decided to take a holiday in Europe and, while there, Irwin bought a Bentley, played polo against Lord Mountbatten's team and received a gold cup from Princess Elizabeth. On their return they agreed the main house was the Springfield homestead and should be renovated.

They wanted to make it comfortable to live in while retaining as much of its character as possible. That meant changing some of its Victorian interior. Bobbie and Irwin engaged Sydney architects Fowell Mansfield and Maclurcan to draw the plans and John Mansfield supervised the work. The changes were designed to open up some of the rooms to make them more practical.

A detail of the wallpaper.

167

The library on the left of the hall, which Florence had used as a sitting room, was converted into an office; two maids' bedrooms were turned into a billiards room; and a new inside staircase was built to the upstairs bedrooms. A new bathroom was put in upstairs and a balcony was taken out.

The main drawing room was redecorated and refurnished under the guidance of interior decorator John Richards. The biggest change was to build a new kitchen in what had been the old church room, next to the dining room. A new oil stove and hot water system was installed.

Mains electricity had become available so the whole house was wired and 60 new lights installed as well as power points in every room. The house was also centrally heated.

The outside was left largely unchanged, although the covered verandahs that had joined the back of the house to the kitchen were pulled down and the area turned into a grassed courtyard. While all this work was going on, Bobbie cleared out stuff that was no longer needed and stored it all in two rooms upstairs which she turned into a small museum. Two trucks took other books and documents to the National Library in Canberra.

Bobbie and Irwin moved into the house in 1953. The renovations had cost more than £25,000, a huge amount then, and that did not include the new wiring. At the same time they demolished the old Cottage because it was in such poor condition.

The extensive gardens were next on the list. Trees and shrubs were removed and a new lawn and a rose garden put in. It became a showpiece.

Springfield again became an important party of society and Governor-General Sir William Slim visited several times. House parties were frequent, particularly when picnic race meetings and polo matches were held.

Irwin, a keen horseman, offered a piece of Springfield to the Goulburn Polo and Picnic Race Club to build a race course and two polo fields. The races were held there until 1986 when they were returned to Goulburn Race Course, which had been rebuilt. Polo is still played at Springfield.

Irwin owned a stallion called Tetreen and it produced several good horses, including one called Alinga. Too good for the picnics, it went on to win a Sydney Turf Club Gold Cup in 1953 and was being prepared for the Melbourne Cup but broke a leg in Sydney and had to be destroyed. The money the horse had won was used to put in a swimming pool at Springfield and a bronze plaque in memory of the horse.

Irwin died in 1964. In 1983 Bobbie, then 84, decided the main house was too big for her so the family played musical chairs. Jim and Pamela moved into the main house, their son Richard and wife Susan moved into the house at Pinea, and Bobbie moved into their renovated cottage, which was originally used by a gardener.

THE MAIN ENTRANCE

Richard, the sixth generation, took over the management of Springfield in 1973. His son James makes up the seventh generation at the helm, taking on a management role in 1999.

Pamela Maple-Brown loves the house and enjoys looking after it. Although she and her husband Jim have lived in the house for more than twenty years, she is still unsure how many rooms there are. 'They tell me there's 33 but I can never get it to 33. I've tried to add them up many times but I think they count things like the linen cupboard, which is a sort of room, and separate toilets, but there's about 30 and we use them all,' she said.

'The thing about the house is the centre part is very condensed. There's just four bedrooms, two bathrooms, sitting room, dining room and kitchen in the middle of the house and that's what we use most of the time. When the family comes to stay you put them upstairs and anywhere else you can find.'

THE ITALIAN INFLUENCE IS EVIDENT.

The approach to the house is along a meandering 1.2-kilometre driveway from the main Goulburn road through copses of pines, elms and poplars.

There is a large formal entrance hall, which is like another large room suitable for entertaining. It has a polished hardwood floor. To the right is the drawing room, left unchanged in the 1950s renovations other than for widening the windows. A doorway was also put in to open into an adjoining small sitting room which the family uses most of the time.

The drawing room has a grand piano, upright piano and an organ and in the hall is another organ and piano. The Faithfull family held lots of musical evenings. The drawing room mirror dates back to about 1880. The curtain holders are gilt tulips.

The sitting room was extended towards the garden in 1951 and has glass doors which open on to an extended porch. There is also a large open fireplace with cedar mantel.

To the left of the entrance hall is the library, now used as an office. It has a traditional paymaster's door at the far end and an open fireplace with marble surrounds.

The billiard room was originally a store room and maid's bedroom. It has an elevated viewing area so others can watch the players. A door leads upstairs to the self-contained west wing with its three bedrooms, kitchenette

THE ORIGINAL GRAIN MILL.

and bathroom. The two rooms above the billiard room were used as the museum until 2005 when the items were given to the National Library, together with the carriage William Pitt Faithful bought.

The dining room is one of the special features of the house. It retains its original 1860s look with warm red-pink terracotta wallpaper, high ceiling and open fireplace. The furniture is mostly cedar and mahogany. The sideboard and table are mahogany. Some of the chairs are original.

The large kitchen area was originally the church room but was divided in the 1951 renovations into a cooking area and

the flower room. There is a separate pantry and storeroom and the traditional Aga stove.

The house has ten main bedrooms. The master bedroom suite is in the main wing of the house. It has an ensuite bathroom and dressing room. There are three more bedrooms with separate bathroom in the wing and a fourth bedroom in the tower.

The homestead also includes jackeroos' rooms, staff quarters and extra bathrooms. Underneath are the cool areas where there is a laundry, and a cellar where meat, milk, butter and other food were kept. Mrs Maple-Brown said although the foundations were put down in 1859, there wasn't a crack anywhere in the house.

Some of the original furniture still remains, particularly the bookcases, which were made for the house, and the 24 dining room chairs. There are lots of cedar wardrobes and the doors are all cedar.

The marble for the fireplaces came from Marulan. It was traditional to put white marble mantelpieces in the drawing room and black marble in the dining room.

The coach-house was built about the same time as the house, in 1860. The coachmen lived in the top. The stone shearing shed was built in the 1830s. Next to it are stone stables, dating from 1840, which were used to lock the special horses up in at night. After the gunfight between the boys and the Hall gang, the bushrangers returned three nights later and stole three horses.

Mrs Maple-Brown recounted that when the family bought their first motor cars, they built two garages. The chauffeur was called Painter and they sent him to Melbourne to learn how to drive. He came back and crashed straight into the front gate.

Horses are an important part of Springfield, and the family has always bred horses for polo, stock work and the racetrack. As Mrs Maple-Brown explains, 'My father-in-law Irwin played polo, my husband Jim played with the Duke of Edinburgh in 1968, our son Richard did, and our grandson James does.

'Horses have always been a popular sport here. My daughter had horses for dressage and jumping and her children have also.'

In addition to the horses, sheep and cattle are still run at Springfield and, while the government took 7000 acres (2835 hectares) of the property after the war for soldier settlement, today it covers 3183 hectares.

Stone Cottage

Lord Alistair McAlpine, who was England's Conservative Party treasurer from 1975 when Margaret Thatcher was party leader, has a long association with northern Australia. He was a pioneer of eco-tourism with his development of Broome, creating the world-famous Cable Beach Club and also a zoo that became known for the success of its breeding programs for the world's endangered species. He bought land, developed some of it and turned other blocks into nature parks. He talked regularly about the need for Australia to develop the vast and unpopulated areas in the north of the country.

Lord McAlpine's public roles have included appointments to the Council of the Royal Court Theatre, Institute of Contemporary Arts, the Contemporary Arts Society and the Arts Council of Great Britain. He has published numerous books, illustrated by people like Sir Sidney Nolan and is also known for his long-running column in the *World of Interiors* and his articles on the auction world in the *Spectator*.

A member of the English building company Sir Robert McAlpine and Sons Ltd, Lord McAlpine arrived in Australia in his early twenties and became involved in building Perth's first luxury hotel, the famous Parmelia. A long string of other projects followed.

He made a foray into Darwin and, in probably what was some sort of experiment, built several small stone colonial-style cottages on prime land on The Esplanade, overlooking Centennial Park, Lameroo Beach and Darwin Harbour. Apparently he had plans to build a hotel on the same piece of land in the 1980s but that did not eventuate and he sold the cottages.

Catherine Paton bought one, and she believes it was originally designed to be a holiday cottage to somehow fit in with Lord McAlpine's plan to develop a hotel on land at the back. 'I don't know why the project didn't go ahead but he sold the cottages and I ended up with one. There were

LEFT: STONE COTTAGE, BUILT BY LORD MCALPINE.

two blocks of land and two roads that came in. We use one road and there's a much wider road next door which would have gone to the block behind where the hotel was to have been built.'

The cottages are on two levels and were built by Multiplex from stone blocks quarried locally. Ms Paton's cottage has not been structurally altered in any way.

Most of its interior woodwork is cedar and, in fact, there were even cedar shingles on the roof when it was first built. Ms Paton said the shingles looked good but they were unable to stand up to the weather and had to be replaced with iron in 2004.

The floorboards are jarrah and the timber in the kitchen is blackwood. Quarry tiles are used on the floor.

The entrance is through a front balcony and louvred double French doors and steps. Upstairs there are three bedrooms mirroring the ground floor with double French doors opening on to a balcony. There is a bathroom and porch at the back.

Building the stone colonial cottages was part of Lord McAlpine's dream of developing Northern Australia, in particular Darwin. They now stand as a reminder of his efforts, which sadly came to an end as the result of a business collapse.

THE DINING ROOM.

171

Strathroy

Cricket's biggest hitter was George John Bonnor who once hit a ball 160 kilometres. In the country city of Orange, he cleared the Wade Park ground and the adjacent street and landed the ball on a coal truck in the railway yards. The hit out of the ground has never been bettered, even forgetting the fact the train and the ball ended up at Dubbo that night.

But probably Bonnor's most memorable hit was in the First Test between Australia and England at The Oval in 1880. The ball went so high he was turning for his third run when caught on the boundary by George Frederick Grace, the youngest of the legendary Grace brothers. Two weeks later 'Fred' Grace was dead from pneumonia at the age of 30. Bonnor the Basher, also known as the Colonial Hercules,

went on to play sixteen more Tests for Australia before retiring to play grade cricket at Orange, bringing the town considerable notoriety and frightening the flannels off many a visiting side. He knocked up a 100 or so every Saturday and finished his last season with an average of just over 200. In one match for Bathurst against the Orientals of Sydney, he made 267 not out in less than two hours. In January 1884, playing for an Australian XI against New South Wales, he hit 64 in 28 minutes, including five sixes and five fours.

The following season, in the Fourth Test against England in Sydney Bonnor made 128, hitting the first 100 in 100 minutes. It was his only Test century but it stayed in the record books as the fastest 100 scored in the first 28 years of Australia–England matches.

STRATHROY, ONCE KNOWN AS
BONNOR'S MANSION.

THE DINING ROOM.

George Bonnor was born at Bathurst in February 1855 but moved to Orange to live with his brother James at his house called Strathroy, known locally then as Bonnor's Mansion. James was a staunch Baptist, but George — a huge man standing 198 centimetres tall and weighing 103 kilograms — liked a drink, unlike his brother, so the story goes he lived in the stables at the back and wasn't allowed in the main house. He died in 1912 from a heart attack, aged 57, and is buried in the Orange cemetery.

James Bonnor had bought Strathroy in August 1897 from a Richard Warren for £2250. Warren had acquired it from the assignee of the insolvent estate of Josiah Parker, an Orange chemist who built the house but went broke and failed to repay the mortgage to Warren.

His father, Josiah Parker snr, was a chemist at the neighbouring town of Bathurst but opened a branch in Orange in 1860 when it was incorporated as a municipality. He had been one of 81 people who had requested the government to do this, so that urgently needed improvements could be made to streets and drainage.

Josiah Parker jnr moved to Orange in about 1865 and traded as a chemist and stationer. His family also had chemist shops at Parramatta and in William Street, Sydney. He had bought 8 acres (3 hectares) of land for Strathroy from Richard Warren and solicitor John Charles McLachlan. McLachlan built Wolaroi mansion in Orange. Parker had Strathroy built in 1884–85 and he, his wife and ten children lived there until 1894.

Parker was actively involved in community affairs in Orange. He was an auditor for Orange Municipal Council

from 1868 to 1874 and was an alderman in 1875, 1883 and 1885–88. When East Orange was made a municipality in 1888, Parker was elected the first mayor. He was also a justice of the peace; secretary of the first building society formed in Orange; was prominent in the establishment of the first hospital, becoming secretary for fifteen years; and was a member of the school board and Licensing Court.

But along the way Parker went broke and Strathroy was released by the insolvent estate assignee to Richard Warren for 10 shillings. He sold it to James Bonnor in 1897, who lived there with his wife Susannah and their children until 1920.

The family was prominent in the Baptist Church. James Bonnor for many years was deacon, treasurer, choirmaster and superintendent of the Sunday School. He was a successful businessman, was active in the agricultural show society and the Farmers and Settlers Association, and was also prominent in an inquiry that looked at Orange as being the site for the federal capital. He was mayor of East Orange at one time.

While at Strathroy, Bonnor filled in the verandah balconies with decorative glass windows, probably to make more room for the large family and servants. He also developed a large garden and a small orchard and planted table grapes.

THE ENTRANCE HALL.

Bonnor sold Strathroy in November 1920 to Anastasia Horrigan, the wife of western New South Wales' grazier Paul Horrigan. They had moved to Orange from Warren after Mr Horrigan lost the use of both legs in a farm accident. Strathroy took up a whole town block and was set back from the street, giving him lots of room to move around in his wheelchair as well as privacy.

Between 1939 and 1955, Anastasia Horrigan sold off housing blocks, reducing Strathroy from its original 8 acres (3 hectares) to 8309 square metres. She relied on this sale of land to maintain the house because her husband was unable to work.

Because of his disability, the Horrigans converted a downstairs billiards room into a bedroom suite and the upstairs area was used by their son Karl. One of the upstairs bedrooms was converted into a kitchen. Mrs Horrigan was a keen artist and one of her sketches is still in an upstairs bedroom.

Mr Horrigan died in 1944 and his wife in 1968 at the age of 94. A doctor visiting the house to treat Karl's mother said going inside was like stepping into a Charles Dickens' novel. There were covers over the furniture, cobwebs, and when Mrs Horrigan died, Karl locked the door to the bedroom and it stayed that way for more than 20 years.

Strathroy was listed with the National Trust in July 1973 after moves by a grandson of Josiah Parker jnr, Alan Turner.

Karl Horrigan became the owner of Strathroy in September 1985, by inheritance. He was a keen benefactor of the Catholic Church and once sent a taxi to bring nuns to the house for morning tea.

Sister Pat Lennane tells the story that one Friday as a young novice she visited the house with her Mother Superior and Karl Horrigan made them ham sandwiches. She didn't know whether to offend him by not eating them or to offend the church by eating them. (As a Catholic, she should only have eaten fish on Fridays.) She looked at Mother Superior for guidance who whispered, 'Eat them, he's going to give us some money …'

The young novice ate the sandwiches. Karl left the room and came back with £5.

Karl never received visitors after 4pm because he considered it was not the done thing. If he wanted to visit neighbours, he would phone first to make a time rather than just turn up.

He also liked a drink, and whenever an Orange garage received a morning call to go to Strathroy to get Karl's old car going because it often had a flat battery, the mechanic was always greeted with a glass of port.

Karl Horrigan submitted a development application to Orange City Council seeking to subdivide the land. The house would be cut off and two other sections would be set aside for the construction of villa units and cottages.

About 30 people lodged objections and the council refused the application. In January 1989 Trevor Gazzard bought Strathroy, which was then in a state of disrepair, and with the help of old photographs, set about conservation.

THE PIANOLA ROOM.

The glass verandah walls were taken out to reveal the original cast-iron columns, the floor coverings pulled up and the Baltic pine timber floors were polished. The original cedar skirting boards had been left untouched but Mr Gazzard scraped back the paint on the walls and found the original friezes. He had them copied for the other walls. The original venetians were renovated.

Mr Gazzard added ensuite bathrooms to the upstairs bedrooms, relocating an original cast-iron bath from a downstairs conservatory to one of them. His intention was to turn it into a guesthouse and reception centre but this plan didn't go ahead.

While living there, Mr Gazzard found a corset box of toy soldiers stamped 1908 hidden in a secret cupboard in the library. He believes the Bonnor children put them there.

Andrew and Deanne McDougal bought Strathroy in 1997 from Mr Gazzard. They were interested in preserving the house and also wanted a place big enough for them to be able to get their extensive collection of Australian artefacts out of storage.

'Our main intention was to protect the house from development and the three parcels of land at the back of the house that could have been sold off. Our commitment was

for that not to happen,' Mr McDougal said. 'Although much of the restoration was done, we concentrated on making more improvements. It had always been a property that was locked up.'

Mr McDougal's family history was another factor. His grandfather John Keith McDougal held the seat of Wannan and was a significant Labor figure and poet. That had contributed to part of their collection: certificates, postcards, photos, needlebooks, and a solid silver spoon commemorating the visit of the American White Fleet that came to Australia in August 1908. The four squadrons of warships, all painted white, were manned by 14,000 sailors and marines. All had embarked on the biggest naval deployment ever attempted by any nation: the first round-the-world cruise by a fleet of steam-powered steel battleships, calling at twenty ports on six continents in the 43,000-mile (68,800-kilometre), fourteen-month circumnavigation.

'One of our visitors was the American consul general and here's this mad bloke in country New South Wales with a collection of the American White Fleet. It's probably one of the better collections in Australia,' Mr McDougal said.

'My grandfather had one of the invitations to attend a reception in 1908. It was one of the biggest events in Australian history with 380,000 people at Sydney Heads to watch the fleet enter the harbour. When former US president Clinton came to Australia, the official gift from the New South Wales premier was photographs of the fleet coming into the harbour.'

THE UPSTAIRS KITCHEN.

PAUL HORRIGAN'S WHEELCHAIR.

Most of the original fixtures and fittings of the late Victorian house have survived, including the ornate ceilings, cedar venetians, pelmets and wallpaper. The staircase, doors, skirting boards, built-in bookcases and cupboards are all cedar. A lot of the period furniture in the house came from Mr McDougal's aunt, while the bedrooms, lounge and dining rooms have original marble fireplace surrounds and decorative overmantels.

The dining and lounge rooms are divided by large cedar folding doors. The grand front door has four panels and the fanlight and sidelights are fitted with glass etched in decorative patterns, including the house name Strathroy.

There are four bedrooms upstairs, one with a balcony overlooking the garden.

The kitchen, although extended and remodelled, still has its original cast-iron stove. A microwave oven has been hidden behind the doors of the pantry.

In the library, green walls are covered with framed photographs, documents, paintings and service medals as a backdrop to the huge bookcases. There is an Italian marble fireplace and a pianola, which Mrs McDougal plays in her spare time.

Sydmouth Valley

After Gregory Blaxland, William Wentworth and William Lawson became the first Europeans to find a way across the Blue Mountains in May 1813, it was only a few months before surveyor George William Evans followed their footsteps to have a look at the new country that had been opened up. The colony needed more land to expand and the mountains until then had been an impassable barrier.

As an apprentice to an engineer and architect, Evans learned surveying while young, but in 1796 he emigrated to the Cape of Good Hope and after British forces withdrew from there, came to the new colony of New South Wales in October 1802. His first job was a grain storekeeper at Parramatta. In August 1803 he became acting surveyor general of lands, and six years later deputy surveyor at

Port Dalrymple. Evans was sent to Hobart in 1812 as deputy surveyor but was recalled to Sydney in 1813 because his services were needed now the mountains had been crossed.

Accompanied by five men, one of whom had been with Blaxland's party, he set out on 19 November to follow the same track, arriving at the western edge of the mountains seven days later. Being curious he went farther and reached the Fish River, following its course for a week until he reached Campbell's River.

About 7 miles (11 kilometres) past the river he came upon a picturesque valley, which he named Sidmouth after the English home secretary at the time, Viscount Sidmouth. Lord Sidmouth had been the parliamentary speaker and then prime minister after William Pitt resigned. There

SYDMOUTH VALLEY, BUILT DURING THE 1820s.

THE EDISON GRAMOPHONE.

THE SITTING ROOM.

is also a coastal town in Devon with the name Sidmouth.

Evans pressed ahead, and on 9 December came to the present site of Bathurst, which he named the Bathurst Plains after Lord Bathurst, the British secretary of state for the colonies. He also named the Macquarie River after Governor Macquarie.

He went farther west before returning to Sydney to report to the governor and received £130 and a grant of land in Tasmania in recognition of his work. The discovery of so great a tract of good land was of the utmost importance to the colony.

Macquarie then accepted a tender from William Cox to build a cart road over the mountains as quickly as possible to open up what he described as the 'champagne country'. Cox had 30 men to do the job and a guard of eight soldiers.

In a government order in July 1814 Governor Macquarie said the people building the road were 'not to be interrupted unnecessarily by others out of an idle curiosity'. Nor could anyone use the road until it was declared passable for carts or carriages. People disobeying the order were to be arrested and sent to Sydney as prisoners.

William Cox finished the road in January 1815 and in April Governor Macquarie and his wife Elizabeth and their

official party went for a look. Sidmouth Valley was one of their camping spots and the governor's tent was set up under a large gum tree.

Artist and naturalist John William Lewin was in Macquarie's party and he did a series of paintings and sketchings along the way. Sidmouth Valley was one of them.

Lewin had arrived in Sydney in 1800 and produced two books on the colony: *Prodromus Entomology* in 1805, which was about insects in New South Wales, and *Birds of New Holland* in 1808. An 1813 edition was the first illustrated book to be engraved and printed in Australia.

Governor Macquarie also commissioned Lewin to draw plants collected by surveyor general John Oxley on expeditions past Bathurst and in the north around Tamworth. In 1814 he appointed him city coroner.

When Macquarie arrived at the road-building party's depot on the west bank of the Macquarie River in May 1815 he proclaimed it the site for a town, which was to be named Bathurst. Later that year a government domain comprising soldiers, government personnel and convict labourers was established there. Surrounded by a large government stock reserve, it was used as the launching pad for explorations of the interior by Evans in 1815, John Oxley in 1816, Allan Cunningham in 1823, and Charles Sturt in 1828.

On a second trip west in 1820, Macquarie again camped under the same tree in Sidmouth Valley. He had stopped at the Fish River the previous night but sent a cart ahead with provisions for breakfast so it would be ready when he arrived there.

Macquarie resigned his post soon after and Sir Thomas Makdougall Brisbane was appointed the new governor. He encouraged agriculture, land reclamation and exploration but had poor financial sense and was recalled in 1825. Brisbane was named after him.

In 1823, Robert Lowe, a magistrate at Campbelltown and Bringelly, was granted by Governor Brisbane 2000 acres (810 hectares) in Sidmouth Valley, along with twenty convicts. He built a house on the property — which he called Sydmouth Valley, spelt with a 'y' — although he didn't spend much time there.

In February 1827 Captain William John Dumaresq on a trip to Bathurst wrote in his diary about negotiating the Fish River Hill: 'It was the worst between Sydney and Bathurst. Never having been to Bathurst before, I could not help saying to myself, "This Bathurst ought to be a fine place to come all this dreadful way to see it." The sight of a four-rail fence in Sidmouth Valley after this weary hill was the first symptom of humanity for nearly 90 miles [144 kilometres] and gave me unfeigned pleasure. It was pleasing to see this beautiful new cottage and substantial barns and outhouses.'

Mr Lowe died in 1834 and his son James Willard Lowe took over Sydmouth Valley and lived there until 1871. He bred cattle and horses but not a lot is known about him. However, he apparently fell on hard times and the bank took the property. Anne Webb, the great-grandmother of present owner Kevin Webb, bought it in a mortgagee sale in 1871.

Mrs Webb and her husband William had come to Australia in 1840 from Cornwall in England. They worked for a Dr Ramsay near Tarana and eventually bought some land of their own. William Webb was killed in 1851 in a wagon accident and Mrs Webb opened a store with her sons and daughters at Muttons Falls, near Tarana and not far from Sidmouth Valley.

Kevin Webb said his great-grandmother bought Sydmouth Valley for her youngest son and his grandfather, Thomas Bernard Webb, who was born about the time her husband was killed. Her son was away working at Narromine with another brother Robert who had land there. He had also been on several trips with the Duracks of north-western Ord River fame. The Duracks had land in Queensland and he spent a good deal of time with them. 'She apparently bought the property to coax him home,' Kevin Webb explained. 'And it worked. Later in 1881 he married Scottish girl Mary Irvine, the daughter of Dubbo police officer John Irvine, and Sydmouth Valley is where they lived.

'They were married at Dundullimal at Dubbo [see Dundullimal], which was owned by Thomas and Alice Baird at the time. Alice Baird was my grandfather's eldest sister. She had lived at Bellaringa, at Warren in western New South Wales, and had been the only white woman for miles before she moved to Dundullimal.'

Thomas and Mary Webb had nine children: Ada Violet, Alfred Richard, Elizabeth Pearl, Herbert Sydmouth, Ernest Lachlan, Clarence Raymond, Arthur Thomas, William Irvine — who was Kevin Webb's father — and Frederick Donald. All were raised in the Sydmouth Valley house, which is relatively small.

The kitchen was separate in those days and some of the living rooms were used as bedrooms. The back verandah was added in the late 1890s.

THE DINING ROOM.

William Irvine Webb and his brother Clarence Raymond Webb fought in World War I. They enlisted in 1917 against the wishes of their father Thomas and went overseas. About a week after they sailed, Thomas Webb died in his sleep at Sydmouth in November 1917. William and Clarence fought on the front line and William was wounded at Hindenburg on 30 September 1918. Just weeks later, on 11 November, the war ended and the brothers came home.

Ernest, a bachelor, was running Sydmouth when they returned. William married in 1937 and wanted first offer to buy Sydmouth if Ernest decided to sell. However, William had to wait 25 years until 1962 before he became Sydmouth's owner and he and his family were able to move in.

Kevin Webb, who was sixteen at the time, said the house needed a great deal of work. The kitchen was rough but was renovated, and the family quickly made the rest liveable. Most of the house hadn't been used for a long time and had fallen into disrepair.

Sydmouth, now owned by Kevin Webb and partner Lynn, has undergone more extensive renovations. Built from bricks made on the property, the outside walls and the main wall in the middle of the house are three bricks thick. The other

A ROYAL DOULTON LAMP.

dividing walls are two bricks thick, plastered and stuccoed to resemble stone.

The roof was originally shingles but was replaced in the late 1890s with corrugated iron, which is still there. There was a heavy snowfall in June 1900 and 80 centimetres was measured at the house. There was concern the roof would cave in but when Thomas Webb replaced it he put extra supports underneath.

Kevin Webb has not altered the general shape of the Georgian-styled house. The back verandah was closed in to provide more living space. A new kitchen was built in a small bedroom or dressing room and a new laundry and bathroom added.

It's doubtful plans were used to build Sydmouth Valley. The twenty convicts given to Lowe obviously had all sorts of skills but it is also obvious some of them had few skills. The old kitchen has one wall 30 centimetres longer than the other side so it's not square at one end. A bedroom door is also crooked but the main house is fairly straight.

All the timber is local hardwood. Most of the joinery inside the house and the shutters are all original red cedar. All the doors, fireplace surrounds, skirting boards in the front section are also all cedar, but the back section of the house does not have as much.

The ceilings were originally lath and plaster and were falling out so they were replaced with plasterboard in the 1920s. A picture rail was put on at the same time.

THE MAIN BEDROOM.

The house has six fireplaces and three double chimneys. All the original rooms have a fireplace. Mr Webb put in slow combustion heaters in three rooms without doing any major alterations. No walls have been pulled out or altered.

Some items of furniture are original and others have been collected by Mr Webb. He has a 1905 model Edison gramophone, which still works, and a lounge suite that was owned by his grandparents. Watercolours on the walls are Lewin copies of Sidmouth Valley from when the artist made the trip across the mountains with Governor Macquarie.

Mr Webb and his partner are also keen collectors of kerosene lamps. A lamp on the mantelshelf in the dining room is Cranbury glass and another on the dining table is a 1920s double-burner banquet. A Royal Doulton lamp dates back to around 1860.

A built-in cupboard by the fireplace in the dining room is an original piece made from cedar. The table came from the Family Hotel in Bathurst and a chiffonier has been in the family for many years.

A piano still used was bought by Thomas Webb for his two daughters. The pencil drawings of a cow's head and deer were done by Mr Webb's aunt Elizabeth Pearl.

A cellar with two rooms runs underneath the lounge and dining rooms. The ventilators have iron bars because, like other early homes, that was where the owners locked up the convicts. Kevin Webb plans to renovate these two rooms.

The stone-terraced cottage garden was run down but has been revitalised by Kevin Webb. He has put in more stonework and, in the process, unearthed the remains of a convict-built carriage drive.

Strangely there are no really old trees. Pines predominated but they were dying so he took them out, and the poplars along the entrance driveway are only 50 years old. There are also several pepper trees.

Tennis was a popular pastime in the early days so Thomas Webb decided to build a court in the 1890s. He dug it out with a horse and scoop and members of the family and friends would sit on the front verandah of the house and watch the games. The tennis court is still there.

Kevin Webb and Lynn run sheep and cattle on the 750 acres (304 hectares) still belonging to Sydmouth Valley. They also grow hay for winter feed.

Thornthwaite

LEFT: FIVE GENERATIONS OF THE FINLAY FAMILY LIVED AT THORNTHWAITE.

BOTTOM LEFT: THE FRONT STEPS.

BOTTOM RIGHT: THE WINE HOUSE, ONCE A SHELTER.

A man with less vision than Peter Bracher would have put the bulldozer through Thornthwaite, an historic stone homestead built 158 years ago by a former New South Wales postmaster general.

White ants had almost eaten through the roof and floor timbers, the attic rooms were occupied by several families of possums and the foundations were in poor condition because of water and salt damage. But Mr Bracher, a Canadian-born lawyer, has made the conservation of old homes a new lifestyle challenge and Thornthwaite is the latest he has overseen.

As a director of the Paspaley Pearling Company, a family-owned enterprise that has bought historic properties, Mr Bracher's attraction to old homesteads has made him a driving force behind the company's restorations.

Thornthwaite was settled in 1835 by Joseph Docker, who later became a member of the first New South Wales Legislative Council and for several years was the New South Wales postmaster general. He bought the 597 acres (242 hectares) of land at auction for the minimum price of £149, or five shillings an acre. With four convicts assigned to him, Docker built the central rooms of the existing homestead first and, by 1847, the present homestead had been completed.

The Dockers farmed Thornthwaite until they found themselves deep in debt around 1870 and were forced to sell the then 9600 acres (3888 hectares) to the George Finlay family for £7500.

Five generations of that family worked Thornthwaite until 1994 when Paspaley bought it.

The property was experiencing a drought and the homestead, although still occupied by a member of the Finlay family, was in poor condition. Restoring it proved to be a complicated project. As Mr Bracher explained, 'Although Thornthwaite is not governed by any legal restrictions, we have rebuilt it strictly in accordance with the International Council on Monuments and Sites' charter for conservation of historic reconstruction under the supervision of heritage architect Alan Croker of Design 5 Architects. So all the work has been carried out to a strict standard. First we had the homestead properly assessed to find out what work was needed, and it wasn't an easy job.

'When we looked under the roof we found most of the rafters were destroyed by white ants, and when we got the roof off we found that was also the case with most of the ceiling joists. The decorative metal ceilings were askew and when we had a look the timber was about as bad as it could be.

'So the way to proceed was to identify the sound timbers and where possible leave them in place, because everything shifted together and if we pulled everything off and tried to build it back up square, it just didn't work. We had to leave as much as was sound there, some members reinforced, but if you try to swing with the curves and dips that have come with time, you put it back together slowly.'

Mr Bracher said they rebuilt the homestead from the tops of the walls up, using all the existing sound timbers they could while at the same time finding and controlling the ants' nests, getting rid of the other vermin, and stopping the water leaks. A lot of damage was caused when the gutters disintegrated and water seeped into the foundations. In fact, when the engineers looked under the house they found extensive decay. There had been some partial repair work to

THE FRONT VERANDAH.

THE SPACIOUS DINING ROOM.

the foundations probably 50 years earlier but the stone was etched away. There was a huge amount of debris — scrap timber and rubble — under there too, so it took weeks to clean that out just to see what was going on. Then the foundations had to be rebuilt little by little.

Mr Bracher said all the work had to be done using the right materials. The homestead was built using lime mortar and that had to be specially ordered. The more modern cement mortar wouldn't have worked, as the building would have ended up with stronger and weaker areas moving at different rates. The builders had to stay with materials that had the same rates of expansion and moisture absorption otherwise they would have created more problems than they solved.

With the major reconstruction work done, the finishing touches took many more months of work. Just the painting took more than a year as the painter insisted on working alone, doing all the preparation and intricate work himself.

The main house and most of the outbuildings are in stone. This was mined and taken to the site by ox cart and put together by the Dockers' convict labour. They proved to be skilled artisans as the house was constructed to a high standard.

It has six bedrooms, two of them large attic rooms and four on the main floor. There is a large dining room and living room with box rooms on either side. Other rooms include a TV room, study and kitchenette. Two small bedrooms off the verandah were probably used for travellers.

There is a separate kitchen connected to the main house by a covered walkway, probably built around 1900. It has cast-iron bread ovens and a rather ancient stove.

A PEDAL ORGAN.

182

THE WOOD-BURNING KITCHEN
STOVE.

THE VIEW TO THE HILLS.

The floors in the main house are cypress. They are not original and were probably put in around the 1900s when some restoration work was done. The ceilings, however, are original, dating back to the 1840s.

Outbuildings include a wine house where it was convenient to make and store wine as well as serving a secondary purpose of providing protection from attacks by unfriendly natives. A small dairy was used for the distribution of milk to staff in the early days and another stone building known as the store was probably used for distribution of food. There is also a meat house. Away from the main homestead

THORNTHWAITE'S CHURCH.

are contemporary stables still not restored, a chicken coop, a disused tennis court and cricket pitches on the flats.

'Conservation of the homestead was a project dear to me. There had been some unsympathetic additions through the years and the restoration gave us the opportunity to put things right,' Mr Bracher said.

In the grounds an old English oak was near death but a tree surgeon salvaged it. There are some old fruit trees, pomegranates and oleander. A rose bush is more than 50 years old and pines were planted more than 100 years ago. The old vineyards are gone, however.

Thornthwaite now covers 6500 hectares.

THE SHEARING SHED.

Toorak

This two-storey stone house was built around 1865 on 20 acres (8 hectares) of land at Breakfast Creek for Brisbane businessman James Robert Dickson. The name Toorak apparently came from Toorak House in Melbourne which was designed by Dickson's cousin, James Jackson.

Born in Plymouth in England, Dickson came to Australia in 1854, living first in Victoria and then moving to Brisbane in 1862.

He was an auctioneer and land agent in partnership with an Arthur Martin until 1864, when the partnership was dissolved.

Martin continued under his own name but Dickson formed a new partnership with a James Duncan. The two firms appear to have been responsible for most of the land subdivision and sales in Brisbane in the 1860s.

Dickson was also a director of a string of companies, including the Royal Bank of Queensland, Queensland Trustees, Queensland Insurance and Land Mortgage Company, and the Brisbane Permanent Building and Banking Society. He entered the Legislative Assembly in 1873 as the member for Enoggera and held various

THE IMPOSING STONE MANSION OF TOORAK.

portfolios until he resigned in 1887. After failing to gain re-election in 1888 he stayed away from politics until 1892 when he won the seat of Bulimba.

Dickson became premier of Queensland in 1898–99. He was a strong advocate of federation, and was a member of the Australian delegation that travelled to England to see the Commonwealth of Australia Bill passed by the British parliament.

He was a member of the first federal parliament and was appointed the first Commonwealth minister for defence. He was knighted on Federation Day, 1 January 1901, but died on 10 January, just nine days later.

The design of Toorak reflects the influence of the English picturesque movement on Australian architecture of the late nineteenth century. When Toorak was first built, photographs show it was only single storey but the original plans had provided for two. Dickson added the second storey in the 1890s because of his large family of thirteen children. There is a single-storey brick and corrugated iron wing at the back.

Located in Annie Street (named after Dickson's wife), Hamilton, Toorak is an impressive Gothic house with a steeply pitched slate roof decorated with fretwork timber barges. A three-level castellated tower stands over the entrance. It, too, had an upper section added in the 1890s.

Two marble lions at the entrance of the house come from an overseas trip Dickson made with four of his daughters in 1890. He also hired Italian artists to carry out decorative work inside the house.

When he died, the land was transferred to Power and Agnes Dickson, two of his children, as trustees. Toorak by then stood on 4 acres (1.6 hectares) of land.

In 1907 the Sisters of Sacred Advent leased Toorak for use as Eton High School, later St Margaret's, but although regarded as a healthy environment for boarders, it was considered too great a climb for day students to get to, so the Sisters moved the school in 1910.

Grazier George Moffatt bought Toorak in 1916 and sold it in 1929 to John Gibson of the pioneer sugar family. Later owners were Brisbane businessman Patrick Woulfe; and grazier, philanthropist and art collector Harold de Vahl Rubin. Pastoralist Sir William Allen bought it in 1963 and it remains in his family.

Inside, Toorak has four large and two smaller rooms on either side of a central corridor. There are also four large and two smaller bedrooms on the upper floor. The entrance hall has frescoes on the walls and ceilings and is divided with a decorative arch.

The rooms on the ground floor have marble chimney breasts and rich plasterwork and cornices. The joinery is mainly cedar.

Timber stairs provide access to the first floor and a sheeted storage area at half-landing level through coloured glass doors. The ceilings in the upper level are half-raked and follow the lines of the roof. The main rooms have dormer windows and French doors opening onto small balconies. A

TOORAK'S TOWER.

small room at the end of the corridor has narrow timber stairs leading to a platform at the top of the tower where there are 360-degree views of Brisbane.

The single-storey wing at the back is in brick with timber windows and louvred French doors opening onto a verandah. The building has been extended and modified and comprises a kitchen, several bedrooms and an office accessed from a central corridor.

The corridor and rooms on the western side have flagstone floors with timber floors in the eastern-side rooms. The western rooms have been extensively refurbished but those on the eastern side still have pressed-metal ceilings.

The gardens are extensive. An oval rose garden circled by an oval driveway creates a formal front entrance. The eastern garden is terraced and the northern garden is lawn with a mature hedge. Trees include mature palms, camphor laurels, jacarandas, liquidambars and Moreton Bay chestnuts.

185

Vaucluse House

William Charles Wentworth, born at sea on the voyage to Sydney in June 1790 to D'Arcy Wentworth, later the principal surgeon of the Civil Medical Department, and Catherine Crowley, a convict, well and truly made his mark in the new colony. After spending six years on Norfolk Island and then returning to live at Parramatta, his parents sent him to school in England in 1803.

He returned to Sydney in 1810, was later appointed acting provost-marshall and granted 1750 acres (709 hectares) on the Nepean River. With Gregory Blaxland and William Lawson he was the first to find a way across the Blue Mountains in 1813, opening up the lush new grazing lands of the western plains.

He was granted another 1000 acres (405 hectares) of land before he went to London in 1816 to study law. He returned to Sydney in 1824, and with Robert Wardell founded the *Australian* newspaper but surrendered his shares in 1828. Wentworth used the newspaper to campaign for a free press, trial by jury, representative government and to attack the established autocracy.

He inherited more property on his father's death in 1827, including an estate at Homebush. He bought Vaucluse in 1827, later enlarging it to 500 acres (202 hectares), and built the stately mansion Vaucluse House. Wentworth, who married Sarah Cox, the daughter of emancipist blacksmith Francis Cox, in 1829, also acquired big pastoral interests as a landowner and squatter.

In one daring feat in 1840, he tried to buy nearly one-third of New Zealand from the Maoris but was frustrated by Governor Gipps. He had sold many of his squatting runs by 1854, including Belltrees, a freehold estate near Scone, but retained others.

When the Colonial Office agreed that New South Wales should have responsible government Wentworth became chairman of the Select Committee, which drafted the 1853 constitution. The Constitution Act passed the British parliament in 1855 and responsible government came to New South Wales in 1856.

Wentworth died in England on 20 March 1872, but at his wish was buried at Vaucluse in 1873. The Blue Mountains town of Wentworth Falls and the western Sydney suburb of Wentworthville are named after him.

One of the most treasured estates in the eastern suburbs of Sydney, Vaucluse House is surrounded by 10 hectares of picturesque gardens and grounds stretching down to Sydney Harbour. Located in one of Sydney's most exclusive areas, Vaucluse House is a stately mansion nestled in a nineteenth-century leafy estate with a kitchen wing, stables and outbuildings.

Wentworth and his family lived there from 1827 to 1853 and again from 1861 to 1862. The house depicts the social aspirations and lifestyles of the Wentworths and their servants.

The mansion comprises three levels made up of sixteen rooms. Now owned by the Historic Houses Trust, most of the rooms are furnished in the style and opulence of the times. Many of the original fittings have been retained.

Part of the original kitchen garden has been re-established. The project was initiated to recreate the kitchen garden as part of the continuing restoration of the historic home, and every effort has been made to preserve its authenticity by using heirloom varieties of vegetables and garden design of the period.

LEFT & BOTTOM LEFT: VAUCLUSE HOUSE, BUILT BY WILLIAM CHARLES WENTWORTH.

BELOW: THE EXTENSIVE GARDENS SURROUNDING THE HOUSE.

Villa Donati

Architect John Augustus Bernard Koch certainly left his mark on Melbourne. He designed many of the city's fine buildings and was mayor of the inner-city suburb of Richmond in 1882–83.

Koch was born in Hamburg, Germany, in 1845 and came to Australia when he was eight. Following his love of design, he became articled to Francis Moloney White and stayed with him as his assistant until 1873 when he established his own architectural firm.

He bought land in Church Street, Richmond, in 1883 and designed his own home, believed to have been built in 1885 by a G.W. Freeman. Typical of his work, the house was Italian Renaissance derived, boasting an arcaded façade with a balustraded parapet and balcony, with arches supported on cast-iron columns. Koch called the house Helenville and lived there until about 1896 when he sold it to the Church of England Widows and Orphans Fund. The fund initially let the house to a Dr Bertha Main.

Around the same time as he built his own home, Koch was commissioned by extensive landowner Alexander W. Robertson to design the 'most magnificent house in Melbourne ...'

Completed in 1890 it was a French Renaissance mansion, significant for its extravagant decoration and finely executed interiors. It was called Labassa and is now owned by the National Trust.

Koch also designed Castlemaine Hospital and a string of hotels in Richmond. He won a competition in 1908 for his design of a new Melbourne Hospital, coming up with an elaborate plan for a whole city block, but the project never went ahead. Later other architects were commissioned to design the hospital on its existing Lonsdale Street site.

In the late 1890s, Helenville, which had briefly been used by the Widows and Orphans Fund for administration purposes, became the home for the Anglican bishop of Melbourne, Field Flowers Goe. He was only the third Bishop of Melbourne.

LEFT: THE ITALIAN RENAISSANCE VILLA DONATI.

Bishop Flowers Goe, who consecrated St Paul's Cathedral in 1891, was quite notable and was regarded as the lucky member of his family because his brother was christened Wild Flowers Goe. He died in 1901.

Helenville had several private owners after the bishop. Probably it gained the most notoriety in the 1970s when it became the Moulin Rouge brothel. Operating from 1974, it offered clients — besides a massage from $5 and beautiful escorts — a gymnasium, sauna, photographic studio and sun lamps, but there was no evidence of any of this in the building. The only change made by the brothel operators was the installation of bars on the windows.

The next owner was Dr Barry Christophers, an ardent campaigner for a better health deal for Aborigines. Dr Christophers was a foundation member of the Federal Council for the Advancement of Aborigines and Torres

THE ENTRANCE HALL.

Strait Islanders, formed to bring about basic human rights for Aborigines. Its members included some prominent Australians, including former South Australian premier Don Dunstan, Oodgeroo Noonuccal, Joe McGinness, and other dedicated people.

He sold Helenville in 1998 to present owners Gayle Lamb and Trevor Finlayson, both university lecturers.

The couple have undertaken a complete restoration and changed the name from Helenville to Villa Donati. 'We wanted an Italian name because the architecture is Italianate and because we like most things Italian. We came up with Villa Donati, which is a family name meaning "to give or donate". The architect left a legacy and we will too.'

Ms Lamb said an upstairs bedroom had a full-length window and small balcony and they believe there was a

THE UPSTAIRS SITTING ROOM.

temporary structure there that burnt down, although they have been unable to find evidence of this. A small kitchen upstairs was not original and was taken out.

There was a red light on one of the front posts, but Ms Lamb did not know what it related to. It could have been something to do with the doctor's surgery, or it may have been left from the brothel.

The front of Villa Donati is all original, including the iron front fence, gate, and black and white marble tiling on

A VESPA IN THE DINING ROOM.

THE MARBLE FIREPLACE.

THE KITCHEN.

the path. Features of the house include marble fireplaces, a large wine cellar and a loft. The loft is really only a small cupboard with an opening.

The ground floor has a bedroom, bathroom, study/office and kitchen at the back. Dr Christophers used the front room, now the breakfast room, as a waiting room for his patients. The floor was covered in a 1970s brown carpet and there was only a small electric heater. Ms Lamb believed he rented out the upstairs as residential accommodation.

'Our bedroom was the surgery. It had a small hand basin with cold water when we moved in so things were pretty austere, but the doctor was here for about twenty years. He apparently had a big following in an off-beat way.'

Upstairs there is a sitting room opening onto the balcony, three bedrooms with marble fireplaces, and a bathroom. The pressed-metal ceilings are 11 feet (3.4 metres) high. The staircase is original and the timberwork is all cedar. The floors have been sanded and polished.

There was a shed at the back of the property that had gone by the time Ms Lamb and Mr Finlayson took over, but they believe it was used to sell rabbits in the Depression. Their next-door neighbour also had some tales to tell.

He had lived there a long time and told them he had a niece who was a nun. On one of her visits in the late 1970s she had engaged in some cleansing ritual in the front yard of Villa Donati to ward off the evil spirits. He thought the brothel closed soon afterwards. The neighbour also said one of his brothers thought there had been a tunnel from Villa Donati under the road to a property on the other side of the street. That could not be verified.

THE ELEGANT STAIRCASE.

Ms Lamb noted that if one took a slice of the front of Labassa, its similarity to Villa Donati became apparent. 'This is an elaborate and embellished building but it is a good example of the detail of the work Koch did.'

THE WINE CELLAR.

Waugoola

Former managing director of Channel Ten Ian Kennon believes he is fortunate not to be part of television any more. Mr Kennon and his wife Suzie are now seasoned farmers, running cattle and merino sheep, and growing canola, wheat and oats on their historic property, Waugoola, in central western New South Wales.

Waugoola, at Woodstock, near Cowra, was owned in the early 1900s by the son of one of Cobb and Co's founders, William Whitney, who had invested in pastoral interests as the introduction of trains and motor cars gradually put the coach company out of business. Mr Kennon bought the property from the Whitney family and is privileged to be only the second owner.

'This is where we live, and although I've been offered consultancies and projects to do with advertising and marketing in Sydney, I don't believe you can be a little bit pregnant,' he said. 'You are either in or out and this is now my sole enterprise and main interest.'

Back in January 1854, an enterprising young American called Freeman Cobb and three other twenty-year-old Americans established an efficient transport business. They imported coaches and ran staged services between Melbourne and the Victorian goldfields.

They made their fortune quickly and sold out in May 1856 to a Thomas Davies for £16,000. The company changed hands again five years later when Davies sold to a consortium led by James Rutherford and Canadian-born William Franklin Whitney for £23,000.

Cobb and Co, as well as its coach line, acquired extensive pastoral interests and bought Coombing (*see* Coombing Park) at Carcoar in 1881 on the recommendation of William Whitney. By 1886, he and James Rutherford were the only partners left in the company.

Whitney died in 1894 and several years later Cobb and Co's assets were divided between James Rutherford and William Whitney's estate. The Whitney family company retained Coombing.

After his father's death, A.W. Whitney managed Coombing Park on behalf of the executors and in 1907 the estate was merged into the Whitney Pastoral Company. Waugoola was another of Cobb and Co's properties.

A.W. Whitney sold his Coombing Park interests and bought Waugoola, which comprised 17,000 acres (6885 hectares). He built the present homestead and modelled it on Coombing Park. The home took two years to build and cost £15,000.

Waugoola was heavily infested with rabbits. However Whitney had no faith in poisoning, so after he bought Waugoola he fenced it off and destroyed all the burrows and rabbit warrens.

The last Whitney to live at the property was William, or Bill, who died in an accident in the 1990s. His wife Elizabeth and four daughters kept the property going for

ONE OF THE HALLWAYS.

a few years before they decided to sell, and Mr Kennon bought Waugoola from the Whitney estate.

Mr Kennon has always had a fondness for the country and, after finishing school, worked for two years as a jackeroo on the northern New South Wales property owned by Ian Sinclair, who later became a federal member of parliament. But he decided he was never going to own his own place earning £3 a week, so he moved back to Sydney and became involved in the media. 'First I worked in suburban newspapers on the upper North Shore, then for Channel 7 and later I established the Melbourne office for the then new network Channel Ten,' he said.

'After becoming sales director and deputy general manager, I was appointed managing director in the good old days of shows like *No. 96*, *The Box* and Graham Kennedy's *Blankety Blanks*. It was a tabloid TV station and very successful, and those shows, which the board of directors had looked on with horror, turned Channel Ten around and saved it from oblivion.

'We used to work hard, have fun and make a lot of money, but it's a very different business now and is more statistical with less personality and there is greater competition from pay TV and DVDs.'

When Rupert Murdoch took over Channel Ten, Mr Kennon left and started an advertising agency which he ran for thirteen years before selling to English agency Saatchi and Saatchi. While he had the agency, the major accounts included David Jones, Mitsubishi and ABC-TV.

In the meantime, Mr Kennon had bought a property near Berrima but he sold that to a neighbour and then bought Waugoola at auction in September 1997. Although structurally sound, the homestead was in need of a lot of work and a painter was kept busy for twelve months. The verandah had sunk and 65 cast-iron columns holding it up were rusted and covered with thick paint. Mr Kennon brought in a huge sandblaster on a semi-trailer, protected the house with tarpaulins, and took every column back to metal through 100 years of paint in order to restore the patterns. Property yards and fences needed work, weeds were eradicated and fertiliser spread. He and his wife spent seven years putting everything back into shape.

Suzie Kennon also has a rural background. Her parents have a property called Gunningra in the Monaro close to Bombala. So they both enjoy the country and appreciate the joys and sorrows it can bring.

Surrounded by rolling hills on all sides, great views from the verandah, a huge garden, swimming pool and tennis court, Mrs Kennon said living at Waugoola was a wonderful lifestyle. She had been a nurse in Sydney and lived at Camden for many years. 'I absolutely love the house. We didn't have to do a lot but we have restored it to an original condition because we didn't want to change anything.'

The nineteen-room homestead, built mainly from materials made on site, comprises 85 squares. It has six bedrooms, three bathrooms, a dining room, a great hall (now used as a billiard room), pantry and store. There is an entrance lobby and a courtyard at the back.

The main bedroom has its own dressing room and bathroom. There are eight marble fireplaces, each with a different marble. In the heydays of the Whitneys, a man was employed to collect, chop and store the wood to keep the fires burning.

THE SITTING ROOM.

THE ENTRANCE HALL.

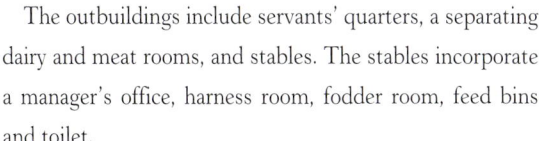

THE LARGE DINING ROOM.

THE GREAT HALL, NOW A BILLIARD ROOM.

Architect J.J. Copeman of Bathurst specified the floor joists had to be 18 inches (46 centimetres) trimmed round. The roof struts are made of well-seasoned Oregon pine, 4 inches by 3 inches (10 centimetres by 7.5 centimetres). The iron roof is original.

All skirting boards are moulded cement throughout. Copeman's instructions for the plasterer included the provisions that all mortar was to be mixed with clean sand and fresh-burned lime, well tempered and allowed to cool for at least two weeks before use. All the lime was to be slaked.

The ceilings are lath plaster. To keep them waterproof, the floors of the two main bathrooms had to be covered with 4-pound lead turned up 4 inches (10 centimetres) against the walls and flashed.

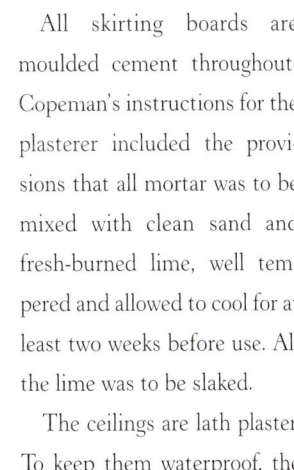

Within the homestead is a cellar with 14-inch (35.5-centimetre) thick walls. It originally was a store for vegetables but now is home to the Kennons' fine wines.

The outbuildings include servants' quarters, a separating dairy and meat rooms, and stables. The stables incorporate a manager's office, harness room, fodder room, feed bins and toilet.

Another small building was used to produce acetylene gas to run the lights. Lime was burnt which emitted the gas. There were 36 wall lights and ten ceiling lights in the house and five wall lights to the stables.

Originally 23 people were employed by the Whitneys, including cooks, maids and servants, station hands and gardeners to look after the extensive grounds.

The woolshed, no longer a part of the property, is about 1 kilometre away. It is still used and originally had 27 stands driven by a steam engine. Only six stands remain now.

The garden has been given a total facelift. It has been made larger and new trees have been put in to augment the original plantings, which included a Scottish elm and date palms. A vegetable garden has also been established.

The tennis court has been renovated and the Kennons have installed a new swimming pool.

Waugoola is an Aboriginal word meaning 'never-ending water'. About half a kilometre from the homestead, on Waugoola Creek, is a waterhole used years ago to change, rest and water horses for the Cobb and Co coach on its way from Sydney to Forbes. The name is still appropriate today, as the freshwater facilities are second to none. Water from all the roofs goes to a 10,000-gallon (45,460-litre) underground tank and is then pumped to a storage tank and gravity-fed back to the house. The storage tank, on a hill, holds 60,000 gallons (272,760 litres).

THE KITCHEN.

132 Windermere Road

LEFT: OLD ENGLISH-STYLE
WINDERMERE ROAD.

BOTTOM LEFT: THE GROUND
FLOOR STONEWORK.

BOTTOM RIGHT: THE HOUSE SEEN
FROM THE GARDEN.

Brisbane architect Eric Percival Trewern was credited with introducing and popularising the Spanish mission, Californian bungalow, Georgian and Tudor revival styles of homes in Queensland in the years between the two world wars. The house at 132 Windermere Road in the Brisbane suburb of Hamilton is an excellent example of the Old English style.

It was built for Cliff Isles, a partner in the Brisbane drapery firm of Finney Isles and Company, which was founded in the late 1880s but bought out by rival department store David Jones in 1955. Most of Trewern's new-style houses were built on speculation but Windermere Road was specifically built for the Isles family by a B. Hollingworth. Later the Isles moved around the corner and built another.

The houses Trewern built between 1921 and 1935 in the same area were all different. One was Georgian, one federation. This one in Windermere Road comprised Tudor-revival elements. All the houses were brick and tile and all were on large blocks of land.

Most of the old colonial houses in Brisbane had been built in the early 1900s from timber with tin roofs. Architect Robin Dodds in the 1920s took the Queenslander look and combined it with a federation style.

132 Windermere Road was built in 1928, the same year Charles Kingsford Smith arrived in Brisbane in the *Southern Cross* after his epic 11,000-kilometre flight across the Pacific. This was an era when Trewern changed his construction methods. The ground floor combines brick and stone while the upper level is stucco with half timber. The chimney, which dominates the façade, is stucco and brick, topped with tall terracotta chimney pots. Terracotta tiles are used on the roof, which has a series of intersecting gables.

Present owners of 132 Windermere Road, Kevin and Julieanne Miller, said the house was always known by them as 'the Murphys' ' even though it was owned originally by the Isles, then two generations of the Cottee family. The Cottees sold to an unknown owner and then the Murphy family bought the house and lived there for about 30 years.

Spencer Cottee in the late 1800s carved a dairy farm out of virgin scrub near Lismore, in northern New South Wales, but when dairying fell on hard times in the early 1900s, he began to grow and process passionfruit. Along the way he developed the now famous Passiona soft drink and a range of other beverages under the Cottee's brand.

The onset of World War II saw Cottee's commissioned to produce jams, juices and concentrates for the army, and some of these contracts are still in place today. In 1970, General Foods Corp USA and Cottee's Ltd merged to form Cottee's General Foods Limited. Cottee's Foods was acquired by Cadbury Schweppes Pty Ltd in 1984.

KEEPSAKES ADORN THE HALL TABLE.

The Millers bought the house in 2000. They lived around the corner in Sutherland Avenue and went for walks every night past the Windermere Road house. They knew the Murphys lived there and they knew Mr Murphy snr had passed away.

'We kept an eye on it and Julie kept saying, "If that house ever comes up for sale, I would like to buy it." I just rolled my eyes,' Kevin Miller said. 'But I was out refereeing football one Saturday morning and she phoned just as I finished and said, "I'm the highest bidder on this house, quick come home." So I went home and we bought it.'

The house had been empty for ten months and the garden was overgrown. It had a timber fence that wasn't original and other changes had been made through the years, such as the fitting of aluminium windows in the kitchen.

While the Millers tried to do extensive renovations in sympathy with the original, there was no concept of heritage listing then. The house had no ceiling lights — all the lighting came from the floor — and to put in ceiling lights the Millers had to take out the ceilings. Instead of disturbing the oak ceilings in the living rooms, they took out the floor upstairs to access that area.

When builders climbed under the floor downstairs they discovered there were two floors, one timber and a concrete one under that, so they ran big ducts and rewired the whole house without disturbing the structure. All the plumbing was replaced. The final rebuild cost $500,000.

'But we left things like the bell buttons for the maids,' Mr Miller said. 'There was a multitude of funny little rooms that we got rid of. Then we had to leave the dining, living and sunroom pretty well intact.

'Upstairs there was a large foyer around the bedrooms but in those days nobody had an ensuite so we rebuilt the paneling, matched it exactly, and created a second ensuite bathroom out of that foyer area.

There are three bedrooms and a sunroom upstairs. Downstairs there is another sunroom, living and dining rooms, a kitchen, a fourth bedroom, study and dressing room. The Millers extended with the addition of a double garage with guest loft upstairs, a sauna and wine cellar.

EXPOSED BEAMS LEND WARMTH TO THE SITTING ROOM.

They relocated a tennis court and put in a new surface. They also built new fences and driveways. The front gate is original but two pillars holding it up had cracked. These were taken apart and rebuilt with more porphyry found in the garden. The excess was used in the pathway.

The Aboriginal name for Hamilton was Mooroo Mooroolbin, meaning 'long nose'; the Millers have lived in the Hamilton area of Brisbane all their lives. Kevin Miller is vice commodore of the Royal Queensland Yacht Squadron and has always been involved in sailing boats. He competed in the tragic 1998 Sydney to Hobart race and was third in his

THE TENNIS COURT

THE SITTING ROOM FIREPLACE.

class on *Industrial Quest,* which he owned and sailed. Of the 115 yachts that started in the race on 26 December, fierce storms and violent winds battered the fleet and only 44 boats made it to Hobart. Five sank, six sailors died, 55 were taken off their yachts, most by helicopter, and 66 boats retired. First across the line on 29 December was the US maxi yacht *Sayonara* owned by Larry Ellison.

Mr Miller is also a keen motor racing fan, competing in two Targa Tasmania road rallies in a Porsche GT3. He also has an open-wheeler Formula 3 racing car. Besides his core business of building industrial sheds and subdivisions, he grows lucerne on a farm at Roma and on another smaller farm in the Brisbane Valley where he also runs some cattle.

Julieanne Miller said the main concern when they bought the Windermere Road house was to create a good environment for their two then teenage children, Hilton and Dominique, who went on to do property economics at university. They also wanted a home that wasn't a museum

THE WEATHERVANE.

'We wanted a few conveniences and a low maintenance garden because Kevin is busy with his company most of the time. But it was a great home to start with and what we have done is to enhance it.'

Wolston House

When land close to the new settlement of Brisbane was opened to free settlers, Dr Stephen Simpson bought a site on the banks of the Brisbane River at Wacol, about halfway between Brisbane and Ipswich. He had been the first commissioner for Crown Lands for the Moreton Bay settlement and held a string of other government posts.

After completing his university medical studies, Dr Simpson had become the personal physician to the European nobility and was able to travel extensively. In 1838, he married his cousin Sophia Anne Simpson, after an eighteen-year engagement, when he was 47. The couple came to Australia in 1840 but, despite letters of commendation, Dr Simpson was unable to secure a job with the colonial government. Attempts to open a practice were unsuccessful, his baby daughter died at birth and his wife died six days later. Several months after this tragedy, Dr Simpson went to the Moreton Bay penal settlement and became acting colonial surgeon and then commissioner for Crown Lands and police magistrate. When the parliament for the new state of Queensland was formed, Dr Simpson was appointed for life to the Legislative Council.

When the government cancelled the decree that no stations be formed within 50 miles (80 kilometres) of the penal settlement, Dr Simpson was able to buy 640 acres (259 hectares) of farmland. He paid 20 shillings an acre.

William Pettigrew was employed by Dr Simpson as property manager, gardener, assistant surveyor and draftsman, because of his knowledge of surveying and building. It was

SANDSTONE WOLSTON HOUSE WAS BUILT IN 1852.

he who designed Wolston House and its outbuildings, but he did not build it. Pettigrew was a free settler and had arrived in the district in 1849. He set up a sawmill in Brisbane in 1852 and became a successful businessman but he regularly visited Wolston and kept an eye on its construction.

Dr Simpson built his home in 1852 — at that time, proclamation of the state of Queensland was still seven years away. He called the house Wolston after his birthplace in Warwickshire, England.

In 1982, Queensland National Trust architect Ray Oliver researched the history of Wolston House and believed it was not a homestead residence built for Dr Simpson but had evolved over time. He said it appeared the central brick section was the earliest and then it was modified by the addition of sandstone enclosed rooms and finally by the addition of an annex at the back.

The central block was built on sandstone foundations, planned as cellar rooms. The house had two main rooms with one of them divided into a pantry with access to the dining room and a small bedroom.

From his research, Mr Oliver believed the kitchen had been added by second owner Matthew Buscall Goggs, who bought Wolston in 1860. But a later survey by architect Stephen Murray showed that Dr Simpson could have added the kitchen before he sold up and returned to England.

Wolston was sold to Grindles Limited in 1906. The farming company carried out a number of major changes, including covering the timber shingles on the roof with corrugated iron and putting in new verandah posts. A timber fernery shed was also added.

THE MAIN LIVING AREA.

THE BACK OF WOLSTON HOUSE.

Robert Hurley bought Wolston in 1956. By then, it was in a poor state as the elderly Grindles had been unable to run the property. The Hurley family made some repairs to the house itself, but spent most of their time returning the property to good shape. However, Mr Hurley faced an important decision. Should he demolish the old house and build a new one or spend thousands of dollars in its conservation? Fortunately, he didn't have to decide because the Queensland government stepped in and bought the property. It cut off the house and garden and gave it to the National Trust.

Robert's son Norman Hurley remembered a verandah off the kitchen that had a slate floor and a half-latticed wall at one end. It was used for ironing and a butter churn was also kept there.

The laundry was also the bathroom, with a porcelain bath under the shutter. Water was warmed in a copper and transferred to the bath with a galvanised dipper.

The house was structurally unsound because of lack of maintenance. The roof leaked, termites had attacked the timber, verandahs were falling apart and creepers had invaded most of the building. But the Trust, after lots of research, was able to save Wolston and return it very close to what it was like when the Goggs lived there. The verandah has been rebuilt to preserve as much as possible of the roof structure.

The huge fig trees planted when the farm was built are still there, after recovering from storm damage in the 1990s, and the house still stands in fields at the end of a country road as it did back in the 1800s, despite the construction nearby of a prison farm and Department of Primary Industries complex.

Wolston House is now the only remaining example of its kind. It projects the image of an early pastoral company and a way of life long gone.

Yarralumla

Most Government Houses in Australian state capitals were built in Queen Victoria's reign and were elaborate buildings, but Yarralumla in Canberra, home to the governor-general, began its life as a humble stone farmhouse. Yarralumla was the name of a sheep property and supposedly comes from an Aboriginal word meaning 'where the cry comes back from the mountain'.

The land, comprising 2560 acres (1037 hectares), was first granted to Henry Donnison in 1828. In 1831, Donnison sold it to Francis Mowatt, who worked for Customs in Sydney.

Mowatt built a long stone house with French windows opening onto wide verandahs. It was known as a hunting lodge because Mowatt had brought a pack of foxhounds from England and used them to hunt kangaroos and dingoes at Yarralumla.

In 1829 Terence Aubrey Murray, who arrived in New South Wales with his father in April 1827, took up a land grant at Lake George. He inherited the adjoining grant on his father's death in 1835 and bought more adjoining land, calling the consolidated property Winderradeen and building a homestead there.

In 1836 he bought Yarralumla from Mowatt, and in 1843 he married Mary Gibbes, the daughter of the New South Wales collector of customs, Colonel John George Gibbes. They lived in the stone house at Yarralumla.

Hostile Aborigines often attacked the farms in the unsettled districts and were killing and taking cattle. The squatters were unable to stop this from happening and many went back to the more populated areas. Murray, who became president of the Legislative Council and was knighted in 1869, gave up squatting in unsettled districts

in 1846, but continued to lease large areas of Crown land in settled districts. But times in the pastoral industry were tough, and in order to avoid losing his land if he went bankrupt, Murray signed over Yarralumla and part of Winderradeen to his wife.

She died in 1858 and left most of the property to her father, Colonel Gibbes. He had lived in a harbour-side house at Point Piper but in 1842 bought 5 acres (2 hectares) of

THE NEW STATE ENTRANCE.

land on Kirribilli Point and built a magnificent mansion, now called Admiralty House and the Sydney residence of the governor-general.

In 1881 Colonel Gibbes sold the Yarralumla property to sheep farmer Frederick Campbell, grandson of the merchant Robert Campbell who built Duntroon, now the Royal Military College at Canberra. By 1891 Campbell had demolished most of the original stone house the Murrays had lived in and built the three-storey house that is now the main section of Government House. The Campbell crest of a bow and arrow is still on the gables.

At this time, Australia was still divided into six self-governing colonies with their own laws and parliaments, but people were increasingly agitating for federation. Australia eventually became a nation when the colonies, now states, united in 1901.

The Commonwealth of Australia was inaugurated on 1 January 1901, in Centennial Park, Sydney. In March, elections were held for the new federal parliament, and in May the celebrations focused on Melbourne, where the first federal parliament was opened in the Royal Exhibition Building. The Duke of Cornwall and York declared the parliament open in front of 12,000 dignitaries and guests.

It took years before an agreement was reached on where the new federal capital should be, with the Australian Capital Territory officially being declared on 1 January 1911. The city was formally named Canberra on 12 March 1913, and in the same year the government bought the Yarralumla property. However, little progress was made on the construction of the capital up until 1921, due to indecision and a shortage of funds because of World War I. The government chose not to renew the contract awarded to Chicago architect Walter Burley Griffin to design the city, and appointed a new Federal Capital Advisory Committee under John Sulman.

In 1923 the government agreed that after the 1926 federal election, parliament would move permanently from Melbourne and sit in Canberra. Construction of a 'provisional' Parliament House began, not where Griffin had originally intended but at a flatter site further down the hill to save money.

Development in Canberra gained pace during this time with the construction of the prime minister's residence, two government office buildings, numerous other buildings, and the beginnings of several suburbs. Public servants also began to be transferred compulsorily from Melbourne to live and work in Canberra.

In 1925 work began on Yarralumla so it could become the official residence of the governor-general. John Lawrence

THE DRAWING ROOM CAN HOLD 150 PEOPLE.

THE 64-DRAWER JEWELLERY CABINET.

THE AUSTRALIANA FUND BUYS SOME FURNITURE FOR THE HOUSE.

House manager Mark McConnell said there was a possible misconception that the governor-general lived in the whole house. The house is actually owned by the Australian people and their excellencies live in a one-bedroom apartment within the house.

Yarralumla now sits in the centre of 53 hectares of land. Private gardens surround the house and are maintained by twelve gardeners.

Around 70 kangaroos live on the property; they have all been named so vets can track their health and know how each one is faring. The kangaroos were popular with Danish Crown Prince Frederik and Crown Princess Mary when they visited Yarralumla in March 2005.

A number of trees on the property are of historical value. Some have been planted by heads of state or royalty during their visits, and some of those VIPs — such as Princess Margaret — have since died.

Yarralumla is known as the Australian House because it represents Australia in a number of different forms with its artwork and artefacts. As Mr McConnell explained, for many overseas dignitaries, heads of state or royalty, visiting the house is one of their only opportunities to see what Australia has to offer, so they look at the artwork and the artefacts, which showcase a cross-section of talented Australians.

Most of the artwork throughout the house would be classed as traditional and is from the National Gallery of Australia. Several paintings are by Arthur Boyd, two of them reverse painted on perspex.

While some of the furniture belongs to the house, some is from the National Gallery, and some pieces have been bought by an organisation known as the Australiana Fund, which was set up by Mrs Tammy Fraser, wife of former prime minister Malcolm Fraser. The fund buys special pieces for Yarralumla, Admiralty House, Kirribilli House and The Lodge. The main aim is to buy really unique pieces of Australiana so they can be retained for all Australians to see.

The piece that causes the most interest is a 64-drawer jewellery cabinet made by Geoffrey Hannah, a master wood craftsman, who comes from Lismore. It's the only one of its kind in the world and represents Australian flora and fauna.

Hannah used a combination of two forms of woodwork — marquetry and parquetry — and incorporated 22 types of wood into the piece, ten of them Australian. Every piece is hand carved.

Baird, the first Baron Stonehaven, was the first governor-general to live there.

A three-storey addition was built facing what is now Lake Burley Griffin and a private entrance was put in at the front of the original stone house. The Vista Suite, used by the Queen when she visits Canberra, was added above the private entrance in 1934 as a sitting room for Lady Isaacs, wife of the first Australian-born governor general, Sir Isaac Isaacs.

But the house was still too small to cater for all the official duties required of it so more extensions were carried out in 1938–39. The dining room was enlarged to seat 50 people at the table and the drawing room made big enough to accommodate up to 150 people for receptions. A new State Entrance was built and more bedrooms were added upstairs.

A new kitchen and services wing was built in 1993, and two years later a separate new building with offices for the governor-general and staff was opened a short distance from the house. Some members of the household staff live on the grounds.

'The house depicts Australia in a number of different ways, certainly in the artwork and some of the pieces, like where the wood has come from, the style of furniture and who made it,' Mr McConnell said. 'From the State Entrance you get the feel of really unique pieces, including a huge painting at the entry by Rupert Bunny called "Lady on a Balcony".

'Over the fireplace the painting is by Hans Heysen, the South Australian artist. Some of the books in the cabinet in the main passageway haven't been cut, meaning they haven't been read. They have historical value.'

The house has had a number of extensions to reach its present size of about 70 rooms in total. Of these, 23 are bedrooms. Because it was never originally designed to be the house of the governor-general, it doesn't have a ball-room or reception room for entertaining. However, there is a drawing room, off the main passageway to the left, which is continually converted to meet the requirements of about 295 functions a year. These range from heads of state or royalty signing the visitor's book and ambassadors and high commissioners presenting credentials to receptions or the awarding of medals in the investiture program. The Blue End of the drawing room is where official calls take place. In 2004 US President Bush appeared there and in 2005 the Sultan of Brunei.

A CORNER OF THE DRAWING ROOM.

To the right can be found the vestibule, and also the original staircase. A staircase at the other end of the passageway was an addition during the time Bill Hayden was governor-general.

Mr McConnell believes Yarralumla is quite an eclectic home. 'Certainly in its style, but over time we have tried to blend the rooms so they flow, although they were not built in the same period. The only room that is slightly different in period is the State Dining Room, which is quite art deco in how it looks compared with the rest of the house.'

The State Dining Room seats 52 people. Made from Queensland maple, there are fourteen leaves to the dining table. The carvers in the centre are where the governor-general and his wife sit, with the governor-general on the left. To the right of them sits the guest of honour. Traditional artworks by Frederick McCubbin and Hans Heysen hang in the room.

The governor-general's study is still used even though a new chancery was built during the Bill Hayden period. The

THE VIEW TO LAKE BURLEY GRIFFIN.

governor-general still uses the office for official calls from people like the prime minister, royalty and other VIPs. Chesterfield lounge chairs and leather give the room a strong masculine feel. This was the room where John Kerr sacked Prime Minister Gough Whitlam in 1975. Photographs show some of the callers, including George Bush and his wife.

One of the special features of the house is that every window or door offers a view of the gardens and surrounds. From the study the views include Black Mountain tower and Lake Burley Griffin.

Mr McConnell said while it was not as opulent as perhaps some of the palaces or grander homes in Europe and overseas, many visitors found Yarralumla inviting, homely and comfortable, and that was really the premise of an Australian house.

RIGHT & BELOW:
THE GOVERNOR-GENERAL'S
OFFICE.

First published 2006

Cameron House
An imprint of Bookwise International Pty Ltd
174 Cormack Road
Wingfield
SA 5013
Australia

National Library of Australia Cataloguing-in-Publication Data

Gregory, Denis, 1940– .
Great Houses of Australia: 50 homes with a story to tell.

ISBN 1 920743 56 1.

1. Historic buildings – Australia. I. Manciagli, Alf,
1944– . II. Title.

720.994

10 9 8 7 6 5 4 3 2 1

Designed by saso content & design
Printed in China through Colorcraft Ltd., Hong Kong